# THE TRUTHS

OF

# SPIRITUALISM.

---

## IMMORTALITY PROVED BEYOND A DOUBT

BY LIVING WITNESSES.

---

By E. V. WILSON, The Seer.

COMPILED FROM TWENTY-FIVE YEARS EXPERIENCE OF WHAT HE SAW AND HEARD.

---

"For there is nothing covered that shall not be revealed, neither hid that shall not be known."

---

CHICAGO:
HAZLITT & REED, PRINTERS, 172 AND 174 CLARK STREET.
1879.

TO THE

**Band of Workers in Spirit Life,**

WHO HAVE,

BY THEIR ADVICE AND COUNSEL, EVER SUSTAINED AND UPHELD ME IN MY

WORK FOR HUMANITY,

THIS VOLUME IS RESPECTFULLY DEDICATED, BY

THE AUTHOR.

"AND THE SPIRITS OF THE PROPHETS ARE SUBJECT TO THE PROPHETS.'

# PREFACE.

---

Dear Reader: We present you this volume of facts — tests from Spirit Life, given in every part of our country, and approved by those to whom they were given.

They are but a few, selected from many thousands we have registered in our diary. The dialogues and discussions occurred just as they are related.

We give you facts just as they occurred, and you can prove their correctness by writing to any of the places we refer to. One thing the reader can rely on, and that is, the facts speak for themselves. We are continually giving tests of Spirit presence wherever we go.

E. V. W.

# CONTENTS.

# THE TRUTHS OF

# SPIRITUALISM.

---

## CHAPTER I.

Charlotte Stewart Keeps her Promise and Shakes Hands after Death — Order to Make Medicine — It is Made — Our Position on Reform —Who am I? What am I? Where am I?—Why I am not a Christian —What the Spirits Tell Me.

### *SPIRITS SHAKING HANDS. KEEPING HER PROMISE.*

In May, 1854, our dear friend and sister Charlotte Stewart, of Toronto, C. W., took a severe cold, and being of a frail physical form, with strong pulmonary tendencies, she fell into a decline, and ultimately died of consumption. During her illness, she was frequently at our house, and we had frequent conversations upon the subject of death, the future, and the powers of the soul in the other life. She was a good musical medium, and many is the time we have heard the angels discourse sweet music through her mediumship. She continued failing and wasting away until

September, when she gave up and laid down to die. We called on her one day, and when sitting by her side, she said to us: "All is over; I must die. My physicians tell me I cannot live. But, my brother, I am not afraid; death has no terror for me; I shall not sleep in the grave."

A little after this conversation, we took our leave and meditated long upon this life and its relation to the future life.

About ten days subsequently, when standing at my desk writing a business letter, my old and tried friend, John Swain, came to me and said: "Our Indian friend Jim says we must have a circle to-night at the house of Sister C. S.; that the Indian medicine spirit will make medicine for our sister, the sick squaw, and has ordered our circle to meet at her house this evening at eight o'clock. Can you attend?"

"Yes," we replied, "we can; but have not time to notify other members of the circle, but will call on Miss S., and notify her."

"Very well," said Brother S., "then I will attend to the rest of the circle," and he left. We continued writing.

Soon after the departure of Brother S., we were again interrupted by Dr. A., who said, "Friend Wilson, I have just left Sister C. Stewart, and your old spirit friend, Jim Black, the Seneca, has been with her, and said, 'call the circle together this night, at her house, and the big spirit medium will make medicine for sick squaw, that will cure her.'"

"Who did Jim say must come?" we asked.

Dr. A. answered: "He said my squaw and her chief, big man and little squaw, and several others, members of the circle."

We said to Dr. A., "Keep this to yourself, do not let any one outside of those named know anything of what is going on."

When night came we were, in accordance with the order of the spirits, at our friend's house, and found the house full of people. We called a council of the spirits, and they determined who should remain in the circle and who not. As our memory serves us now, there were present in the room, Mr. and Mrs. John Swain, Mrs. S. being the medium, Mr. and Mrs. J. B. Caulkings, Richard Arnold and Lady, Thomas Anderson, Thomas McClear, Dr. Aulflick, Mr. Stewart, brother of the sick woman, E. V. Wilson and Mrs. Wilson, and one or two others. We were ordered to clear the room of all but those named, to set in the circle.

Said the spirit: "You will now take the sick woman and lay her on the sofa in the parlor, after which, you will place some distilled water on the table in an earthen pitcher; also a tumbler. You will then reduce the light, not put it out, and form the circle around the table on which stands the water;" all of this was complied with. Soon there came many loud and continous raps, with shaking of the table; then the tumbler began a rotary oscillating motion, frequently striking heavy raps upon the table. The pitcher was taken from the table and tipped over the tumbler until the glass was filled half full of water. The glass continued shaking and oscillating for ten or fifteen minutes in a violent manner, throwing some of the water out on the table. Then the motion moderated down to a gentle rotary oscillating one, and all this without contact of human hands. Then came to the rim of the tumbler small globules of light, some sparkling like diamonds, some blue, some white, others red and yellow. These continued to come and drop into the water in the tumbler. Sometimes we could hear a slight noise such as might be made by dropping a small spark of fire into water. Soon there came a very strong but pleasant aroma, filling the whole room; this continued full twenty minutes. We were then ordered to fill the room with light, which was done, and we found in the glass a little over a gill of liquid of the color of pale brandy and as heavy as castor oil, and of a sharp, pungent smell, peculiar and undesirable, with a biting taste like potash or alkali.

The spirit then said: "Give sick squaw six big drops at sun up and sun down, and when medicine gone, me come and make more." Our circle was then over.

Sister S. took the medicine as directed, and soon began to mend.

The reader will bear in mind that the medical faculty had given this woman up as incurable. She had been confined to her room, and had to be brought down by her friends to attend the circle. Ten days subsequently, we met her on the street in her carriage, and on shaking hands with her, she exclaimed, "Brother, is it not wonderful — this spirit power, and what they have done for me?" Her countenance changed, and in a sorrowful tone, she said, "Do you know, brother, that my friends are opposed to my using this medicine, saying that they fear that it was from the Devil?"

Later a portion of this medicine was submitted to a chemist for analysis, and found to contain the common properties of water; after which the friends of the lady withheld the medicine, refusing to let her take it. She failed rapidly, and soon was unable to be about.

Late in December we called on her, and found her very low, when she told us, under marked excitement, "They declared that the medicine was the work of the Devil, and took it away."

We went to her mother and brother, demanding to know what had been done with the spirit medicine. The mother replied, "We have submitted the medicine to able doctors and to our minister, and concluded not to give Charlotte anything that we do not know what its composition is, and to be frank with you, sir, we think the medicine was made by the Devil, and are afraid that it will cost her her soul. Our minister thinks it wrong to take the medicine."

Shortly afterward we made a tour through the West, expecting to be gone two or three months. The evening before we left, we called on our sick sister, and she promised us faithfully that if she passed away before our return, that she would come to us and let us know of the fact.

On the 30th of December, 1854, we left for Cincinnati, Chicago and other Western cities, returning February 27th, 1855. Our first call was upon our sick sister, Charlotte Stewart. We found her alive, not able to speak aloud — only in a whisper — or to raise her hand to her head. She told us that the angels were with her continually and that she could hear them talk and see them. We asked her if she was afraid to go into the unknown land ?

"No fear whatever, there is no death," she replied.

Again we asked her, "Do you remember your promise to us last December ?"

Her countenance glowing with celestial light, she said, pressing our hand, "I do, and I shall keep my promise."

Thus things continued for several days. One afternoon, in March, we called on her and found her as she had been for several days past, gradually failing, with the prospect for the next ten days as it had been for the past ten days. As we were taking our leave, we felt a gentle pressure of the hand. We held our ear close to her lips and heard her say, "I shall keep my promise," and then we left for our home.

On that evening, we had a good deal of writing to do, and continued at it until late into the night. In the evening, at a late hour, we heard raps on our desk, faint but distinct. We listened, and they were repeated. We then asked, "Are these raps made by a spirit?"

"Yes."

"A relative of ours?"

"No."

"A friend?"

"Yes."

"Were we well acquainted with you?"

"Yes."

"Will you rap how many years you have been dead?"

"Yes."

"How many?"

No raps.

"Have you been in the Spirit World a year?"

"No."

"Six months?"

"No."

"One month?"

"No."

"One week?"

"No."

"One day?"

"No."

"Twelve hours?"

"No."

"One hour."

"No."

We took out our watch and found that it was ten o'clock and fifteen minutes. We then said, "We do not believe you. We have no friend that has died to-day."

Loud and continuous raps was the rejoinder.

We asked the spirit to rap out the exact time of death; and then was rapped out 9.15 P. M.

"What," we replied, "you died this evening at 9.15?"

"Yes."

"And was our friend and acquaintance?"

"Yes."

"Well, spirit, we do not believe you, and as we are anxious to complete the writing before us, we will be obliged if you will leave us."

At this request there seemed to be a mournful pause and then a few solemn raps as if the power was disappointed, after which all was still.

On and on we wrote until late into the night, and when we were done, we arose and started for bed. The raps came again, passed through the house with us to our room. We questioned them a little more, but with no satisfactory result, and retired.

After we were in bed, the raps came clear and distinct upon the head board of the bed. We again questioned, asking for the first time, "Is it the spirit of a woman?"

"Yes, yes," came in quick response.

At that moment, we for the first time thought of Charlotte Stewart, and following the thought came a shower of raps. We then asked, "Is this our friend and sister Charlotte Stewart?" and in response there was a perfect fusilade of raps.

I startled, lost in wonder, for we were young in the knowledge of Spiritualism ; we were silent, and the raps continued. We then laid our right arm and hand on the outside of the bed, and as we did so, we said, "If this is the immortal part or spirit of our sister and friend Charlotte Stewart, take our hand and shake it."

Instantly our hand was taken by two hands in a

gentle but firm manner, and was clearly and distinctly shaken.

Reader, we cannot describe our feelings. Suffice it to say that we were out of bed instantly, and slept none that night. Early in the morning we called at our friend's house and was informed that Charlotte Stewart had taken her departure at nine, the evening before, for her Spirit Home; was with us at ten and a quarter, and a little before, and again at three in the morning, thus keeping her promise.

Are we not surrounded by ministering spirits?

## *OUR POSITION ON REFORM QUESTIONS.*

We are for reform, consequently intend to continue to be a thorough reformer through this life, and in the other life, too, so long as we have the power to think.

We are in favor of universal suffrage without distinction of color or sex, based on educational qualification. "If we were President of these United States," we would, in a special message, advise Congress to legislate on this subject as follows:

*First*—That in 1880, November election, every person above eighteen years of age, out of jail, who could read understandingly, and write their name legibly, should be entitled to the right of suffrage without reference to sex or color, for within three years, every person in the United States can learn to read and write.

*Second*—Thereafter, no person or persons should vote or exercise the divine right of suffrage, who could not converse in English sufficiently well, to be understood in the common-place affairs of life.

*Third*—Brain intelligence, not property, should be the true standard of suffrage.

*Fourth*—All officers should be elected by the people at regular annual elections held for that purpose—from the President to the post-master, including the judges of every court in the land. In fact, every civil office, or office of trust, should be elected by a majority vote of the lawful voters in the district, where such an office may be required.

*Fifth*—The abrogation of the Electoral College and Grand Jury are necessary for the well-being of the Republic, and the prosperity of true Republican principles. Let the people elect every officer in the Union, by a fair majority vote.

*Sixth*—In every case of jury-trials, a majority vote should determine the case, whether civil or criminal.

*Seventh*—In every case where woman is on trial for life or liberty, let her elect to be tried before a court whose judge and jury are women. Let her have a woman to plead her case, and if imprisoned, let the wardens of the prison be women.

*Eighth*—Make woman eligible to any office in the gift of the people. Let her occupy the holy place of office from the President to the post-master. If England is proud of her Victoria and Queen, and justly so, why not America be proud of Mrs. President. Mrs. Livermore is better qualified to be President of the United States than Logan, Blaine, Morton, Thurman or Tilden; and Mrs. E. Cady Stanton would make a better senator than Chandler or Harlan.

These statements will place us before the people on our record, and we "intend to fight it out on this line," if it takes us our natural life time.

Freedom of speech, freedom of thought, freedom of the press, and the right to worship God after the dictates of the soul in its individual nature, is the just fruit of Republican principles.

Let us have freedom to do the right — not license to do the wrong.

We recognize no law as obligatory and binding on us that deprives our sister woman of privileges that we enjoy. Then let us have universal suffrage.

## *WHO AM I? WHAT AM I? WHERE AM I? WHERE DO I LIVE? AND, WHERE AM I GOING?*

Questions enough for one Chapter, is it not, dear readers? Who am I? Well then, we are not a myth, but a real fact,— real and tangible, fifty-eight years old March, 1876, three and a quarter o'clock, A. M. 16th day, according to the best of our memory; and weigh two hundred and fifty pounds.

A Pennimite writes to us asking, "If we are a myth?" By no means, "If the court knows herself, and she thinks she does," we are not a myth, but a solid fact, and think we demonstrated that to the full satisfaction of the aforesaid Pennimite at Farmington, Ohio.

What am I? The church says that we are the Devil. Ministers teach it, and thousands believe it, and we have been told to our face that we had a devil. Well, one day when we were alone, we felt a little queerish like, having been told a little while before that we were possessed of the evil one; so we thought we would look into the matter a little, and put our senses into use.

*First*—We smelt of ourself, and were actually alarmed, for we smelt sulphur; but when we began to reflect, we remembered that the day before in riding from Buffalo to Rochester, we sat in the same seat with a minister, thus accounting for the smell. We felt relieved.

*Second*—We carefully felt of every part of our body, found no extraordinary heat, and we were pleased.

*Third*—We pulled off our boots and examined our feet carefully, and after using our senses according to the best of our ability, we came to the conclusion that we were not a devil.

A friend or foe writes us: "Long may you live, brother, for you are the Jesus of this age." This we emphatically deny. We are simply what we are, and no more. We claim no leadership; make no promises, and never fail.

Where am I? This is readily answered. We are here to-day, was there yesterday, and will be yonder to-morrow. We are lecturing, teaching and writing all the time; no idle moments for us. We do not beg for places, are well paid, well treated, and have no occasion to abuse or misrepresent committees, societies, or speakers.

Where are we going? This is the question of all questions, and who can answer it? Not the Theologians, for they frankly say they do not know; only believe. Not the Materialists, for they deny a future existence. "You are going to the devil," is dinned into our ears continually, and is devoutly prayed for.

We are anything but an angel in the minds and thoughts of some; and by others we are damned; hence, taking it altogether, it is a little mixed. One thing, however, is clear to us; we prefer to go with the multitude, whether they go to hell or heaven, for from the Theologian's stand-point, the devil gets the wholesale trade, and God gets the retail custom of this world, and as we have always taken first-class seats and paid full fare, we expect to go with the multitude. But candidly, in the hearts of the people, we have an abiding place, and that place is sacred to us. We know our friends and love them, and hate not our enemies. We love those that despitefully use us, and we can say with Jesus: "Father, forgive them, for they know not what they do."

We are opposed to settled speakers and all other fossil conditions, and mean to do the right.

We live at home a portion of the year with Mary and her pets, and the balance of the time, we are on the wing.

Thus we answer a few of the many questions asked us. In the future we shall answer other questions not quite so personal.

## *WHY AM I NOT A CHRISTIAN?*

*First*—Because the churches do not agree among themselves in regard to the future.

"A house divided against itself cannot stand."

*Second*—Because they bow before images, and Deify a man, and follow not the teachings of their Deified man in their fellowship one with the other.

"Thou shalt have no other God before me."

*Third*—Because they teach of heaven and the mercy of God, and his power to save, and yet the Christian world concede the tremendous truth that their God is not able to cope with the Devil, and that the Devil gets the great majority of mankind, and their God gets but a miserable minority of His own created works.

"And God saw everything that he had made, and behold it was good."

*Fourth*—Because Christians have no tangible idea of heaven or the condition of man after he is in eternity.

"In my Father's house are many mansions; if it were not so I would have told you. I go to prepare a place for you, that where I am ye may come also."

*Fifth*—Because they preach of God as a God of love and yet declare Him to be angry with the wicked and full of revenge.

"God so loved the world that he gave His only begotton Son to save it."

*Sixth*—Because they have no charity, and exercise not mercy, having no peace among themselves.

"For his mercy endureth for ever."

*Seventh*—Because they teach man, that morality and reason are the very worst enemies man's soul can encounter, and that man can only be saved by faith in the atoning blood of Jesus Christ.

"Faith without works is nothing." "Work out thine own salvation."

*Eighth* — Because the church and Christianity are at loggerheads with science, and have denounced every progressive idea that has come before the world.

## *WHAT THE SPIRITS TELL ME.*

"My Brother. Think seven times before writing once, and when you write let your room be cool, your dinner light, and your feet warm."

"When you blame your brother, or find fault with him, be sure you are not to blame yourself."

"Never speak evil of a woman, for she is the dependent being under your laws, and while you make the laws for her, you have no right to find fault with her conduct, for in so doing you find fault with yourself."

"Be just in all things and you will be just to yourself."

"There is something to do in the Summer Land; hence, something needed to wear and food to eat."

"The ornaments and associations of your home in the Summer Land you will take with you from this life, then be careful and freight your bark with the true and the good of this life."

"There are family circles, social reunions and social relations in the Spirit World. Matehood depends upon the Divine law of affinities; hence there is no marriage, or giving in marriage in the Spirit World."

"You will understand yourself and others in the Spirit Land, not alone from speech but by intuition. You will not be always a resident in one sphere; you may live in many."

# CHAPTER II.

E. V. Wilson at Morrison, Ill.— Remarkable Revelations — Interview with Cropps, the murderer ; His Claims — A Talk with Spirits — J. Antis, M. D.; L. Grasmuck; John Mayhew, and others.

### *E. V. WILSON IN MORRISON, ILL.*

Below we give the crude report of our seance in Morrison, clipped from the *Reform Investigator*. The editor is a live man, a brick, and knows how to publish a newspaper. We like him, and all he lacks is a thorough knowledge of Spiritualism. Come out, Brother, and make friends with us, "for the children of this world in their generation are wiser than the children of light."

"E. V. Wilson, of Chicago, has been giving a series of lectures and tests on Spiritualism, at Concert Hall, during the past week. As a speaker Mr. Wilson is logical and convincing, as a test medium he is hardly surpassed by any 'humbug,' from Balaam, who, 'falling into a trance, yet having his eyes open, saw a vision and heard the words of God,' to Simon Magus who would 'pay in coin,' for the 'right' of mediumship. We could, if we deemed it expedient, offer quite as convincing proofs of the existence of spiritual communications as Mr. Wilson himself; but, comprehending as we do, the prejudices and illiberal spirit of 'sound divines,' and good Christian people, and the skepticism of the age, we are content to wait for conservatism to break its shell by the slow process of 'hatching,' and come out a full grown chick. One thing, however, we do not hesitate to assert — that the individual who believes the teachings of the Bible, and yet rejects Spiritualism, is either ignorant of one or the other, or else he is 'no philosopher at all.'

"The key to the interpretation of the Bible is Spiritualism. It is the attempt to marry the Orthodoxy of the nineteenth century to the angel that came down from heaven, at whose 'presence the earth was lightened,' and to reconcile creeds and dogmas to the teachings of the inspired Word, that makes such logical minds as Henry Ward Beecher Christian in name and Infidel in belief. They tell us that Modern Spiritualism is of the devil. We have never doubted the agency of the devil in mixing up in the affairs of mankind and 'crowding in,' among good company, from the day he seduced Eve to the time when he tempted Christ, by offering him all the kingdoms of the world to fall down and worship. Had he succeeded we should not now be staring poverty in the face by advocating financial, social and political reform in a demoralized government. The devil is in Modern Spiritualism, as well as in the Christian churches, and what we are working for is to get him kicked out. There was One the devil could not buy with money — let us, whether Spiritualists or Orthodox Christians, follow him."

### *REMARKABLE REVELATIONS—INTERVIEW WITH CROPPS, THE MURDERER. HE CLAIMS TO HAVE BEEN ENGAGED IN FIVE MURDERS.*

A large audience assembled at the Calvert Assembly Rooms, corner of Saratoga and Calvert streets, Baltimore, for the purpose of listening to the arguments of Mr. Wilson, the celebrated Spiritualist of Chicago, in defense of Spiritualism. His defense of the theory of Spiritualism was taken from the New Testament, and if his deductions did not fully satisfy those present, they went a great way in shaking the belief that Spiritualism is not a myth, but a peculiar something, which cannot be clearly understood by all persons. His arguments indicated that he has been a profound student of theology, his Biblical quotations and knowledge of the different forms of religion being voluminous and unlimited.

But the feature of the evening was his reading of character, what persons had experienced in their early days, what their ailments were, and other matters, were truly remarkable, and created at times considerable excitement. The first subject magnetized by Mr. Wilson, was Mr. Crosby of this city, the magnetic influence being obtained by the lecturer extending his left hand, into which was laid the right hand of Mr. Crosby, that is, all of the hand with the exception of the thumb. The two hands remained passive for about two seconds, when connection was broken, and Mr. Wilson proceeded to analyze the character, feelings and antecedents of his subject. He was informed what portions of his features resembled his mother, and what portions resembled his father, the dispositions of the parents and the disposition of the subject, all of which Mr. Crosby pronounced correct. Mr. Wilson also informed Mr. C. that there was standing by his side a large man, weighing probably two hundred and sixty pounds, a lawyer by profession, who deceased fifteen years ago. Mr. C. declared with astonishment that such a friend had died precisely fifteen years ago, and when a gentleman in the audience verified this assertion, the people began to talk among themselves, and wonder what kind of a man Mr. Wilson was.

The next subject was a lady. She was informed that she had strong characteristics; she could be coaxed but not driven, and that if her husband attempted to rule her there would be a merry row in the house. The husband, who was a portly gentleman, greatly to the astonishment of all present, replied, "That's so!" The lady was told that two years since, she had a quarrel with a lady friend, and that she professed to be a friend, but in reality she was an enemy. The subject admitted the truthfulness of all that Mr. Wilson had said, with the exception of the false friend, but when Mr. W. replied that the quarrel originated at a pic-nic, the lady instantly remembered the circumstance, declared it correct, and voted the lecturer a seer.

The next subject was also a lady. She was informed that she had a peculiar fluttering at times about the heart; that it greatly annoyed her, and that she was compelled at times to sit up in bed in order to rid herself of the violent thumping; that about four years ago a pain suddenly made its appearance under the right shoulder and has taken up its abode under the lung. The lady was asked if the symptoms had been correctly portrayed, and she replied, "Correct."

At this stage of the proceedings, Mr. Wilson stated to the audience that, while walking upon the streets yesterday, he was approached by the spirit of a demon bearing the semblance of a man. The man said that he had been hanged eleven years ago, in this city, for murder, and that he had been implicated in five murders, and on two different occasions had assisted in attempting to destroy the city by fire. The spirit said that on one occasion, with the assistance of one Patrick Burke, he robbed and murdered a man twenty miles east of Baltimore; that fourteen years ago he assisted in killing and robbing a stranger and throwing the body into one of the wharves on Pratt street. This restive spirit stated that his last victim when encountered was in his shirt sleeves, and that he was stabbed in the side; that he was a resident of Philadelphia, and was on his way home from Washington when he encountered the murderers on Pratt street. Mr. Wilson described the sanguinary man of blood as a stout man, low forehead, bristling hair, high cheek and jaw bones, massive shoulders, showed his teeth when laughing, muscles of iron, ponderous fists, and a pugilist of some note. When Mr. Wilson had ceased giving these outlines, voices from all parts of the hall ejaculated, "That's Cropps, who killed policeman Benton." The lecturer concluded with this spirit by saying that the spirit before leaving, remarked :

"Tell the people at your lecture to-night that for five years I led the Plug Uglies."—*Baltimore American*, 1870.

## *A TALK WITH SPIRITS.*

E. V. Wilson, an Illinoisan, who has for several weeks been lecturing before the Spiritualistic Association of this city, concluded his labors in Lyceum Hall last evening. His subject was the Law of Influence, or Magnetism. We have neither time nor space, to give an extended report of his discourse, which was rather discursive, as well as original. In a strange way he would stop in his lecture, saying occasionally that the spirits were troubling him. One of these said his name was Willis ; that he sailed the schooner Wiltsie; was wrecked off Madison dock at Cleveland, in 1836; that he sank with her; was found in the cabin dead; that some men took $800 out of her; that men in Ashtabula knew all about it. After the defunct mariner had had his say through Mr. Wilson, the latter continued his lecture, describing persons likely to fall in love at first sight, or become converted at revival meetings. They generally had blue eyes, brown hair, small limbs, round plump forms, and range between fifteen and nineteen years of age.

Lloyd Garrison was the man who wielded the greatest influence in this world. He brought about a four year's revival meeting (of blood), and converted a whole nation into Abolitionists. He was the greatest character in the tragedy of the American Revolution.

Mr. Wilson devoted considerable time to the delineation of the character of some of the ladies and gentlemen in the house. He claimed to have nothing to do with phrenology or physiognomy, but operated by means of a subtle fluidity pervading the material space. Out of about thirty persons only one had the hardihood to deny the description of the character. He told a Mrs. S. that her dead husband was present, and the lady wanted to know what he had to say. He says, answered the lecturer, "Tell my wife she's a fool to submit to all that she does — she is oppressed and down-trodden by a domineering man, who married more for money than woman." And the lady said that it was so.

Another spirit-man acknowledged that he had cut his own throat in Buffalo, thirteen years ago. The offence was not forgotten, but the offender had been forgiven. Another, named Joe Waters, told a story about a number of Lake captains who years ago at a Commercial street saloon wagered that their stomachs could not be turned.

One spirit that had been hovering around for two nights, said he was murdered fifteen years ago, "and the man that murdered me was in this house last night, but is not here to-night. He is in the city. I shall not point him out to have him arrested, but I wish him to know that I am on his track; and that is hell enough for any one man in life."

This sensational announcement closed the lecture. —*Buffalo Paper.*

MORRIS, ILL. Dr. J. Antis writes: "Brother E. V. Wilson has just concluded here a series of four lectures to large and appreciative audiences. They were handled with the skill of an expert and were gleanings from the great book of Nature. Fertile in thought and rich in expedients, he seems the right man in the right place. Holding his audience as by enchantment, while the deep and turbid waters of error and superstition, handed down through the vistas of the past are being filtered, cleared and made to respond to those rich effusions of thought based upon science, knowledge and truth. It is noteworthy that among his most attentive auditors, were the most developed and matured minds; and that though cherished opinions and sacred ideas were handled without gloves, yet there loomed up before the mind of the enraptured auditor so clear an elucidation of the idea which was wont to be conveyed through the influence and power of science as revealed through the aid of powerful instruments and experiments, flanked with historical data and past reminiscences, that he seemed chained to his seat in breathless silence, drinking in largely and with gusto from that celestial fountain treasured up in the archives of our brother's exhaustless mind. There were over one hundred public recognized tests given, unmistakably and without reserve. Incidents and events with data in the lives of individuals, were recognized and publicly acknowledged. It was a flow of spirit and feast of soul! A love feast with the Angel World. The seed sown in Morris is taking root in good ground and will yield in abundance, exemplified by the persistent demand for more of the same kind. It shall be gratified when the first shall have been properly digested. With those minds there will be no more hankering after the flesh pots of Egypt, but their aspirations and demands will be for more light."—*July*, 1870.

WESTON, MO. L. Grasmuck writes: "According to promise, I write you to report the success of our meeting here last week. Brother E. V. Wilson spoke to large and attentive audiences four evenings. The house was full, although we charged fifty cents admission at the door. The result of his engagement here has been a complete stirring of the mental world among us—it is the subject of conversation in all places and on all occasions, and the bitter tirades of the clergy after he left, only add fuel to the fire he kindled. Some how the impression has got abroad that Brother Wilson is a good medium, but an eccentric speaker. Nothing could be farther from the truth. His power and eloquence are something truly wonderful, as admitted by all who heard him here. In his delineations of character, he was correct to a fault—never failed, but quite a number of incidents of the past in the lives of persons were not recognized at the time, while many have, upon mature reflection, brought them to mind afterward. Several of the descriptions of spirits were very startling, and were at once recognized. Two ministers of the Christian church were present and gave respectful attention, and have acted fairly with us, while others were too holy to attend, but not too holy to misrepresent and abuse him when gone. The actions of one of our Methodist brothers on last Sunday showed that he was badly hurt — his fine church was almost empty, while Wilson had a full house. We were successful financially and have some money left. We want another good speaker at once. They will be welcome and have large audiences, for the people are hungry."—*January* 1, 1870.

---

## CHAPTER III.

The Angels came to our house — A Beautiful and Affecting Test.

### *THE ANGELS CAME TO OUR HOUSE.*

The angels came to our house, and mother went away with them, to their home in the Summer Land.

On the morning of January 22, 1869, at nine o'clock, Lois Emerson, relict of the late William Emerson, of Emerson Farm, Du Page county, Illinois, went away amid songs and joy with the angels to their home in the Spirit World.

Our mother had suffered much for months before she left us; but knowing that her Redeemer was with her continually, she bore her trials with the patience of a true Spiritualist, and with a smile resting on her face, she left her normal body without a struggle, calmly and peacefully entering into her spiritual life. She passed over the river in company with those who had preceded her. On Thursday, the 21st, we noticed a change in her, and saw that she was pressed for breath, and Mary, her daughter, said, "Mother, I feel that you are to leave us."

"Do you?" she said.

"Yes, mother, I do, and have you any fears?"

"No, no, why should I," she answered.

She spoke this so calmly, and her words were so full of peace, and with a sweet smile on her face, she said, playfully, "Maybe I am not going now."

Mary said, "Mother, you are, and what will I do?"

She held her close to her and kissed her many times, saying, "Darling, darling child, why do you wish to keep me here to suffer? I am willing to go or stay. 'Not my will, but thine be done,'" we heard her say many times. She thus continued sitting in her chair through the day. She often asked for spirit counsel and advice, and messages were sent her through Planchett and other ways. The angels spoke unto her words of comfort. Thus was she consoled, and thus encouraged. In her last hours she was made very happy.

Late in the day, she said she would lay down once more, and did so. Her mind was clear, her voice full and strong, talking much with us, sending kindly words to all, and thus she continued through the night.

A little while before she passed away, she asked to have her head turned to the West. This was done, and the end was at hand. Mary then took her in her arms, and the angels told us to sing; and Mary, Sarah and Dora, daughter and grandaughters, with eyes filled with tears, sang the "Beautiful River," until she was over its waters.

So peacefully she left us, we scarcely knew when the birth was completed. Mary continued to hold her, when Sarah said, "Mary, lay her down."

"No," said Mary, "sing once more."

We continued singing when mother's lips moved once more as though trying to speak, and then were motionless. And our mother was an angel.

No stranger's hands were allowed to touch her form. Mary, Sarah and Dora, dressed her for the last time. There was no noise, or confusion, for the angels were present, and they did not like noise and confusion.

Sunday came, a bright and beautiful day, indicative of her cheerful nature, and beautiful spirit life. We placed her form in a beautiful casket, and the casket on two frames by the side of the piano, and those sweet singers, Mr. and Mrs. Hillis, of Elgin, and Mr. and Mrs. Spaulding, of Chicago, grandchildren of our mother, were the singers on this occasion.

By her request, her old minister, Father McChesney, and the Rev. Mr. Tompkins, of the Union church, were called to officiate at her funeral. Mary called Mr. T. to her side, and handed him the selections for the singing, saying to him, "Mother wished us to meet at this time, not to mourn for her, but rather to make it a season of rejoicing over her birth into the Spirit World. She charged us over and over, not to mourn, but to rejoice that her sufferings were over." Mr. T. received the Spiritual songs, reading the first piece, "Our Mother," Spiritual Harp, 28th page, which was played and sung with masterly execution, and listened to with profound attention, for it was "Our Mother," and her favorite song. Mr. T. said, "I will read one more song as very appropriate on this occasion," and read with fine affect, from the "Spiritual Harp," "She crossed the Shining River," after which Mr. T. made a few remarks in regard to the sublime beauty of these songs and how appropriate they were on this occasion.

Father McChesney made a short and beautiful prayer, after which the choir sang "The Beautiful River," with great effect. Many were overcome by its gentle strains.

Mr. T. then read a few choice selections from the burial service, after which he made some excellent remarks, speaking of her great love for her friends and enemies, of her pure life, her patience and resignation, enduring the greatest suffering without murmuring, and that it had done him good through the two months preceding her departure for her future home. He called our attention to her wish that we should rejoice instead of mourn, and that to him, in view of her great suffering, it did seem meet to rejoice. He then referred to her joining the loved ones gone on before her, and of her anticipating meeting them, and that in his own opinion, there was not a doubt but she had met them, and that there were recognition of friends and relations in heaven.

The choir then sang, with fine effect, the song, "Shall we Know Each Other There," after which the congregation, which was large, passed by her, many weeping as they bid her loved face farewell, and then we kissed her good-bye.

Then came her oldest friends and carried her tenderly to the family burying ground, followed by her children, and grandchildren, and a long train of loving friends, to the last resting place of her mortal remains; and, as they were lowered into the ground, the choir sang that grand old hymn, "There is Rest for the Weary." All was done in quiet — no confusion; harmony pervaded all, and all felt that it was a season of joy and not of sorrow.

She has promised to come back, and she will, and will bless us from her spirit home with pearls of wisdom and words of cheer.

Dear mother, thy loved face is no more with us, but thy spirit is; and may we live as thou hast lived — a pure life — and in our last moments rest as thou resteth — fearless, firm, loving, cheerful, and willing to go hence — and then may we say with thee, "Thy will, not mine, be done."

Mother was eighty-two years, ten months, and twenty-seven days old. She was born at Lynn, Mass., February 26, 1786.

We thank thee, and bless thee, dear mother, and will remember thy loving words of counsel in thy last moments until we meet thee again, "Beyond the Rolling River."

She has left a large circle of relatives and friends,

who will rejoice in her great gain, and, in consideration of her great age and pure life, we do not mourn her going away from us, but we shall miss her very much.

*A BEAUTIFUL AND AFFECTING TEST.*

Just before our dear old mother passed away, last January, she called her daughter to her and said, "Mary, I want you to remain near my body until you are satisfied that I am free from it. Will you do so?"

"Yes, dear mother; anything you wish me to do, I will do."

Well, after mother had ceased breathing for hours, Mary remained in the room near her until late at night. Mary says: "I felt that my mother was near me, and then I heard her step, felt her breath on my cheek, and then I heard her say in a whisper, close to my ear, 'Mary, open the door and let me out,' and I arose, went to the door, opened it wide; I felt her pass me, heard the whispered good-bye, and I knew then that mother had left the form, and was with father, once his bride, pure and unsullied; and I knew they were happy in their home in the Summer Land, and then I closed the door, locked it, and retired to rest. I had let dear mother go, after eighty-three years sojourn here, and now I know that she is happy, and with my father, her lover and husband. God is good."

Thus spoke the wife and daughter to us on our return from our winter tour.

Mother is not dead, but an angel in Heaven, and the place where we laid the casket away we are ornamenting, and intend to make of the ground a beautiful flower garden, with a monument of roses, beneath which, by and by, we will lay away our forms, and our immortal part join those that have preceded us.

Remember us, dear ones, in your own beautiful homes.

---

# CHAPTER IV.

## *THE GAMBLER AND THE SPIRITS.*

The following dialogue occurred on the steamer Jasper, in December, 1868, on the Mississippi River, between St. Louis and Hannibal:

*Gambler.* Gentlemen, now is your time to make a fortune. This game is authorized by act of Congress. Five hundred dollars for one, and the lowest you can win in this game is two for one.

*Minister.* Gentlemen, do you know that you are offending against God in this gambling operation you are now engaged in, and that at each throw of the dice you are mortgaging your souls to the devil?

*Gambler.* Are you sure of this fact, Mr. Minister?

*Min.* Yes; so sure that I have taken the responsibility to admonish you of your error, and now tell you, in the name of my Savior, that your calling leads to death here and hereafter.

*Second Gam.* My dear sir, if your Savior is offended, and you are in danger, you have our permission to retire to the ladies' cabin, where you will find company more agreeable to your taste than the gaming table.

*Min.* But, my dear sir, it is my business and my duty, as a minister of the living God, to enter my protest against your gambling here in this public manner.

*Gam.* Why do you sanction church raffles, cake lotteries, and Paschal House schemes, or Chicago Opera House enterprises; for, to my certain knowledge, the ministers of our churches invested some thousands of dollars in these gambling schemes, and if I mistake not, your name is D——, of W——, and you ordered five tickets in the Paschal House scheme. Am I correct?

*Min.* (With confusion.) I believe I was over-persuaded, and invested in that affair, but—

*Second Gam.* Permit me, my dear sir, to over-persuade you again. Put down your money and win your pile.

*First Gam.* And permit me to say that this is as fair a game as any lottery in America, and as honest as Methodist Drew's, of New York, in his stock gambling to the extent of a national panic, and far more reputable. For while our scheme will, at the most, ruin but a few, his will ruin thousands, not only men, but their families. And dare you open your head to him? Not a bit of it. You and your churches hold your peace, and accept an hundred or more dollars, with a "thank you, sir," and "may the Lord prosper you, sir."

*Min.* That does not justify your gambling here in a public saloon, where all have rights in common.

*Spiritualist.* (Modestly.) May I ask, Mr. Minister, if it was just for you to buy tickets in the Paschal House enterprise, or to sanction a cake raffle, or lottery for missionary purposes? May not this throwing of the dice be justified, on the ground that these men pay fifty per cent. of their winnings into the coffers of the church?

*Min.* Sir, are you an advocate of the gamblers' profession?

*Spirit.* It does not follow that I advocate gambling, but that I am criticising your engaging in it, as you evidently have on your own confession, of the purchase of lottery tickets.

*Second Gam.* Good for you, old man! Take a chance?

*Spirit.* Yes; but before I do so, let me ask you a question. Would you advise a young man, who was the only support of a widowed mother and two orphan children, to risk that which they depended on for their winter's support, when you know that the chances are ninety in every hundred against him?

*Second Gam.* No; I would not. You have asked a square question, and I give you a square answer.

*Spirit.* I like that; and now I am going to put a

second square question; it is this: Have you won from this youngster one hundred and ten dollars this evening?

*First Gam.* Well, what of it, old man? Is it any of your business? We risked our money for his, and would have paid it if we had lost.

*Spirit.* I grant all that, and I am not finding fault. I have an object in view, and expect to make five points in the game I am playing; and I tell you frankly that I intend to use you two gamblers as my right and left bowers, and the minister here will be my counter.

*Min.* If you please, sir (freezingly), do not mix my name up in your gambling operations.

*Spirit.* Why not? You opened the game, and I am following your lead. Am I right, gamblers?

*Gam.* That is according to euchre. Follow suit when you have it.

*Min.* Sir, you are taking liberties with me. I cannot allow it.

*Spirit.* True, sir; but you took liberties with these gentlemen, and why may I not take liberties with you? Are we not all sinners together? We are all gambling; you and I for souls, these men for greenbacks.

*First Gam.* But, my friend, you are losing sight of this game in which we are to play the parts of right and left bowers. What are you going to lead off with?

*Spirit.* I shall lead this young man as my first card, you having won from him one hundred and ten dollars. Mr. D., you are a minister of God, and ought to be well posted in his affairs, tell us this young man's history.

*Young Man.* (Sharply.) By what right do you interfere in my affairs?

*Min.* And why do you call on me to read his history? Am I his keeper?

*First Gam.* I say, old fellow, are you not getting your hands full?

*Spirit.* Yes; and I am going to play trumps soon, and call the game. Now, Mr. D., you stated, a little while ago, that you were a minister, and, as such, had a right to call these men to an account, and, as God's minister, you ought to know more than those around us, hence I call on you to lead a winning card and end this game.

*Min.* (In temper.) I deny your right to use my name, or call my holy profession in question, and shall not permit you to do so any more.

*Spirit.* Then I shall play trumps, and this young man is the card I shall play.

*Y. Man.* Again, sir, I ask, by what authority do you call me in question?

*Spirit.* By the authority of your father, now a spirit, who left you in charge of his wife and two little daughters — your mother and sisters. You are now returning to them penniless. What was to have supported them through the winter you lost, and you have only five dollars left out of your long voyage from the pinery. How will you account to them when they ask you for the things you were to bring them when you returned? Am I right, my young friend? Answer me, on your soul's truth; I command you to answer!

*Y. Man.* (Weeping.) Yes. Father, forgive me, and I will sin no more.

*Min.* (Excitedly.) In heaven's name, who are you?

*Spirit.* One crying in the midst of the churches. Repent, ye ministers and Christians, and make ready for the great day of the Lord. "For we came to our own, and they knew us not."

*Gam.* Look here, young man; is this true?

*Y. Man.* (Sobbing convulsively.) Yes! Oh, mother! mother! what shall I do?

*Spirit.* And now, my friends, the spirit father of this young man asks you to refund the money you have won of him to-night; and, in addition to his request, the spirit of Mary, the one you loved best on earth (and when in the earth life her word was law to you), asks you to keep your promise, and grant the first request her pure spirit makes from her spirit home.

*First Gam.* (Speaking sadly, while his fine blue eyes were overflowing with tears.) Yes, Mary mine, I will, for thy pure soul ever sought to bless me. Here, young man, here is your money; take it, go home, and when you see your mother and little sisters, tell them all, all that has taken place; and, Mary dear, remember me in your angel home.

*Min.* Amen! Bless the Lord!

*Spirit.* Work out thine own salvation, young man;

be wise hereafter, and never gamble again. And you, Mr. D., minister, try the spirits, and all will be well.

*Min.* I don't believe in your spirits; they are of the devil.

*Second Gam.* Well, we do; and they have done what you could not — made us pay over one hundred and ten dollars.

*Y. Man.* (Sadly.) I thank you all, and mother will pray for you.

*Tableau.* Young man weeping, and counting his money. Gamblers packing up. Passengers grouped around us, many of them weeping. Ladies crying, and some of them asking the angels to watch over their sons.

*Colored Waiter.* Dat am ob de Lord, shuah.

*A Lady.* (Taking me by the hand, and saying.) Will you let a mother thank you, sir, for now I know that there is a hereafter?

*Old Farmer.* (Excitedly, to minister.) You don't believe in spirits, do you? Kin you do this? and if you can, why don't you? I say, old feller, you come to my house, will you? and you may stay jest as long as yer a mind to.

*Spirit.* Bless the Lord, James; my bowers have told, my counter has done well, and I have won the game.

And there was no more gambling that night.

## CHAPTER V.

*A SEANCE AND ITS RESULTS, AT HANNIBAL, MO., DECEMBER*, 1868.

Yesterday morning I met my friend, Colonel L., and, after the compliments of the morning were over, he said to me:

"Brother, where are you going, and what are you going to do with yourself to-day?"

My reply was, that I had business that would occupy my attention most of the day, but shall be at liberty this evening for a social chat with you.

"I am glad to hear that; and we will be pleased to see you at our rooms, at the National. Come early."

So the day passed off, and at 7:06 I found myself at the National, with my friend, the Colonel, and his excellent lady. After the salutations were over, the Colonel said to me:

"B., E. V. Wilson, the spirit lecturer and reader of character, gives a seance at the Court House this evening; would you like to go?"

Well, Colonel, to be plain with you, I do not take any stock in Spiritualism, and I do not believe that there is a spirit medium in the world who can give a square test to a perfect stranger, unless posted before hand.

"Are you not a little prejudiced, Mr. B.?" said the Colonel's lady.

"I may be, and yet am willing to own that I wish Spiritualism was true."

So we determined to go; and others in the parlors of the hotel were infected by our conclusions, and joined us. On reaching the Court House, we found at the door a pleasant-looking man, ready to take our *quarters*.

"Ah," said I, "sir medium, you have an eye to the finances of our mortal life as well as to the joys of our spirit world."

"I am not the medium," said the door-keeper, in a very pleasant voice. "And Mr. Wilson said to me: 'Let the poor in without pay.' Will you walk in?"

"No, no, I thank you; I am not a beggar." So I paid my quarter and went in.

After being seated, with about one hundred others, I cast my eyes about for our medium, expecting to see a sallow, gaunt, long-haired, spectral-looking sort of Grahamite, but saw no one that answered my expectation. After a little, to my very great astonishment, the one of all others I had taken not to be the medium came forward, in a very off-handed manner, and said, in a pleasant, full voice:

"When I was a little boy, an old friend said to me, 'My boy, learn to know yourself, and you will be qualified to know others; study man more, and God less, and you will know more of earth, and heaven, and the inhabitants thereof, than by studying God alone.' And, my friends, I have followed that advice. And now, with the help of my spirit friends, I propose to take a walk with you through the past. I do not ask you to favor me, but to shut me out entirely; close up the door of thought, and seal up your memory; make yourselves as positive to me as you can. Do n't accept a thing unless it is true, for I shall tell you facts from the book of your lives, and prove it by you."

At this, he turned sharply to a man by my side, and said :

"Thirteen years ago, you were walking in a city many miles from here. It was ten o'clock at night. You were in an unpleasant mood, for you had bitter words with those you did not like. You were nearing a corner, on the shady side of the street, when a man sprang from a hiding-place and struck at you with a dagger. His blow missed its aim. You escaped, but the man is dead. He was a Frenchman."

"My God!" exclaimed the stranger, "how do you know this? For it is true; and I know the man is dead."

"Yes," said the seer, "he is dead; and tells me other things."

Turning to the right, he went half way across the room, and, pointed to a young man, said :

"I see you in the early winter, with others, on the ice. It is in a city. The ice is thin, gives way, and there are five of you in the water. You were then fourteen years old. One was drowned; he is here, and tells me this. Is it true?"

"Yes; every word," replied the young man. "I was fourteen, and it was in Chicago."

"Thank you," said the seer. "I wish all would

answer 'yes,' or 'no,' for I want to occupy all the time myself."

Wheeling right about, he pointed out a fine-looking old man, and said:

"There is with this man a First Lieutenant of the Confederate Army, and says, 'This man is a friend of my dear mother, and knew me well; go and tell her that her son still lives—is now an immortal—and has not forgotten the loved ones of this earth life."

The seer then described him minutely, and looking straight at the old man, said: "You know him?" With a faltering voice, the old man said: "Yes, I do; and will tell his heart-stricken mother."

Walking through the house, to another man, he said:

"Fifteen years ago, you and three others entered into a business operation involving time, distance, money, and application. You lost by the operation, and had to step out." He then described the leader of the party. "Yes, or no?" "Yes," answered the man.

Going to another part of the house, he pointed out a lady, and said:

"There is a bright-eyed little girl of four summers with you. She went to the Summer Land nine years ago last summer. She holds up to you a rose-stem—two unfolded roses, and one bud on the stem. She says you laid them on her little bosom when they put her into the coffin. And she says: 'Mamma, don't cry, for I am very happy.'"

"My child! my child!" cried the mother, excitedly.

Again the seer turned around, and, pointing to a woman, said:

"Seven years ago, the storm whistled around you, and darkness — thick and opaque — enveloped you; and one left you — he is now in the spirit land. You last heard from him four years ago this fall. Yes, or no?"

"Yes," said the woman, with tears in her eyes.

Crossing the room to as healthy a looking lady as any in the house, and one of our company, he said:

"This lady has a sore and tender spot here, on the left side, between the heart and skin, caused by exposure and hurt, three years ago this spring."

"True," said the lady; "and I feel it to-night."

Turning to a very pleasant, mild-looking woman, he said:

"Ordinarily, this woman is good-natured and well-disposed, but there is kill in her, and, when angered, she is phrensied and dangerous."

Those who knew her affirmed it to be true.

Then he continued to give test after test, until he had given fifty-six. Then, pausing for a second, he said:

"Ladies and gentlemen: I have kept you here two hours, and have given fifty-six tests; fifty-three of them have been identified; and I will now close by giving you a startling test:

"There is in the room a spirit; he is about the size of this man, light complexion, and, when in health, full-fleshed and fair; he was buried yesterday. He says: 'Tell my wife that it is best that I passed away, both for her and myself. For the last nine years, I have been of no help to her, and now am at ease. Tell her that, for nine years, my palsied form has been but a dead weight and incubus, hanging upon her skirts, and I a prisoner in my body. Now I am free. My long and painful illness prepared my spirit so far for spirit life that I can readily return, and am here to-night. And now I want to send to my late wife two incidents, as tests: First—I was with her last night, and she awoke from a dream; I awoke her. Second—Three years ago, I had a sinking turn, and all thought I was surely dying. I recovered, contrary to the expectations of all. My name is Dick.'"

And many exclaimed: "Is not this Dick Hager, we buried yesterday?" And one lady said: "I knew him well, and before his sickness, which had been of nine years duration; and I could not have described him as well as the seer has done."

The seer then said: "Friends, this test has a shadow of collusion about it. I heard of this man's burial, but nothing more. And I now challenge the audience to find collusion in any one act. Ladies and gentlemen, good night."

And the seance was over.

"I came, I saw," and I am compelled to yield the point. And now I ask my clergyman to do these things, or explain them, for I have found a man that tells me all that I ever did. B.

# CHAPTER VI.

A Dialogue between a Christian and a Spiritualist—A Conversation on the Cars—A Test: Reading of Character.

### *A DIALOGUE BETWEEN A CHRISTIAN AND A SPIRITUALIST.*

*Christian.* "Thou shalt not suffer such as have familiar spirits to live in the land!" There, Mr. Spiritualist, you say you believe the Bible, and there is the Bible law for you; what are you going to do with it?

*Spiritualist.* I am going to do with it just what you do with the following law: "Neither shalt thou wear garments of mixed material, for whosoever does is an abomination in the sight of God." Now, I see you have on garments of mixed material, hence you are an abomination, and common nuisance, in the sight of God. There is Bible for you, Mr. Christian; what are you going to do with it?

*Christ.* O, well; the law you have quoted was for the Jews only, and not for us Gentiles; hence, not binding on me, or the Gentiles. Therefore, the application is not good.

*Spirit.* Both of these laws were given by the same God, and to the Jews, and for the purpose of separation from the Gentiles, to designate them, as a peculiar people; and if one law is not binding on the Gentiles neither is the other; and if you have a right to make an abomination of yourself before God, I have a right to commune with familiar spirits.

*Christ.* But familiar spirits are evil spirits, and it is not right to do evil.

*Spirit.* How do you know that familiar spirits are evil; and where do you get your authority?

*Christ.* The law made to suppress witches and wizards is evidence of their being evil.

*Spirit.* Yes, yes; but we are not talking about witches and wizards, but about familiar spirits; nor can you find in the Bible, one who has a familiar spirit that is called a witch. You will notice that the disjunctive conjunction, "or," is used every time, thus: "Such as have familiar spirits, or wizards, or necromancers," etc. Thus far your rulings fall to the ground, and we will come back to familiars.

*Christ.* Well, you will admit that they are forbid, and that it is not lawful to commune with them?

*Spirit.* I admit that they are forbid; but *that* does not make it unlawful, or evil, for us to do what the Jews could not do under the law. For instance: the law against swine flesh, among the Jews, is not recognized by us; therefore, because the law forbids the use of pork to the Jew, it is not obligatory on us.

*Christ.* Would you advise the seeking unto these mediums, familiar spirits, what good can come of it? Will you tell me?

*Spirit.* My dear sir, you are dodging the main question. It is not, Would I advise it? but the application of the law, as well as what constitutes a familiar spirit. For instance, Saul says to the woman of

Endor: "Divine unto us by the familiar spirit." Not thy or my familiar, but some other spirit; and she did so. Who opposed? Samuel, the prophet of God; one of Judah's noblest sons; and Samuel is a familiar spirit. Moses and Elias was the familiar spirit of Jesus, and Elias of John the Baptist; and Jesus of Nazareth became the familiar of Paul. Read the twenty-second chapter of Acts; also the ninth. Thus I might point out to you a score, or more, of familiars in the Bible, who are angels, immortal, and yet helpers of man. What do you say to this, Sir Christian?

*Christ.* I say, sir, that you are wonderful in sophistry, and that the Devil can quote Scripture. I do not believe in Spiritualism, nor you cannot convince me; for Spiritualism is evil, and of the Devil, and none but the spirits of wicked men ever come back to earth.

*Spirit.* I thought you did not believe in Spiritualism, and here you are admitting the whole thing.

*Christ.* You are mistaken. I do not admit your position. But I must bid you good-bye. The boat is near our landing. But before I go, let me tell you, my friend, to find Jesus; he is your only Savior.

*Spirit.* When, and where, was Jesus lost? Will you tell me?

Exit Christian, with a very long face, growling about the Devil. And I go to my dinner—which is a good one—and, while eating, may hear of Jesus.

## *A CONVERSATION IN THE CARS.*

On Tuesday, February 2, 1869, on our road to Eddysville, the following remark was made by a gentleman in the seat before us, to a lady by his side:

"It is all bosh—positive foolery—an imposition."

"What is it, dear?" asked the lady.

"Why, this account of a talk with the spirits, in Buffalo, last night," said her dear.

"Why," said the lady, "I thought that the horrid thing was dead—exposed long ago. You know, dear, our minister exposed it, over seven years ago, and we have heard nothing of it since."

"No; it's not dead, by a long sight," said her dear.

"What do you refer to," we inquired.

"This article," he said, pointing to a column in his paper headed, "A Talk with the Spirits."

And before us we saw an account of our seance in Buffalo, on the evening before. The account was garbled, and far from correct, and yet was well calculated to attract attention. After reading it, we asked, "Where is the bosh, for this article testifies that these things did take place?"

"Well," he said, "suppose they did; does it follow that they are spirits?"

"Yes, certainly; and who is better qualified to determine this than the phenomenon itself? You are a phenomenon. A bull looks at you, and you say to the bull, 'Mr. Bull, I am a man;' and the bull turns to the cows, and says, 'My dear cows, that's nonsense; here, our dear calf stands up on his two legs, trying to make us believe he is a man.' 'It is bosh,' says the cows. 'Yes,' says Mr. Bull, 'positive foolery,' and the cows and bull go away satisfied that your testimony is worthless; and you have no right to testify to the bulls and cows what you are; and just so you say, 'Bosh! bosh!' and give the lie to an everlasting truth, and that, too, in the face of the fact that the phenomenon has never denied itself, and when even left to speak for itself, it has ever said, 'I am a spirit,' or, 'We are spirits.' No matter whether skeptics, Christians, or Spiritualists, deal with the phenomena, the universal answer is, 'I am,' or, 'We are spirits.'"

"Are you one?" said he.

"Yes, everywhere."

"And so am I," said a lady, just behind me.

"And I," said a man in front of the "dear."

"And here, too," said another, on the opposite side of the car.

"Do you think Spiritualism is dead?" said we.

"Well, we have not heard anything about it in a long time," said the dear.

Our station was at hand, and we had to leave.

### *A TEST: READING OF CHARACTER.*

A friend placed in our hand a letter, and, as he did so, said: "What do you think of the writer of that letter?" We held it a few moments, and then read:

"The writer of this letter is a male; about five feet two inches in height; weighs one hundred and sixty-five pounds, or thereabouts; is between forty-five and fifty years of age; his hair is short and thick on his head, of dark color; his beard short — say two inches long — and thick, and nicely trimmed. He is well made — strong of limb, flesh of fine fiber, nerves well organized and very firm. His temperament is in a scale of seven: bilious, six full; sanguine, six minus; nervous, five plus; lymphatic, four minus. He is firm in purpose, strong in will power, clear of mind, far-seeing, and possessed of remarkable courage; and yet is not reckless of his own life, or of others. He is very reticent in all public or important matters; says but little, and writes less; in private, however, he is sociable, genial, and frequently quite mirthful. He is a good eater, and likes his meals in good taste; enjoys a sumptuous dinner, but is not an epicure; can live on hard tack and fat pork, if required. Seldom finds fault; firm as a friend, strong in enmity, but with a kind and forgiving nature. He has a clear head, and remarkable executive abilities; possesses economy without parsimony; loves money but for its use. Is a firm, kind, and indulgent father and husband. Is a great man, and does well whatever he has to do. Is a genius, and needs but the opportunity to make his mark in the world. He has fight in him, and can kill, if required. He is a man of action; has now, and will have, many personal as well as public enemies. He has passed through great dangers; has been in great commotion; his life is a success. The assassin has been close to him. If he lives through this year, he will live for many years."

We know of but one man living that this character

resembles, and that is General U. S. Grant, the President of the United States.

"What are his religious views?" asked our friend.

He is liberal and religious, but we doubt if he belongs to any church.

"Who is he?" we asked.

"It is General Grant, President of the United States," he replied.

---

## CHAPTER VII.

The Fire Test; or, Tried in the Fire and Found True—A Fear ful time, the 8th, 9th and 10th of October, 1871—I opened the door and all came out—Pa, Lincoln is in the house!—Papa, I shall be burned up—There came upon us a wave of living fire—I fell forward with my babe in my arms, all on fire—It was fearfully sublime—There at my feet lay a little form roasted to a crisp—She came into the fire saying, "Oh, where are mother and baby?"

### *THE FIRE TEST.*

Readers, when you have read the following wonderful experience, you can fully understand the royal beauties of our gospel, as well as the wonderful and exceeding delights of clairvoyance, the rock on which Jesus built his church.

The kind of prayer exercised by my brother Eames is the prayer, and the only prayer, we believe in. We have never known it to fail in man's extremity, and we believe that any soul, in time or eternity, which, when in soul extremity, appeals to the All Father for aid, will find the aid to be forthcoming.

My brother-in-law is now at my house, my honored guest, with his motherless girls. Weeks and months must pass on before he can help himself, and ours the task to feed, clothe and comfort him. Oh, how glad we are that we have a shelter for him; and we only wish we had room for a few more from the ruins of Birch Creek, Peshtigo, and the Sugarbush settlements:

DEAR BROTHER: Here I am, at home, with the remnant of my family — the two oldest girls — in answer to your kind letter, telling me to come with my two motherless children. God and his angels be with you, to reward you and yours for the kind welcome extended to us on our arrival.

We reached your home on the morning of the 8th, leaving Menominee Tuesday evening, the 7th ultimo. I desire to give you some account of this terrible fire, which we have passed through. Leaving my wife (your Mary's sister), and our two youngest children — aged, one thirteen months, and the other seven years — behind us — gone on before us to the other shore; and why we were spared, and I in particular, burned as I am, is more than I can tell; but God knows. Oh! the horrors of that night! No pen can portray, or language express, and we who suffered can hardly realize, what we have passed through.

Sunday, October 8, was a cold, chilly day. The atmosphere was very remarkable — still, and filled with a dense, blinding smoke, fearfully increasing toward night. Still we felt no real alarm, as I was confident that if the woods were on fire, and the fire approaching, I could save my family and my buildings, as we had prepared for such fires, and were in a clearing of twelve acres. Through the day I had been out in all directions, looking for fire, or any signs of actual fire approaching, but there was none; therefore, on my return home, toward night, I felt no more alarmed than usual; and yet, could not rest, on account of the dense smoke and peculiar smell accompanying, making it very unpleasant to inhale. However, my wife and children went to bed, as usual. I laid down on a lounge, and was up and down, through the night, watching, as had been my custom since any talk of fires. At a quarter to ten in the evening, I was up and out in the darkness. Nothing was to be seen or heard, hardly a leaf stirring, but oh! the smoke! The smell — one could hardly endure it. I feared, I knew not what. I laid down until the clock struck eleven, when I was aroused by seeing lights approaching our house. I woke up my wife and children, and told them to dress themselves, and then went out to see who was coming. It proved to be my next neighbor, Mr. Blauvett and family, coming over, so that we might be together in case of fire, as there was more clearing around my house than theirs. By the time they had got to my house, my family were up and waiting—feeling the approach of some unseen foe. We knew not from whence or where to look for danger, and yet felt this ominous stillness—this dense smoke and stench, together with the cold, and intense darkness, all combined, portended something fearful, and we waited in silence its approach, Mr. B. and myself outside, and our families inside. I had closed the doors, to keep out the cold and smoke. While standing a few feet from the door, all at once I saw a bright light approaching, in size as large as a half-bushel measure, and, as it came toward us, it appeared like a ball of fire, approaching from the southeast, and I saw it pass directly over my house to the northwest, just high enough to clear the house. The night being so very dark, as it passed over it dazzled our eyes, and I watched it out of sight. All in the house saw the same light, as it approached and disappeared, from the windows. Next, we heard a tremendous explosion, which was so great that I can compare the sound to nothing I ever heard. The ground shook and trembled beneath our feet; the house jarred to its foundation, and the window-glass rattled in their place; and while we stood in breathless silence, not knowing which way to look or turn, or from what quarter the danger was coming, for, as yet, we saw no fire approaching; we heard a low, rumbling sound—a sullen roar, like an earthquake; this lasted only a few moments, after which came a change of atmosphere, with slight puffs of wind, and growing warmer every moment. Suddenly my house took fire overhead. Remember, I was out doors, in the midst of this intense darkness; and, as I looked, my large barn was also on fire — the flame crawling along like a fiery snake, on top of the barn, on top of the house, in the tops of the trees, in the air, and yet no fire on the ground.

I opened the door, and all came out, and we started for the hill. You remember the ridge west of my house. We had selected this place to go to, in case of fire, and from this fire we knew no better place to go. House and barn on fire — we must go somewhere. All this took but a moment, and we left the house — our happy home — forever, only to be united again beyond the River of Death.

Mr. B. and family, together with my children, proceeded ahead. At this time all was instantaneously light as day; darkness had disappeared, and the whole heavens seemed one vast wave of fire. I took the baby out of my wife's arms, and we followed the others toward the hill. O, God! Such a scene as now presented itself cannot be described. Not only in an instant had my house and barn taken fire on their roofs, but the whole air was one bright wave of flame-fire, and, as yet, no fire on the ground; only later, as it caught from this shower of fire in the air.

We hastened on. When about sixty feet from the house, my wife spoke:

"Pa, Lincoln is in the house — our only son."

I placed the baby in her arms, saying, "You follow the rest to the hill, while I run back and see, and if he is there, I will bring him to you, dead or alive."

I entered the burning house, which was all in a blaze overhead, and fire falling through in every direction, so rapid had been its progress. My search was sharp and rapid, but he was not there. I ran back to where I had left my wife, supposing she had gone on, when, to my surprise, I found her standing just as I had left her. I said to her:

"He is not in the house. Give me the baby. He must have gone on with the rest."

I took the baby on my left arm, and just then saw our boy coming toward us. He came running up to me, saying:

"Papa, I shall be burned up. What shall I do?"

I replied, saying: "Give me your hand, my boy, and we will go to the top of the hill; but do n't try to get away from papa."

I saw that his terror was very great. I feared for him. I also said:

"See, pa has got the baby and mother here, and we will go together."

Thus, having him by one hand, and the baby on the other arm, I said to my wife:

"Take hold of my vest collar," as I had no coat on. She did so, but never spoke from the time she thought our boy was in the house. She was perfectly paralyzed with fear for his safety, and stood gazing at the terrible fire in the heavens. I noticed, as we hurried along, that the wind was increasing at a fearful rate, great trees bending like withes before it. A few steps more, and we would have reached the top of the hill, where the children, and Mr. B. and family, were. At this point, my son let go my hand, and bounded away like a deer toward his sisters, and at the same instant there came upon us, from what quarter I know not, a wave of living fire, completely enveloping us in its embrace, and prostrating us all to the ground. It struck me in the face, blinding me in an instant, and my long beard and hair was in a blaze. I fell forward, with my baby in my arms, all on fire — my wife falling across my feet, and rolling over on her back — not a sound from her or the baby — myself in flames. The roar of the fire tornado was more than deafening, it was grand; it was like the sound of the cataract, the thunder, and the roar of the sea, combined. It was fearfully sublime. I laid my baby down, drew up my feet from beneath my wife, and, in the midst of this fearful ruin, prayed Almighty God to let me die with my family. Why had he passed me by? "O, take me, too," I cried. I had no desire to live, for I supposed that all was gone, and that this sheet of flame had swallowed all, and, in agony of spirit, I prayed to go too. But I was not allowed to die. A voice came to me, so distinct and clear that I heard it — I am not mistaken — saying: "Get up; get up, and look for your children." I could not resist. I arose to my feet, went forward a few steps, and there, at my feet, lay a little form, roasted to a crisp. I supposed it was my darling boy. "Oh! my boy," I cried aloud. My senses were suspended for a moment — I knew nothing. I groped my way along, I knew not where. I thought I saw some object moving. I pulled my eyes open, called my eldest girl, and, brave child, she came to me into the very face of death; she came into the fire, saying:

"Oh! where are mother and baby?"

I replied: "Mother and the baby are dead. And where," I asked, "are Mary and Lincoln?"

She answered: "Mary is here; Lincoln is dead."

I was blind and on fire. She led me where Mrs. B.'s children and Mary were. Mr. B. and part of his family were gone, we knew not where.

I said to them: "We must all lay flat on our faces, that we may breathe," the air being full of fire falling all around us.

The wind had increased to a hurricane, the largest trees bending and being uprooted before it. The roar of the wind, the blazing and falling timber, the glare of the fire, the whole heavens being one vast sheet of flame! One must see, to fully know and understand the horrors of that terrible night. There is no use for me to attempt to describe it; it cannot be done. There is no danger of any pen, or speech, exaggerating the scenes of this fearful hour, for all of this happened in less time than I could tell it. In less than one hour, my wife and children were dead at my side, my property all destroyed, and only the ashes of my home left. And this was the foe that had come upon us. No one could guard against fire from over our heads, and we fell before it.

Can you imagine my feelings, brother, as with my girls, now motherless, myself still burning, we lay there? God grant that you may never pass through such a night!

Soon the wind decreased in violence, and the force of the tempest of fire and wind had passed on; we could hear its terrible roar, and we were in its awful trail. We now began to fully realize our condition: All of us cold, and nearly naked; I fearfully burned, from the top of my head down to the soles of my feet, suffering the most intense pain. I felt that I could not endure and live; my face one mass of burns; my body burned deep in many places; my hands, legs, and feet fairly roasted. I had on two pairs of pants; they were tucked inside my boots; they were burned clear off, and up inside the boots, leaving the leather, burned to a crisp, on my roasted feet. Can you realize what I passed through and suffered — suffering ten thousand deaths, and could not die, as I had desired to, with my wife and babies?

I then called on the little group — six of us in all — and said to them: "Here is all there is left of our two families, so far as we know. We know not where your husband and the other children are; my wife, baby and son are dead. Now, in this hour of sorrow, let us all, with one accord and united voices, pray earnestly to Almighty God, our Father, as we never did before, that we may have grace and strength to endure this terrible affliction that has come upon us, that in this fearful pain I was suffering I might be sustained and strengthened." And as our voices mingled, ascending in prayer, all at once I felt surrounded with a host of angelic beings; they were on my right and on my left, before me and behind me; I felt their presence so clearly, that I thought, if I moved either way, I should touch them. And we prayed on without ceasing, until, in a moment, I felt my pain had left me entirely, and from that moment I have never felt the least pain from my burns; and all who were with me, and have nursed me for the last thirty days, can testify to my condition when with them.

And I call upon my God to witness, that this is the truth, and that I am this day a living demonstration of his power to heal through ministering spirits. Although, brother, you know I have never professed to be a Spiritualist, neither have I been a member in the church for many years, I know not who these beings were. I recognized none of them. It mattered little to me who they were. When they came, my pain left me; and more — they lifted from me the great weight of sorrow that weighed down my soul. They bid me look up, not down, on those lifeless forms; they are not there, in those charred and marred bodies; they have passed on, are now (resting in the Summer Land) above, and will be with you soon; they suffered not as you think, but in a moment, in the twinkling of an eye, at the sound of the tornado's trumpet, they were born into immortal life. Turn now to the living; there is your duty. Mourn not for those who have passed on; you are to live and go from here.

From this united prayer I rose up free from pain, and strengthened to endure my loss. We remained there until near daylight. Beginning to feel cold, I was led to some half-burned logs, which they turned over, and we sat between them, trying to keep warm, as there was not fire enough left to keep us warm.

It had come upon us like a flash of lightning, and left us as quickly, with our dead, and the ashes of our homes, as tokens of its visitation.

Morning light came. I wished once more to look, with my motherless girls, upon our lost and loved ones. My two girls led me back to where their mother and baby sister lay. I pulled my eyelids apart, for my face was so swollen and blistered that I could not see, only as I opened my eyes by force, and looked upon their faces for the last time on earth. Somehow, their faces were not much burned; but I cannot dwell here; they were dead, and their bodies roasted. My wife lay as she fell, with arms extended toward heaven, as if imploring aid. A little farther on, we found our darling boy, the one on whom I had hoped to lean, for support, in my old age, not burned as the others, but, we supposed, died from inhaling the hot air. We turned from our dead in silence, and passed on by the ashes of our home, no longer a home to us; all, all had gone!

I turned, with my children, and started for Menominee, seven miles away, not thinking for a moment that all, between our little settlement and the town, had shared our fate. But such, we found, had been the force of the tempest, that the State road was blockaded; huge trees, torn from their roots, lay across the way in every direction, making the road almost impassable. Fire had passed over the ground, leaving its traces all around. Every house was burned between ours and the town but one, and this was five miles away; we reached it about seven o'clock in the evening. All that day I was led by my girls, and our neighbors, over and under trees, groping along in darkness, for I was blind, and all of us hungry, thirsty and nearly naked. Glad were we when we reached Judge Ingalls' farm. We found an old Frenchman in charge, who welcomed us, and supplied our pressing wants. Just then Dr. Sherman met us, having come down as quickly as possible after getting word from my neighbor, who had gone ahead. The doctor, seeing how bad I was, and being so tired, thought best to have me rest until morning, when they would send the teams again for me. Tuesday morning came, and I was carried on a bed, in a wagon, to Menominee, two miles, and found friends, who kindly welcomed me and dressed my wounds. I remained with them for thirty days, until able to come to your home with my motherless girls, where I was welcomed by your family. God bless you, my brother!

I have told you I got to Menominee Tuesday morning, October 10, and, while there, was cared for by Dr. Sherman, who, after cutting off the rags — remnants of my clothes — proceeded to dress my burns — roasted feet and hands, and swollen eyes. I cannot tell you how bad I was. You know Dr. Sherman well; and to any who doubts my word, write to him as to my condition, and then they will realize fully what the Lord has done for me, through his angels.

Drs. Shepard and Dodge took charge of me after the first few days. I was tenderly cared for, and nursed with brotherly and sisterly love by all with whom I met. I have experienced nothing but kindness to myself and children. Friends of long-standing, and strangers, vied with each other in acts of kindness to us, in our helpless condition, and have our grateful thanks. Drs. Sherman, Shepard, Dodge, Judge Ingalls, Messrs. Grimes, Abbott, Brooks, Bagley, and others, will testify that, when I reached Menominee, my condition was such that none thought I could live; and all who came in contact with me, will testify to the truth of my statements, that I have suffered no pain, and that they have heard no complaints, or groans, or flinching, when my burns were being dressed.

On Tuesday night, the 10th, while lying at the Taylor House, I saw my wife, in a vision. Others came with her; and it was said to me, from these spirits — I could not distinguish whose voice:

"You will live, and go to Illinois."

I awoke, and felt refreshed, and have ever since felt surrounded by these unseen friends, helping me all the time. I could not, at the time, comprehend how I was to go to Illinois in my present condition. You may judge of our surprise, on the receipt of your and Mary's letter to Judge Ingalls and myself, with love, sympathy, and your home open to us. Brother and sister, it quite overcame me; and yet I felt and knew I was to go to your home with my girls, expecting to have to ask you for a home, through the winter, and, instead, came the invitation, a free-will offering from you and yours. So, at the end of thirty days, the promise of those heavenly visitors was fulfilled. When I left kind friends procured me a pass to Chicago;

they saw me on board the steamer for Green Bay, where other friends — strangers to me — many of of them friends of yours — saw me on board the cars; went with me to the Mayor's office, who kindly greeted us; then countersigned our passes, and bid us God-speed. Who could do more?

All the way to Chicago, conductors, and all others on board of the cars, seemingly vied with each other to help us on our way. It was only necessary for me to mention the Peshtigo and Menominee fires, and point to my burns, for they were my witnesses. On my way, I met many who knew you, and to mention your name to them, was to win, at once, their sympathy and help. One gentleman came to me, inquired about the fire, our condition, where we were going, etc., and took a fine woolen scarf from his neck, asking me to accept it, saying: "Tell E. V. Wilson his old friend, Mr. Hardinge, of Shell Rock, Iowa, gave it to you." He then hurriedly left.

And now, my brother, here I am, in your home, all there is left of my once happy family being tenderly cared for, all our wants supplied, by your Mary, and children, and, after five weeks, I find myself quite helpless. I can see, thank God. My hands and feet are slowly improving, and I am gaining strength, and can move about the house a little. I feel confident that I will regain the use of my hands in time; the nails are all coming off, but new ones will come in their place; I trust to retain all my fingers, and the use of them.

I thank God for allowing us to testify that I have

been healed of pain through the ministration of angel friends; and I here desire to add my testimony to the thousands of other witnesses, that I know our loved ones do return to us, and that men and women are prompted by these, our spirit friends, and theirs also, to help their brothers and sisters of the earth-life.

And now, dear brother, this is the way I have been led to your house, and am made welcome by your family, as well as by many unseen angel friends. I can feel their presence, but cannot always see them, and, since being in your house, have felt them working over my crippled hands and feet, and believe they will restore to me the use of them in good time.

Brother, I am a living demonstration of spirit power, through the laws of God, who came to my help, in my hour of trial, and relieved me of all my pain. I am now a Spiritualist. What else could I be, after seeing, hearing, and feeling, their presence, and witnessing their power to remove pain and restore one back to life, who was so near the grave as I was? And you are at liberty to make use of these facts as it seems good to you.

All I have here stated can be proved, by writing to any of the parties mentioned above, or to the Relief Committee, at Menominee, Michigan; they will all remember me, as the only one, so badly burned, that lived.

God and angels be with you, my brother, and bless you in your work, in the cause of spiritual freedom. And here let me thank all kind friends, who have assisted me through you.

I could add much more in detail, but have dictated enough to give you some idea of what I and mine have passed through, and of the manner my dear wife and children closed up their earth-life, and were borne into spirit-life through fire.

I hope soon to see you, and look forward to the New Year, anticipating your return, for Mary says you will spend New Year's day with the dear ones at home.

Mary, your mate in life, and partner in business, writes this for me, as I cannot.

My girls send love to Uncle Eben, whom they have not seen for over six years.

Accept love and heartfelt thanks from myself and children. Your brother,

PHINEAS EAMES.

*Lombard, Ill.*

---

## CHAPTER VIII.

**The Quincy (Mich.) Wonder, 1860—The Salem (Ill.) Tests, 1868.**

### *A TEST FROM MY DIARY OF* 1860.

In December, of the year of grace 1860, I was resting a few days at the pleasant home of my good friend, Brother T——, of Coldwater, in Michigan.

One day, sitting in the daguerrean rooms of B. M., my helper, Dr. Roberts, called my attention to a communication in regard to Quincy, saying:

"I want you to give a lecture at Quincy on Saturday evening; subject, "The Bible: A Text Book for Spiritualists."

We asked if there were any Spiritualists in Quincy.

"Yes," he said; "two families, A. W. S—— and T., and they can get the Union School House; there is, also, a skeptic, Judge M., in Quincy, who will favor a lecture. By the way, Mr. T. is coming here to-day; is on his way now, and is coming to these rooms."

We here described Mr. T. to Mr. R., who was in the room at this time.

Mr. R. laughed, saying: "You have described Mr. T. very correctly, and, if he comes here to-day, we will see if you will be able to identify him."

Soon, hearing steps on the stairs, we said: "Mr. T. is now on the stairs." Then the door opened, and we met him with, "Good morning, Mr. T.; you are from Quincy."

"Yes, I am from Quincy; but you have the advantage of me, sir. I do not know you."

"True sir," we replied; "we do not know you; but my spirit friend, Dr. Roberts, knows who you are, and has desired me to give a lecture on Saturday evening. You are requested, by the spirits, to engage the Union School House of Mr. S. and Judge M. You can get it; and we will send you the handbills necessary for advertising the lecture."

"But," said he, "suppose I cannot get the School House; what then?"

"But you can, for Dr. Roberts says so."

"I will try," said T., "and if I do get it, I will write to you."

"You will get it," we said, "and we know that you will."

"Very well," said T.; "we shall see if the spirits tell the truth," and then left us for his home.

The next day we sent him the handbills, which read as follows:

"Spiritualism! —— will lecture at the Union School House, on Saturday evening, December —. Subject: 'The Bible: A Text Book for Spiritualists.' He that hath ears, come and hear. The lecture will be free."

On Friday, we were sitting in the store of Mr. W., when there came in a fine-looking young man, asking Mr. W. if the man who published this placard was known to him.

"Yes," said Mr. W.; "there he sits."

The young man came to us, and said, "Father says you had better withdraw this placard, and not lecture in Quincy, as is advertised, for the Christians are preparing to mob you."

"Who are you? and who is your father?" I asked.

"I am Melville M., son of Judge M., of Quincy, and he says you had better stay at home."

"Well, sir, permit me to thank you and your father for the advice given; but say to him, when you go home, that we shall speak in Quincy on Saturday evening, and will take the responsibility of meeting the mob."

"Very well, sir; you are warned, now do as you think best," said the young man.

"We certainly shall," we replied.

Well, Saturday came, and in the afternoon we took a horse and sleigh, and, in company with Sisters T. and K., went to Quincy, reaching the place of meeting a little late. We found the house crowded — not a spare seat in it. On pushing our way through the audience, to the desk, we were touched on the shoulder by our spirit guide, Dr. Roberts, who said: "There, in that corner (pointing to our right), you will find the trouble, if any, this evening. Be on your guard; follow your impulse to the letter, and you will pass through the storm safely. Be cool, calm, and fearless, and all will be well."

On reaching the desk, we took a look at the corner specified, and, from the appearance, we judged that there was mischief there. Announcing our text, we proceeded to define Spiritualism, in our own peculiar way. On reviewing the conversation between Satan and the Lord, in regard to Job, we were batted by a stout, heavy-built Englishman, thus:

"Hold on, sir!"

"Well, we are holding on."

"Do you know what you are saying?"

"Perfectly well, sir."

"Are you responsible for what you say?"

"To the letter, sir."

"Do you mean to be understood that the Bible warrants the dialogue you are uttering?"

"Yes, sir, to the letter."

"You do?"

"Yes, sir."

"You are a liar," he then said; "a black-hearted Infidel liar."

In a moment, half of the audience were on their feet. Calmly, we turned to our questioner, and said: "Thank you, sir. We are much obliged to you; and here let me say, that it is not the first time we have been called a liar by a Methodist clergyman."

"How do you know that I am a Methodist minister?" he asked.

"When coming through the crowd, to the desk, we smelt sulphur in your corner, and, knowing that Methodist clergymen deal largely in that article, concluded you were one of them."

At this, there was a great shout and laugh. Seeing how the tide was turning, we seized upon the auspicious moment, and said:

"Come up to the desk, sir; you are not a bad man; you mean well; come up, and let us reason together."

He accepted the invitation, and came forward. As he stepped upon the platform, we saw spirits around him, and said:

"Hold, sir! we see you in a storm at sea; you are on board an emigrant ship. On a hammock, in the steerage cabin, there lies a dying woman; you are by her side, weeping; she is dead; the storm is over, and preparations are made for ocean burial; the form is ensacked, with dead weights at her feet; the funeral service is read, and she is consigned to a watery grave; and, ere she has found the bottom, you are writing to that pale-faced woman, sitting there, to come to the New World and take her place."

"Some one has told you all this," he cried, in a loud voice, "you lie, and you know that you lie."

"Judge not, lest ye be judged by that judgment ye mete out to others," we instantly replied. As this was said, there stood up a man, in the middle of the house, and said:

"It may be that you can tell me something."

"Yes, we can; we see by you a bright yellow man, of the negro race; he was a peddler; and says, twenty-two years ago, he put up at a new two-story house, about one mile from here, in that direction (pointing with his finger), and he says he went up stairs to bed; he was brought down stairs in a blanket, and buried in a sand hill, some rods from the house; and that, when the railroad was built, his bones were dug out of the hill; and that you know who killed him."

At this, Judge M. stepped upon the platform, saying, "Let this thing stop."

"Leave the platform," we said, "it is ours, and we intend to use it. Are there any others here who wish anything told them?" At this, the party with whom we saw the yellow man, left the house. We waited a moment, and then continued our lecture for an hour. At its conclusion, we were invited to tarry over night at the home of Judge M., and of him learned that all we had said was strictly true, and that he was cognizant of the facts, as related.

Are we not surrounded by a multitude of witnesses.

## *MANY SPIRIT TESTS.*

Lecturing in Salem, Illinois, December, 1868, the following tests were given:

*First.* While speaking, there stood by me a spirit, and said: "My name is Mikey; and I was killed west of this, on the railroad, six years ago." He was identified.

*Second.* Sitting in my chair, near the desk, waiting for the audience to get in, there came in, among the others, a gentleman and lady, and behind them came a beautiful little girl, with her hand hold of the dress of the lady. Looking up to me, with a sweet smile, she said: "My papa and mamma; see, won't you, my papa and mamma." Up to this moment, I thought that it was a child in the earth form, but then saw it was a spirit. Subsequently, while speaking, she came again; and this time showed herself to me in a school-room, full of life and joy, and gave me to understand that she was the favored pupil of the man she had just before called papa; and then she said to me, in a sweet, childish way, "Won't you describe me?" And thus she continued to tease me, until I consented to do so; and then she patiently waited her time, sometimes with the mother, and then with the father I then described her; and when I mentioned

6

the school-room she laughed in childish glee, saying: "Five years ago, papa."

The gentleman answered, and said: "Five years ago, I was teaching school, and the little child you have described was in my school, and my darling little daughter had that winter left me for a mansion in our Father's house." And the voice of the father toned down to the gentle accents of former days, when he used to pet his "wee darling," in the earth-form.

*Third.* To Dr. G., called on by request, I gave the following incident:

"Six years ago, I see you in a cloud; there is a bitter storm of hatred and enmity about you; it is as dark as night; your life is in danger; you move forward, yet deeper into the dark; you halt, retreat, notwithstanding you are urged to go on. I then saw a man in the shadow of the darkness, and others moving to and fro, in the shade of the trees. A change takes place—they recede; you are safe."

"You are right, in every particular; and the affair of six years ago is true, wonderfully true."

I subsequently learned that the Knights of the Golden Circle determined, in their council, to hang the Doctor to a limb of a tree, near his own house, on the occasion referred to, and came in numbers, to carry out their plans; but, by the timely caution of the Doctor, they were thwarted, and his life was saved.

"How do you get these facts?" asked a man in the house.

"From his sister, who is with him, and is one of his guardian spirits," giving the time of her death, and then describing her.

"Is this true, Doctor?" asked the man.

"It is strictly true."

"Do you know the speaker?"

"I have no acquaintance with him; never saw him until yesterday."

"Most wonderful!" said the questioner.

*Fourth.* Here came a spirit — crude, rough, and full of bitter feeling — exclaiming, "They choked me to death."

"What is your name?"

"White. D——n them! they did not give me time to get into ——."

Looking at me, he exclaimed, "They had a hard time with me, and I kept them at bay for some time. I then told the Sheriff that, if he would give me enough to eat and drink, afterward they might hang me in time for me to get to hell before night; and they did so; and then I let them hang me."

Afterwards, I learned that this man had barricaded himself in his cell, and kept the officers of justice at bay for some time, finally consenting that they might take him out and hang him, in time for him to get into hell, provided they would give him a good, hearty dinner to eat, and some whisky to drink, which, I am informed, they did.

*Fifth.* Mr. K., of this place, was sitting some feet from me, and there appeared a haze, or halo, around his head, in which I saw five men. I described two of them so that they were at once recognized. I saw a plan on foot to ruin him. I then described the whole thing, and said the affair grew out of some church matters, and that these men I saw were leaders in the church, and that they had done their best to ruin him.

"What do you know about the matter?"

"It is as true as God," he answered, with a great deal of energy; "and the five men you have described were five ministers, and they have done their best to ruin me."

"Who tells you this?" was asked.

"The spirit of his friend, who has been in the spirit world a number of years."

"Is this so, Mr. K.?"

"Yes, sir; and the description is correct."

"All of these things you may do, and much more." "Shall he not give you in charge of his angels."—*Jesus.*

"I have met a man that has told me all that I ever did. Come and see. Is not this the E. V. Wilson we have heard about, over there in Dupage county, Illinois?"

# CHAPTER IX.

The Lyncher and his Victims—I love Jesus, my Jesus—A German Spirit Test.

### *THE LYNCHER AND HIS VICTIMS.*

At a seance in St. Louis, on the second Monday evening in August, 1867, the following took place:

I was giving readings of character in the presence of one hundred and thirty-five persons. There was a man present who was a stranger to all, and by him a spirit, who said to me, "look," and I saw four others standing with him by the man, and the spirit said: "This man hung us five fourteen years ago this month, down yonder in Texas." The scene changed and there stood by him three more spirits, and said: "This man executed us there eleven years ago next December." Again the scene changed, and there was with the man two other spirits, who said: "This man executed us seventeen years ago, last May, down there in Texas."

We approached the man and said: "Sir, may we tell you what we see, and what took place with you in the past?"

"Yes, sir, (flippantly,) if you can."

"And you will not be offended if we tell some strange incidents in your past?"

"No, sir, I will not be offended; for I do not believe you can tell me anything, for the reason that I know you do not know me."

"Very well, we will see if we can tell you anything. There stands with you the spirit of an Irishman, and with him four other spirits, (describing them,) and he says, "you executed us five in Texas fourteen years ago this month." What do you know of it.

"Nothing. There is nothing in it, sir. Not a word of truth in the statement, sir."

"Sir," we said, "there is beside these three other spirits, who say you executed them eleven years ago. The leader of them is a Spaniard, and says you know him. What say you to this?"

"There is nothing in it, sir. It is not true."

"Sir," said we, "it is passing strange, but here are two other spirits, and one of them is a Southerner, and they say you executed them seventeen years ago last May, down there in Texas. Is this true?"

"No, sir; it is not."

"Sir," said we, there is a conflict here between the spirits, myself and you. I wish to get at the facts. I presume you do, or you would not be here. Will you answer me a few questions?"

"Yes, sir. Ask all you please."

"Were you in Texas from 1845 to 1863?"

"Yes, I was."

"Were you an officer of the law, or associated with the Vigilance Committee?"

"Yes, sir; but any one could tell that by my looks."

"Have you ever helped execute any men as such officer?"

"Yes, I have helped hang a good many men in

Texas, in my time. But any good judge of human nature could tell that by looking at me."

"Did you help execute the Irishman and his four companions?"

"Yes, but it was not fourteen years ago, hence there is no truth in the statement."

"When did this happen? Will you tell?"

"In August, 1853."

"Will you take 1853 from 1867, and tell me what the difference is?"

"It is fourteen years, but then you or any other good judge of human nature could tell this by looking at me."

"Here in fact, you have helped at many executions, and especially at the execution of these men whose souls or spirits are here to-night."

"Yes, I have; but it is not spirits; and if so, why can't I see them. And then you know you might have heard of these things. Besides, any one might know that I was from Texas, and had been a public man."

"Yes, yes, my friend, all this is but gammon on your part, and you know that I know nothing of you whatever, and yet you have admitted every fact related of you, and try to get rid of them by saying any man could tell this from your appearance. This is a poor compliment, and one I do not want to rest at my door."

The people were very much surprised.

Now, dear readers, here is a fact, and a stern one. These spirits were once men. They came not in bitterness, but to enter a protest against the pleadings of men in favor of Judge Lynch and his court.

Judge ye, between these spirits, and their executioners.

## *A GERMAN SPIRIT TEST.*

Monday evening, October 3, 1870, we gave a seance at Beeshop's Opera House, in Council Bluffs, Iowa, when the following incident took place. The Germans demanded tests. We turned to Mr. Beeshop and stated:

"There are with you two beings who once were men in this earth life. They knew you over twenty years ago in the Old World."

We then went into a minute description of each.

"The first spirit speaks in German. I do not understand him."

"Try and tell what he says," said Beeshop.

We replied, "He says, 'Ich bien burgomaster Metzler.'"

"I knew him well," said Beeshop, "now the other, who is he?"

"We cannot tell, for the words he speaks are very peculiar. 'Ich bien der chastier Gotlieb.'"

"My God!" said Beeshop, "I remember him well."

We answered, "He is now singing the chorus of a song, and one that we think you joined in singing with them."

"Repeat it," cried half a dozen voices.

"We will try," we replied.

After listening carefully to the spirit chorus, we repeated as follows, as near as we can write it:

"Litorao, litorao, litorao, litorao,
Willa willa wick, ye hiras so, litorao,
Willa willa wick, ye hiras so, litorao
Willa willa wick com bom."

Beeshop and others, then present, replied:

"We knew both these men in the Old World. The one was what you call a mayor, the other a jester, their names, Metzler and Gotlieb. Over twenty years ago, we parted with them in the Old World. On the eve of our separation, we joined in a song, the chorus of which, Mr. Wilson has rendered as correctly as is possible for one not conversant with the language, to do."

## *I LOVE JESUS, MY JESUS, WHAT COULD I DO WITHOUT JESUS?*

Thus spoke a lady to me, Nov. 28, 1868. And what called out these words? A spirit communication, and the communication from her son and daughter. I saw them and had the name of one, and the son and brother was in the act of giving his name, when I said, "Mrs. ——, your son and daughter are here." "Stop, sir, do not say another word, please don't, I cannot bear it. I do not believe it, I am no Spiritualist, I do not want to be, nor will I ever be one. My views are fixed, unchangeably so, and I am satisfied. Nothing can alter my opinion and belief. I love Jesus, my Jesus, what could I do without Jesus?" And here the mother was lost in her adoration, for the deified Jesus. "Go back, children mine, to your dark and silent grave, sleep on until 'the Resurrection of the dead.' I buried you long ago, and with you I cast into the tomb my love and memory for God and I want you no more with me on earth, for my Jesus is all I ask, and all I want, so don't talk to me of the dead."

I turned in sorrow from the mother, to these little ones from the Kingdom of Heaven, and like little pets of our own dear home circles. They cried, big tears rolled down their little cheeks, and the little boy said in a sweet voice, "Sister, come away, for mamma don't like us any more." "No, brother," said the little angel sister, "It is not mamma that don't like us, for she does, only its her think that don't like us, mamma does." Then there stood with them an Angel Guardian, and said, "Come, dear children, we will go; you must wait a little longer." I closed my eyes and wept, for I, too, have some sweet little angels in the Summer Land, and O, how I like to have them come and visit me. Thanks, Heavenly Father, for the heavenly influence of angel children.

# CHAPTER X.

Woman and Her Mission — Wonderful Case of Healing — Bitten by a Bloodhound.

## *WOMAN AND HER MISSION.*

What is the mission? Has any one any idea? Is it identical with man's? If so, why not admit her to the right of franchise? "O, she don't want to vote; has no taste for political matters, and would not vote if she had the right; and besides, she would always vote as her husband did, and hence she would be a power in the hands of designing politicians, and open the door for corruption."

The above remark we overheard on the cars not long ago.

Now being on the Frontier Line of Progression, we were at once interested in these remarks, and at once took part in them.

*Spiritualist.* How do you know she does not want to vote?

*Stranger.* Because she is not qualified; her sphere is in-door — not out. Let her take care of the house and its contents, is my motto.

*Spirit.* You do not answer my question. How do you know she does not want to vote — of your own knowledge? Has any one woman told you that she did not want to vote?

*Stran.* Yes, there has; and more than one.

*Spirit.* Will you give me their names?

*Stran.* No! I won't.

*Spirit.* Then I infer that you do not know of a woman who does not want to vote.

*Stran.* Yes I do. My wife, for one, would not vote.

*Spirit.* Is your wife on the cars?

*Stran.* Why do you ask? Do you doubt my word?

*Spirit.* No; but I would like to know for myself?

*Stran.* Well, sir, I am good authority, and I know what I say to be true; and again, if she was disposed to vote, I should do my best to prevent her.

*Spirit.* Just as I thought; she has suffered so much under your rule — felt the rod so sharply that you are afraid to grant her the right of suffrage, for fear she will turn the tables upon you, and you in your turn suffer at her hand, thus paying the penalty of your oppressive rule.

*Stran.* Are you a Woman's Rights man?

*Spirit.* Yes, we are.

*Stran.* Did you ever know any respectable woman that wanted to vote?

*Spirit.* We will not answer any question that involves the respectability, for it is no part of the qualifications of a voter. Make male voters respectable, and then ask for respectable women to vote.

*Stran.* Well, then I will drop the respectable. Will you now answer my question?

*Spirit.* Yes. I not only know of one but many; yes, thousands, and among them we count your wife, for wherever we find a man so bitterly opposed to the right of franchise for woman, we are sure to find a woman in that house that is opposed to oppression.

*Stran.* Please answer my question. Do you know, personally, one woman who desires to vote?

*Spirit.* Yes; your wife, my wife, Mrs. Cady Stanton; Mrs. S——, of Michigan; Mrs. E——, of Cleveland; Mrs. R——, of Chicago, and here is a notice of a vote taken in a Methodist church in Chicago, where one hundred and sixty-one votes were cast in favor of lay representation, and eighty-seven of them were women, and this is significant of their interest in the right of franchise as well as their desire to have a representative voice in affairs of the church.

*Stran.* Woman has no executive ability, is not qualified for office, and would be insulted at the polls if she should go there for the purpose of voting.

*Spirit.* *Ipse dixits* are not arguments or answers, and prove nothing. Your reasons are stale and unworthy of your manhood; your first position is an insult to woman. Why is she wanting in executive ability? If she is so, we, the men — her sons have made her so. But we deny it; and refer you to Queen Esther; Cleopatra; Catherine, of Russia; the Empresses Josephine and Eugenia, of France; Elizabeth and Victoria, of England; and Mrs. Cobb, of Washington, besides thousands of other able women of our country. As to their being "insulted at the polls," that is all bosh. They are not insulted at the theater, opera, circus or fairs, and if they should be then kill the man that offered the insult — but there is no need of going to the same polls with the men; let a place be prepared on purpose for them to vote.

*Stran.* Well, sir, you have a right to your opinion, I to mine, and I am opposed to petticoat government in all its phases, and shall vote against it.

*Spirit.* And I have a right to my opinion, and I am in favor of woman's right to enjoy the franchise of our country, and am opposed to pantaloons monopolizing petticoats, and are willing to share the spoils with them, and shall vote for woman's suffrage.

The whistle of the locomotive called our attention to the fact that we were at our destination, and the conversation closed.

### *WONDERFUL CASE OF HEALING.*

In Council Bluffs, Iowa, dwells Dr. —— and his lady, old residents of the place. The doctor is an Atheist; his wife a Catholic. They are well off in this world's goods — are considered rich. They have five children, four with them, one in the Summer Land. Some four years ago, Jesse, their first born son, now thirteen years old, had an attack of fever which ended in hip disease, contracting the cords of the leg, drawing the foot up to the back of the thigh, causing the thigh to shrink and wither and the leg to be useless, and obliging him to walk with crutches for over three years. Last winter and spring the hip became very troublesome and painful — pus in considerable quantities forming along the bone from the thigh joint nearly to the knee, and in such quantities that by placing the fingers on the thigh, pressing hard, and moving the hand down to the knee, the pus would accumulate before the finger as it approached the end of the sack, when the pressure would become so great that the pus would force itself back and by the fingers, and as it passed, you could hear the gurgle as it flowed back to its place. Early last summer, the doctor called a counsel of physicians. Their conclusions were:

*First.* Amputation.

*Second.* Make an incision, opening the flesh from joint to joint, extract the sack and pus, clean the bone, and heal by slow and sure process.

*Third.* To absorb the pus by scientific applications, sever the cords at the knee joint, straighten the leg by force, leaving the boy to pass through life with a stiff knee—"and I accepted the third proposition," said the father, "and offered ten thousand dollars to any one who would cure my son, and make his leg whole and perfect as the other."

Thus much the father of Jesse told me. Said the mother:

"With a sad and sorrowful heart I took Jesse up to his bed on the evening of the day this counsel took place, trembling with fear in view of the trial my boy was soon to pass through. While undressing him and preparing for bed, I felt a strange influence come over me. My hand was strangely moved out and toward the thigh of my boy, and the voice of my father, who was in his day a good physician, but who has been many years in the Spirit World, said to me,

'My daughter, heal your son Jesse,' and then my hand went out to the thigh of my boy, making several passes over it; after which I was told to take the boy out of bed and stand him up against the wall. I obeyed, and then I noticed that the leg was straight. I stepped a little back from him, and bade him come to me. He did so. The next morning he came down stairs without his crutches. The leg was well, full and sound; the gurgling pus gone, the stiffened cords limber and straight. My boy is healed — is sound and well."

"Come hither, Jesse."

And the lad came to us in the perfect use of his limbs. The crooked leg is straight; the withered and shrunken thigh is full, round, and plump as the well one, the gurgling pus gone. There he stood before me, the personification of health. We examined the boy carefully; we saw him walk, work, run, play. There was no halt or limp, no complaint, and no effects of the old disease left. There is no difference in the size, shape, form or appearance of the legs.

We turned to the doctor, and said:

"Are these statements of yourself and your wife true, and may we use them?"

"Yes."

"What say you, madam?"

"Yes."

"Doctor," we asked, "Did you or the physicians in counsel have anything to do with the case?"

"No, sir."

"Who cured this son of yours, doctor?"

"My wife, sir; not I."

"What say you to the spiritual part in this case, doctor?"

"I have only this to say. I did not see the spirit. My wife says she sees, hears and feels, at times, what you call spirits. I know the child was a helpless invalid when he went up to bed with his mother. I know he came down healed, sound and well. You see him as I see him. I did not heal him, nor had any living physician anything to do with his case. My wife healed him."

"Madam, did you heal this boy in and of yourself?"

"No, sir; my father, now a spirit, through me, healed this, my son."

"Have you ever seen or felt the influence of this spirit, your father, on any other occasion than this?"

"Yes, several times. Once he came to me and told me to take my sister out of the convent, and I did so, and I attribute, through God, the healing of my son to the Spirit World, and myself as the vital or living agent used by them."

"Are there other cases in which you have felt this power, and healed the sick?"

"Yes; I was in Missouri this summer, after the healing of my son, and there was in the family with whom I was visiting, a child who had falling fits, and had had them for several years. While there, this child had one of these terrible fits. I felt this wonderful power with me; took the child in my lap, passing my hand over its head and face, and from that time to this, the child has had no return of the fits. So writes one of his parents."

"What do your priests say to these things?"

"They say it is the work of the devil, and that he does these things to deceive me and cause the loss of my soul."

"Do you believe them or the spirits — which?"

"I believe the spirits, and shall continue to believe them."

And in my soul I rejoiced and thanked God that I am free and not a Christian, and that I had lived to see these things.

We are prepared to prove the statements in this communication.

### *BITTEN BY A BLOODHOUND—A MOTHER'S MALEDICTION—SHOCKING DEATH FROM HYDROPHOBIA.*

Has the dog a soul? or, is he immortal? Will some minister of God ask Jehovah, and inform us? We publish the following extract for the double purpose of calling the attention of our readers to the fact, that months after the man was bitten, the dog being killed at once, the dog repeats himself in the man, leaping fences, chasing cattle, barking and growling. In every respect the man is sunk, and the dog is dominant. Has the dog a soul?

*Second.* Did Jehovah God hear the prayer of this Christian mother, and send the spirit of the bloodhound to haunt this young man to death, and thus answer the prayer of this Christian woman in widowing her daughter?

*Third.* If God can thus be moved (and it seems that he can) by the prayer of an infuriated and madly insane woman, what are we, the "children of this world," to expect from these union prayer meetings and Y. M. C. A.? Anything but joy when God stoops to earth and unlooses the bloodhounds of immortality to hunt to the death a trustworthy and industrious young man, to establish the fact that he is a prayer-hearing God. It is time that there was a rebellion on earth, as well as in heaven.

"A melancholy and in many respects singular death from hydrophobia occurred yesterday morning at Yonkers, Westchester Co., N. Y., where the horrifying circumstances are at present engrossing an unusual share of attention. To medical men it is another terrible illustration of the fact that although the poison conveyed in the bite of a rabid animal may remain dormant in the system for an indefinite period, its power to torture and destroy life does not deteriorate.

"The victim, Thomas Lamp, who was in his twenty-fourth year, was by trade an engineer, and employed at a foundry in the village named, throughout which he was well known as a trustworthy, industrious man. During last winter, while employed in a brewery in a neighboring village, deceased was bitten by a ferocious bloodhound, owned by his employer, and although the wound inflicted by the fangs of the brute was not very severe, the animal was at once dispatched, and the affected part having rapidly healed, the occurrence was soon forgotten by the deceased. On Tuesday of last week, deceased was united in marriage with a young woman whose mother had bitterly opposed his attentions to her daughter. Having, by the exercise of a little strategy, realized their matrimonial wishes, the married pair had scarcely reached the domicil of the bridegroom when the mother of the bride made her appearance, and on her knees, after imploring curses and vengeance on the luckless couple, fervently prayed that her daughter might be a 'widow in less than three months.'

"It appears that the diabolical imprecations of the mother had a most depressing effect on the minds of the young people, and on the following day deceased evinced symptoms of the awful malady, the seeds of which had been sown in his system some months previously. Medical skill was resorted to without avail, and on Friday the wretched man, in one of his terrible paroxysms, escaped from his attendants, and after reaching some open lots, displayed cat-like agility in bounding over fences and otherwise disporting like an animal. He was subsequently secured by two of the Yonkers police, who found it necessary to handcuff the madman on arriving at his home in Brook street. Either the sight or sound of water would throw the patient into the most agonizing convulsions, and, as the malady developed itself, he would bark like a dog, snarling and snapping at those who were near him. He continued to grow more violent and dangerous, so that for many hours before his dissolution it was deemed necessary to bind him with strong cords, and while in this condition, his struggles, shrieks and howls were truly shocking, until death ensued, as above stated."

---

## CHAPTER XI.

Tests from Spirit Life — Is it a Delusion and Trick?

*TESTS FROM SPIRIT LIFE.*

E. V. Wilson, of Illinois, now lecturing in this city, was invited to give a private seance at the house of Mr. H. Stevens, 185 Buffalo street, Buffalo, N. Y., on Thursday evening, December 10th, 1869.

There were twenty-one persons present, and fifty-three tests given, not including character reading. A few of these tests we will write out and send you for publication.

*First.* R. S. "Will the spirits tell me my religious views?"

Here the medium drew a perfect history of the character, habits and manners of Mr. S., which was approved both by himself and his brother; then the medium said: You are not a Spiritualist, but a compound of Unitarianism, Universalism, and Comptonianism. You believe in God as a law, man as the only being understanding that law. Hence a God unto himself, and his future state dependent on himself so far as his happiness is concerned. Your incidental life is defined as follows: At twelve years of age, you are fleeing for life before an enraged bull; a red one, with a white spot in his face. At sixteen, I find, or feel (do not see,) you under the influence of drowning. There are four of you together. You rescue another from drowning. At twenty-two, you make an important move affecting you locally, socially and pecuniarily; it is the first great move in your life. At twenty-nine, you are in the midst of operations that involve the interests of thousands, and many, very many, are dependent on you for support. This year is very important in your life. At forty-three, you are in danger of losing your life. With enemies seeking to ruin you, this year begins a long series of troubles and enmities that culminated in very great trial and bitterness. In 1854, I see you land in the evening from a steamer at the foot of Commercial street. You are watched, hunted and followed from the woods up yonder, in the northwest. They are seeking to take your life. They make the attack; but by a remarkable effort of yours, you escape. They wish to have two thousand dollars. The spirit says Geo. L. was one of the prime movers in this. I gather these things from the spirit of your brother, who has been with you all these long years. Mr. S. admitted all that had been told him, and remarked that the assassins did not get a chance to use their pistols.

*Second.* A lady from Canada, an entire stranger,

was told of financial trouble, now in law, and the home and name of the parties given, and a spirit standing by her gave his name as Samuel Zimmerman.

"All true," said the lady, "and I knew Samuel Zimmerman well."

*Third.* Mrs. H. "Madam, my first influence with you is of terrible power that doubles you up, crushes you, and leaves you prostrate, weak and helpless. It is in your twenty-fourth year. Madam, there is a spirit here, I think she is your mother, and tells me an incident that occurred before you were born, and during the period of gestative life. It is in the form of a great excitement from fright, caused by the attack of a wild animal on your mother. I feel it from you, and yet it is ante-natal. You know nothing of this, save from hearsay. Again, madam, I find you at seventeen in great danger of death from a runaway team. I get all of these things from your mother, now in the spirit land."

"All you have said is true," said the lady, "and the fright was caused by the attack of a bear on my mother a few weeks before I was born."

*Fourth.* Mr. and Mrs. C. and daughter. Among many incidents given these persons, was one of enmity of long standing, the party accurately described, and the amount under litigation given. The medium then turned to the daughter and said: "My young friend, you will not be offended at what I now tell you. There stands a spirit with you who says, 'you are my daughter.'" He then described the spirit carefully, and when he left for his home in the Summer Land.

"He says to you, my young friend, 'be careful how you encourage the acquaintance of a young man that you made a few months ago.'"

The young lady answered, "You are right; my mother has been married before, and I am her child by the first marriage."

The other communication was identified also.

*Fifth.* Mrs. H. S. "There is with you, madam, a fine looking little girl, four years old. Calls you aunty, and says she looks like that picture hanging on the wall, but is not the original of the picture."

Mrs. S. replied: "My sister lost a little girl of four years old, who looked enough like the picture referred to, to be the original for which it was taken."

*Sixth.* The medium turned to Mr. G. and said: "Your sister says, 'brother, you are thinking of exchanging property and getting you a farm of eighty acres. Sixty improved, with a good dwelling house; barn not so good. Has a fine orchard and good fences. Look well to the title. Get an abstract of the original purchase, and all will be well.'"

Mr. G. replied: "Some days ago, a man offered to trade a farm to me for some city property, on which there are buildings and orchards, with sixty acres of improvements. I have lost a sister as the medium mentions."

These are but a few of the many wonderful tests given on that evening.

The medium's style or manner of giving these readings, is quick, sharp and pointed. Does not stop to repeat; seldom, if ever, asks questions. Cautions his hearers to ask no questions or tell him anything by word, hint, or action. He approaches his subjects, asks them one at a time to lay their right hand on his, to use no muscular action, then quietly draws his hand from under that of his subject and gives his readings, seldom looking at his subject. When through, turns sharp round and asks of his subject yes or no, and ninety times out of every hundred, we hear the word yes, in answer to his question.

He is lecturing here with great approval to full houses, and his seances are attended by hundreds. He writes all day, talks until ten and sometimes twelve o'clock at night, is an early riser, and is doing an immense amount of work.

There were twenty-one present at the matinee referred to, and our names can be reached by applying to the medium, or to Mr. Stevens, 185 Virginia street, Buffalo, N. Y.

## *IS IT A DELUSION AND TRICK?*

May 15th, 1869, the following conversation was overheard on the cars, during our journey in Wisconsin: "This is all a trick, a delusion of the Devil." As our ears caught these words, and being alive to any and everything pertaining to "our master, the Devil," we turned our eyes toward the speaker, and found the words came from an intelligent looking man of some two score years and ten. He held in his hands Harper's Illustrated Weekly, and his eyes were fixed on the wood cut, representing Mumler's spirit photographs. There were three others beside him, two ladies and a gentleman, and it was quite evident that they had become excited over the matter.

"Yes," said lady number one, "I am surprised that in a court of justice, such things should be admitted as proof."

*Second Lady.* But the man was on trial for an offense against the law, and should be heard in his cause.

*First Gentleman.* True, and yet the law ought not to recognize a delusion.

*First Lady.* They not only recognize a delusion, but the result of the trial tends to encourage it. Only yesterday, Mrs. P. expressed a desire to get a spirit photograph of her dear Flora. Only think of a spirit sitting to be photographed. What nonsense!

*Second Gent.* I for one do not believe it, and the whole crew of mediums and speakers, as well as their dupes, should be sent to the workhouse and there taught to earn their bread and butter by honest labor, — ahem.

*First Lady.* I thank you, Doctor, for your manly protest against the works of Satan.

[This was drawled out.]

*Second Gentleman.* I but do my duty, madam, as every true man should.

*Second Lady,* speaking to First Gentleman. What was that man's name that lectured on Spiritualism in Aurora, on Sunday, two weeks ago, and gave tests and read character?

*First Gent.* I forget his name. He was evidently an imposter.

*Second Lady.* I remember his name well; it was Wilson, and they do say that he gave many wonderful readings and tests, and among others that he read, was Judge P., and he told my aunt that it was true.

*Second Gent.* It is all very easy accounted for. Prof. Grimes, Dr. Von Vleck, Prof. McQueen, and S. P. Leland tell us how it is done, and this man Wilson, no doubt, had visited the cemetery and there learned the death of the parties referred to, just as Leland says they do.

*Spiritualist*, for the first time speaking. Pardon me, but may I ask if Judge P. is dead?

*Second Lady.* Oh, no; he was living and well, yesterday.

*Spiritualist*, turning to the Second Gentleman. How then could this man — what did you say his name was? "Wilson." Wilson read the character and give the history of Judge P. from the tombstones of the cemetery?

*Second Gentleman.* Well, if he did not in his case, he did in others.

[This answer was given in confusion.]

*Spiritualist.* How do you know that Wilson did so?

*Second Gentleman.* Because it has been proved to be so.

*Spiritualist.* By whom, when and where?

*Second Gentleman.* By Leland, McQueen, Von Vleck and others.

*Spiritualist.* Are these men truthful and reliable?

*Second Gentleman.* They are said to be truthful.

*Spiritualist.* Are they? Suppose a man should testify against you in a law suit, and you knew that he was paid one hundred dollars for his testimony; and more, that he had confessed himself a common liar—would you accept his testimony? Would you not as a judge exclude him, and would you as a Christian and honest man ask such a being to testify against your neighbor?

*Second Gentleman.* No, I frankly confess I could not and would not.

*Spiritualist.* Well, sir, such is the character of Leland, and here is a copy of a libel (producing it), he signed to save himself from greater trouble. Grimes is an Infidel, and an avowed enemy of Spiritualism, and cares not a cent for church, Spiritualism or Religion, save as he is paid to abuse the one or the other. McQueen is a State prison bird, and Von Vleck is a worthless villain.

*Second Gentleman.* Can you prove what you say, sir?

*Spiritualist.* Yes; and more. I can prove that the ministers and churches knew the character of these men when they hired them to abuse Spiritualism.

*First Gentleman.* Do you mean that our Christian churches paid these men a price for their expose of Spiritualism?

*Spiritualist.* Yes, and more; that the ministers of the gospel took them into their churches and families, and we can prove that the Christians of Monmouth, Illinois, furnished Leland money to come there, and that, too, when they knew that he was a common liar; and the common law says that the party concealing a crime or criminal, or conniving at crime, or receiving a criminal into his house, is guilty of an offense against the peace, if not a criminal. Again, I have heard you call the Mumler photograph a delusion. May I ask, is that a delusion which is capable of proof?

*Second Gentleman.* No; by no manner of means.

*Spiritualist.* Very well, then, Mumler's case being proved in a court of justice, or the charge against him not being sustained, and he being acquitted, does it follow that he is an imposter, or spirit photography a delusion?

*First Gentleman.* But Rockwood says that he can counterfeit the whole thing, and did it, too.

*Spiritualist.* True; but did that disprove the genuine? by no means. Again: Mr. Gilmore testifies that he detected Rockwood every time, and failed to detect Mumler. Again: wherever there is a counterfeit, it proves that there is a genuine somewhere; hence, Rockwood being the author of the counterfeit picture, Mumler's must be the genuine; Leland, Von Vleck, and McQueen being the counterfeits, West, Wilson, and Mumler must be the genuine authors that these rascals are imitating.

*First Gentleman.* Are you a Spiritualist?

*Spiritualist.* Yes, sir; I am proud to say that I am, and I would now like to parallel a case for your consideration. Will you listen to it?

*Both Gentleman.* Yes; and nothing would please us better.

*Spiritualist.* Very well. We will suppose that A. and B. are brothers, and agreed in everything, socially and educationally. Both go to a revival meeting. A. gets religion and B. does not. A. feels the Holy Spirit and B. does not. A. goes by himself, kneels down to pray at the foot of a great tree, and then in great agony asks the Holy Spirit to come to his help. After a while he feels relief, and all at once he is filled with joy. He has met with a change. He then hears a voice saying, " Get thee up, go and preach my gospel to all the world." He comes before the world, and on this testimony is accepted as a minister of Christ, and you never hear the testimony doubted. B. goes before the world; makes just as good a prayer, preaches a better sermon; confesses to have heard the voice of the Holy Spirit; continues two or three years to preach the gospel of Christ acceptably, and then goes back upon Christianity, and denies it all; comes out and exposes religion; says that he is a ventriloquist, and made it all, therefore religion is a humbug, and A. an imposter; and B. is hired by the Infidels and Spiritualists to expose religion. Now, sir, this is the position I call on you to accept — are you willing to set aside the religion of the age, on B.'s testimony?

All responded: By no means.

*Spiritualist.* Very well, why should Spiritualism be condemned on corresponding testimony?

"Pardon me, madam," turning to Second Lady; "you live far from here?"

"Yes, some four hundred miles."

"It would be impossible for me to know your history."

"I think so."

"Will you permit me to give you a spirit communication?"

"O do, please, will you?"

"We will try." We then said, "there is a beautiful little girl here. She would be nine years old if living now. She has been in the Spirit World four years. She left you in the fall of the year, you called her Violet; and she says, 'Mamma, do not weep, Violet is with you, and you dreamed that you were playing with me last night, and then I kissed you, and you awakened from your sleep, and your dream was over, but you cried, 'Violet, my Violet, sweet blossom of my young life, come to me in dream with your angel love, and bless me,' and mamma, you thought it was a dream.'" The little angel vanished from my sight, and the woman wept, saying through her tears, prayerfully, "Father, care for my little one, my Violet so tender, so young, and yet so beautiful; and I thank Thee, O my Heavenly Father, for this great and unspeakable joy, for I know of such as my Violet 'is the kingdom of Heaven.'" Then turning to the Spiritualist, "It is all true that you have said," and the medium wept, saying, "do not think our Spiritualism all a delusion."

*Lady.* The angels are near us, and sometimes we may grieve them, and it is such a joy to know that they are with us.

The whistle's shrill call rolled back from the

engine throughout the evening air, warning us that our depot was at hand. Bidding them good bye, we arose to leave. "Who are you?" asked the lady. We turned to her and said, "E. V. Wilson." And they were exceedingly astonished.

---

# CHAPTER XII.

Tests at Racine, Madison and Reedsburgh, Wisconsin.

## *TEN DAYS IN WISCONSIN.*

June 15th, 1869, found us gliding swiftly over the iron rails of the M. & C. R. R. A pleasant ride of three hours brought us to the quiet and beautiful city of Racine, Wisconsin, situated on the shores of Lake Michigan, twenty-five miles south of Milwaukee. We lectured here three times to full houses, and held one seance, giving many fine tests and readings of character, in public as well as in private.

At our first lecture, we gave one reading of character of a man unknown to us, which was affirmed as remarkably correct. We saw the changes that took place with him, pointing out the data which occurred when he was fourteen and twenty-three years old. We then stated that, "twelve years ago you had a financial trouble that came near ruining you." We then described the man that was the cause of it, stating, "We get these facts and statements from your sister who is a spirit, and with you," describing her minutely.

SECOND NIGHT.

*First.* Read the character of Dr. W., and saw by him the spirit of a young man who was described minutely, and when he died, as well as his age. Identified.

*Second.* We saw by and with Mrs. ——, the influence of discord and jealousy with great inharmony, describing the person and giving the time; which proved correct.

*Third.* We saw by a man, the spirits of two little boys who were drowned, fully describing them.

*Fourth.* We saw in the life of a lady present the incidents and facts that took place when she was twenty-two years old, describing them very accurately. Acknowledged correct.

THIRD AFTERNOON AND EVENING.

*First.* We saw by a stranger, the spirit of his sister, who left this life long ago, for her home in the Spirit World. This sister said to him subsequently, "All is well with the lad; they say he is alive and you will hear from him."

"That information is the object of my visit here," said the man.

*Second.* We saw by a lady, name unknown, the

spirit of her sister, gave her age at the time of death and when; which were identified.

*Third.* Crossing the room, we spoke to a lady saying, "There is with you a beautiful little girl," describing her. "She is your daughter. There is another, the spirit of a man, but is unwilling to be described or fully seen. Why, we do not know."

"It is my daughter," said the lady, "and I understand why the other will not present himself."

*Fourth.* To a young man, we said, "There is with you a young man," giving age, time of death, and how; fully describing him. He presented himself in a first corporal's uniform. Fully identified.

*Fifth.* We turned to a lady, and said, "May we tell what we see with you?"

"Yes."

"There is over your head a broken ring. The symbol refers to an incident that took place when you were seventeen years of age. One-half of the ring represents you, and the other half, one that is not with you now." We then fully described the one representing the other half of the ring, and what became of him.

"It is all true," said the lady, sharply, "but I do not know what they want to bring up those old things for—they might let by-gones be."

*Sixth.* We saw, by a prominent citizen, the circumstances and incidents of five years ago, fully describing them.

"Yes," said the man, "that is the oil affair, and is correct."

*Seventh.* We saw, by the sheriff of the county, a drowning scene and the date. Fully identified.

*Eighth.* We turned to a young lady and fully described a place, the time, the parties, and what took place. Identified.

*Ninth.* We turned to Mr. S., saying, "There is with you the spirit of your sister, and with her, your son and daughter, all in the Spirit World," describing them. Fully identified.

*Tenth.* We saw by a woman, her son and brother; describing them.

All of the above statements were fully identified, and are but few, of the many that we gave in Racine. In no case was the reading of character denied.

The Spiritualists of Racine are alive and thriving. Among these earnest workers, we may mention the following names who ministered to our wants: The Palmeters, the Stebbins, the Waits, the Burgesses, the Chamberlains, the Trowbridges, and Sister Pauline Roberts—honest and faithful workers. They hold regular meetings on Sunday, in the court house, with fair attendance. Speaking, usually, by Brother Trowbridge, who is a worthy advocate of our gospel. Long may they flourish and prosper.

Friday, June 18th, found us at five o'clock, P. M., in Madison, at the quiet home of Lyman C. Draper, Esq., a true man, scholar and historian. We lectured at night to a small audience, one hundred and fifty in number, in the City Hall. Our subject, "Nine Postulates on the Bible." Of what we said, saw and described, we refer our readers to the following clipped from the *Wisconsin State Journal* of June 19th:

"E. V. Wilson, of Illinois, spoke in the City Hall last evening, to Spiritualists and others, interested in the peculiar phenomena. His subject was, "Nine Postulates on the Bible," briefly stated as follows:

"*First.* Man became like God after the fall—not before.

"*Second.* That Adam was expelled from the garden lest he might become immortal.

"*Third.* That the 'curse of Cain' was really a blessing.

"*Fourth.* That the Bible sustains the claim that disembodied spirits return to earth and identify themselves to their former friends and relatives.

"*Fifth.* That Jesus was not God, and did not claim to be.

"*Sixth.* That Christ was a disembodied spirit controlling Jesus, as a medium; this control beginning at the baptism of John.

"*Seventh.* That the Divine authenticity claimed for the Bible, is not warranted by the teachings of the Bible.

"*Eighth.* That Modern Spiritualism is the key to all revelation.

"*Ninth.* That the spiritual phenomena of the Bible, form the basis of the Christian religion.

"Mr. Wilson undertook to demonstrate these propositions with argument and phenomena.

"To illustrate, he turned to a stranger and said, 'There stands by you a spirit representing herself as a beautiful little girl; says she passed away when three years old; is now a full grown woman in Spirit Land; says she is your sister;' describing the vision very minutely. The gentleman (Mr. Burr) acknowleged the relation, and recognized the spirit.

"Mr. Wilson then delineated the characters of three strangers in the audience, which were fully accepted by the subjects, and indorsed by their friends. One of these gentlemen was, Hon. E. B. Dean, of this city.

"During these tests, Mr. Wilson turned to a gentleman, and said, 'There stands by you a spirit in the uniform of a Federal Captain; knew you before he entered the service; was killed in 1863, before Vicksburg;' then describing the Captain minutely. Fully identified.

"Again: Saw, and described, the spirit of the late Judge Wyram Knowlton; gave the name; fully identified by many present.

"Saw, and described a spirit, purporting to be the late Governor Harvay, a stranger to the medium. With some discrepancies, the description was considered good. The apparition made the strange statement that he did not fall into the river from the boat, as was believed, but was pushed in, designedly, by an assassin."

Saturday, June 19, we lectured at night to a good audience, on "Influences." Gave the following tests:

There is here, the spirit of a lawyer, who lived in this city several years ago, and says he died in the insane asylum, five years ago. We described him as a spare man, well built, pale, very sallow, about five feet ten inches in height, brown hair, oval features, a little dandyfied, wearing a dress coat, plug hat; carries a small cane, and otherwise minutely describing him. We then pointed out several gentlemen that he identified. There was some quibbling over the identity, when the spirit said, "I was compelled to leave my house in Sheboygan, Wisconsin, some years before my death; came here; was here in 1859, '60 and '61; returned to Sheboygan; became insane; was sent to the Lunatic Asylum, and died there; and many exclaimed, "It is Mr. Hiller." One man, Mr. Hamilton, said, "I knew him well, and it is as accurate as I could describe him."

We then left the platform, and went among the audience, being attracted to a group of gentlemen of marked intellectual appearance. They were positive, highly-cultured men. We read the character of two of them; gave several incidents in their lives, as well as marked traits of character, with whom we found the spirit of Hiller. There was a good deal of doubt on their part as to the identity and incidents, as well as spirits seen, and related as with, and belonging to them. The traits of character were accepted. The incidents rejected, in most cases. In our own estimation, we think we failed with these men; and from the fact, that their positive natures conflicted with our own. We went to them, determined to give them tests; and in this failure, we see clearly and fully the development of law, and that the medium must negative himself and depend on the law and the spirit, or fail.

This affair created considerable feeling in the audience on the part of these gentlemen, and ourself. The whole thing was conducted in a spirit of good feeling and manly deportment. We learned subsequently, from others, that many of the points and dates, were identified by those who knew these gentlemen; but, it was not the testimony of the gentlemen referred to; hence, not acceptable to them. Our meeting closed for the day, with the best of feelings, and all went to their homes well satisfied.

Sunday, June 20, we lectured to large and intelligent audiences, at two o'clock, and at a quarter before eight o'clock, P. M., the afternoon subject being, "Why am I a Spiritualist?" The evening subject, "The Law and the Testimony."

During the day, we gave many fine tests and readings.

*First.* We saw a man, when a boy, thrown from his horse, and nearly killed; you are ten years of age, describing the horse fully. Subsequently, the man told us we were right in every particular, save one. You say the horse was a dark bay, which is not the case; he was a dark iron-gray.

*Second.* By a man, who was trying to prove that these things seen and recognized by mediums, "was our double, or the mind wave." We saw him in a boat with two others, and the boat came near swamping, thus endangering their lives. Repeating this to him, he said, "I have no memory of any such thing." We then repeated again what we saw, giving the time and describing the place minutely. He then said, "It is correct, and you have described the place with marvelous accuracy." We asked, "Where now is your 'double or wave mind?'" "I cannot tell," he replied.

*Third.* We saw from the platform, and at a distance of twenty-five feet, by a lady, the spirit of a woman holding in her hand a little box, she said, "This is for this woman, and she is my own dear, dear ——," (here we lost the sentence,) but we fully described the spirit, which was identified by the lady's mother, who was present.

*Fourth.* We pointed to a lady, saying, you are suffering thus and so, these troubles beginning eleven years ago; giving a full diagnosis of her complaint.

"You are correct," said the lady.

Many other public tests we gave during the day and evening, which were fully identified. What is it?

One or two private tests are worthy of a place here.

We saw a beautiful little boy with Mr. C. and Mr. D., describing him very accurately, giving his age. He proved to be Mr. C.'s nephew.

Sitting in the parlor of L. C. D.'s farm house, we heard a voice say, "Helen is here; tell them Helen is here." One said, "Who is this Helen?" We then saw in the midst of a bright band of spirit girls, the one who called herself Helen, and thus she said:

"We come to greet thee, mother, from our home divine; from the land of flowers, we come to meet thee. Our love continues free and unabated toward those on earth, with whom we once were mated. Do not mourn us as lost, dear friends, for we are not dead, nay, nor far from you.

"Father, mother, I greet thee from the Summer Land; greet you in company with my angel band of mates,—these, my companions and I, come to you with glad tidings of great joy, testifying that I still live,—live to bless you, to call you ever by the sweet, endearing names of father and mother.

"And now in joy, and in song, with my angel sisters, I take my leave, away to our arbors of love, in the midst of trailing vines and flowers, whose odor fills the Summer Land. To our beautiful homes, we go awaiting thy coming—dear father, mother, we wait your coming.—HELEN."

NOTE. The above was spoken in part to the parents of this spirit at the time her name was given, and has been repeated to us since. We having seen her and heard her in the spirit twice. And thus our work ended in Madison, the capital of Wisconsin.

Tuesday, June 22, found us in Reedsburg, Sauk county, before a large and skeptical audience. We spoke there four times in two days, to full houses and attentive listeners, giving many fine tests of spirit life, and facts in the lives of individuals present.

Before our coming, the friends of Spiritualism asked for, and obtained the use of the basement of the N. S. Presbyterian church.

The officers of the church informed Mr. Montross that he could not have the use of the same, for the reason that there was to be a conference of ministers of the district on the very days we were to have the use of the building, and that this meeting had been appointed long before our engaging the house, and that they, the officers, had overlooked the fact; hence, we could not have the use of the house. This upset our plan, and looked very much like a "sell," but nothing daunted, our friends came to the rescue, and by dint of perseverance, secured the postoffice hall in which to hold our meetings. A short time before our meeting came off, one of the leading men in the church went to the authorities, and suggested that the church put off their meeting one day and that Wilson speak twice on the first day, and that many persons who wanted to go to both meetings would be accommodated.

With a contemptuous expression of face, with sneer and curl of lips, the reply came, "We shall not postpone—let the spirits look to themselves," (or words to that effect.) This made the theological "nigger in the fence" show his teeth, and the wager of battle was accepted.

"Very well," said the gentleman, "you can do as you like. For one, I, and my family, will go and hear Wilson."

Things looked a little squally. One Spiritualist and medium with his spirits, "demons," according to the church, pitted against six or seven ministers and their Holy Spirit, backed by the authority of the church, to wrestle for the victory in a little town of eight hundred inhabitants. When the battle commenced, matters stood about thus:

Six ministers against one medium; seven hundred

and fifty Christians and unbelievers backed by public opinion, against forty or fifty Spiritualists and sympathizers. They took up position in the basement of the church: we, in the upper part of the postoffice. Each contending party were in position at 2 o'clock, P. M., and began shelling the town. They fired whole broadsides at a time of prayers, psalms and holy bullets of faith; fast and thick they fell. While from our side, we kept up a continuous flow of historical Bible grape, scientific canister, and spiritual bombshells, charged with the names, dates, incidents and facts of, and in the lives of those who were present, as well as of those who had passed away. Rapidly their ranks were thinned, and ours increased. Our scouts reported that at one time, the enemy was reduced to six officers and three men, and one or two nurses. Thus, the battle continued, until Wednesday evening, when Balaam's animal, one Peter Burns, burning with a desire to immortalize himself, came to the rescue, and demanded of us to be heard. We politely handed him over to our hearers, who decided he should stop that braying. Turning toward the audience, he roundly abused them for stifling public opinion, (?) being his individual self.

Things began to look serious, and the cry came from every quarter, "put him out," "out with him," several springing to their feet, when, lo! the arm of justice interfered, and Peter Burns "petered," and peace dwelt again in our midst. The victory was ours, with a house full of "freedom's sons and daughters," willing captives to our merciful and glorious gospel of joy and heaven for all, and sorrow and hell for none; our victory complete, our success grand, with stamps enough on hand at the close of the seven day's fight, to meet all expenses, and no one hurt save Peter Burns, and he but slightly.

Amidst the greetings of all, and the shaking of hands—with the request repeated by many, "Come again,"—we left for our home.

There are good and true men and women in Reedsburg, and we carry with us sweet memories of pleasant hours spent in the quiet and genial home of our host and his excellent lady, Mr. and Mrs. Young. Long may they live to enjoy their happy home.

God is good; the spirits true and faithful, and angels are our helpers.

The following tests were given in public at Reedsburg, Wisconsin:

*First.* Mr. Weaver; we see you in your sixteenth year, or rather we are told that in your sixteenth, you rescued a young friend from drowning; this is positive. It is a boy. Thirteen years ago, you were in financial trouble, caused by two parties. We then described one of them minutely, observing that he was a villain from head to heart. We get this from your sister; describing her carefully.

"Do you know anything about what he has told you, Mr. Weaver?" asked several, at the same time.

"Yes, it is correct," and as he has stated.

*Second.* Read the character of one of the audience, very carefully. Fully identified.

*Third.* Saw, by a person, the spirits of the father and mother, describing them very carefully. Fully recognized.

*Fourth.* Read the character of Messrs. McR. and W., calling attention comparatively to the sharp points in each. This reading created a good deal of amusement, and was fully identified by all that knew them, as well as by themselves. Heard the sister of Mr. W. say that she was present, but did not see her, Mr. D. stating, "I have lost a sister."

*Fifth.* With Dr. Danforth, saw a spirit, who said, "I am cousin Mary, and passed away at fifteen." We then gave a full description of her.

"I lost a cousin of the age and description given." said Mr. W., "and her name was Mary."

We then gave four prominent points or dates in his life, all of which he fully identified.

*Sixth.* We heard a spirit say "Julia is here; I am Julia."

We said, let the audience give no sign of recognition, and we will find the relative of this spirit in the audience. Soon we saw a light settle around the head of a lady, and in the light, the face and name of Julia. We pointed out the lady, described the face; gave the name; all of which was identified by the lady.

*Seventh.* Saw, by Mr. A. ——, a beautiful spirit boy, who came to him, put his hand on the knee of Mr. A., saying, "Papa, my papa."

We said, "Sir, this boy died very young, when a babe."

"Yes," said Mr. A., "I lost a little boy, six months old, some years ago."

*Eighth.* Saw, by Mr. Ellenwood, the spirit of an officer of the army, a second lieutenant; entered the army as such; was promoted; died in the service; knew you well and is now often about you as a spirit. Fully identified.

*Ninth.* We saw by this man, the spirits of an Indian and a white man, describing each carefully; the one speaks, and the other doctors through this man, whose name is Marsh, and he is a medium; all of which proved correct.

Many other readings and tests were given in public, and identified.

The following were given in private, and are good proofs of Spirit Life:

*First.* On entering the house of Mr. Samuel Montross, we saw by Mrs. M., a spirit, who said, "Sally Ann, Isaiah Williams is here with you. Did you ever know him?"

"No, I never knew any person by that name, and my name is not Sally Ann. There is, however, one by the name of Sally Ann in the house, and we know a man by the name of Williams, but not Isaiah."

*Second.* On entering the apartments of Mr. Enos Montross, we were introduced to his family; one his adopted daughter. When we took her hand in ours, we said, here is one who has fine mediumship, and may become a fine writing and seeing medium. It proved true, and she is a fine medium.

*Third.* While at Mr. Young's, we saw by his wife,

the spirit of her father, and entered into a minute delineation of his form and features, age and character. Mr. and Mrs. Young criticised the description sharply, differing with us in reference to the forehead, nose, chin and mouth. We reviewed the features, affirming our position, saying, if you have a photograph of him in the house, we can identify it. Mrs. Young then brought into the room, three albums, handing one to her husband, and holding one out to us, unopened. "His photograph is not in this; give us the other," we said. We took it, opened it, and pointed out his photograph. They then yielded the point.

Thus, are the spirits continually pushing the facts of another life upon us.

"They that believe on me, these signs shall follow them." Christians, what are the signs?

---

## CHAPTER XIII.

A Conversation with Elder Tanner, Mormon, of Salt Lake City, in 1869—A Talk with a Minister.

### *MORMONISM AND POLYGAMY.*

We were drinking water at the well of Brother G——, of Monroe, Wis., on Sunday, Aug. 1, 1869, when there came to the well two men (not angels), who inquired if Mr. G—— was at home. We answered "No." Offering them a drink of water, they partook freely; after which, one of them introduced the other as Mr. Tanner, of Salt Lake City.

*Tanner.* I am two thousand miles from home; have come twelve miles to hear you lecture to-day. I do not deny Spiritualism, for I read of it in the Bible. However, I know but little about it, hence I called to see you.

*Spiritualist.* I thank you. Walk in.

So we entered the house, and were seated; after which, the following conversation took place:

*S.* So you are a Mormon, and an Elder?

*T.* Yes; I am a Mormon, and an Elder.

*S.* Are you on a mission for the Saints?

*T.* No; I am on a visit here to the friends of my wife, who is with me. This man's wife is my wife's sister.

He pointed to the gentleman by his side.

After many questions and answers, on every subject pertaining to Mormonism, we asked, pointedly, if he was willing to talk on polygamy.

*T.* Yes, sir; and will give you correct answers.

*S.* Do you endorse polygamy, yourself?

*T.* Yes; it is right, and we practice it.

*S.* How many wives have you?

*T.* I have four wives with whom I am living when at home.

*S.* Are they with you now?

*T.* No; only one.

*S.* Were the rest of them willing for this one to come with you?

*T.* Yes; and desirous she should come.

*S.* Have you a favorite among them; or do you love them all as one woman.

*T.* My first wife takes precedence of the others, and I think the most of her.

*S.* How do you live — all under one roof together, as one family?

*T.* No; not as one family, but under the same roof; two of them live together in one apartment, and two of them live separately, in rooms by themselves.

*S.* Are your women quiet and passive, complying with your wish and will? Have you any trouble with them?

*T.* Oh! the usual differences of opinion, but nothing serious.

*S.* Suppose your wives, or any one of them, get dissatisfied, and wish to leave you; what then?

*T.* I give her a bill of divorce, and she is free to go.

*S.* Can she be accepted by another man, and taken in honor, according to your customs, as his wife, and retain her position in society?

*T.* Yes; and does so, too.

*S.* Have any of your wives left you?"

*T.* Yes; one of them.

*S.* What did you do in her case? And, if she had children, what was done with them? Who owns the children?

*T.* I gave her a bill. She had one child, and took it with her, she being capable of taking care of the child. Where they are not capable of taking care of the child, then the man retains the same. This woman is married again.

*S.* Will not this system of polygamy tend to immorality and prostitution?

*T.* By no means — but the reverse. There are no prostitutes in Salt Lake City or Utah. Such a thing as a house of ill-fame is not known in our country.

*S.* But is there any jealousies, heart-burnings, or dissatisfactions, with your wives, in regard to the society of the man or husband?

*T.* Yes; but we manage that without any trouble. We teach them to know that this course is for our mutual good.

*S.* Suppose wife No. 1 wants your company and society at the time you desire to be with No. 2 — wife No. 3 also claiming you, as her property, for the time being — what then?

*T.* We reason with them, and show them that it is best to be governed by our judgment. The difficulty is easily managed.

*S.* How many children have you by these wives of yours?

*T.* Sixteen; and sixteen grandchildren.

*S.* Are your daughters married and living under the same system; and do you countenance it?

*T.* They are married under our system, and we countenance it; and I, for one, teach it, by encouraging legitimate polygamy. We also encourage early marriage.

*S.* Are your women permitted the same liberty with men that you take with women?

*T.* We take no unlawful liberties.

*S.* We beg your pardon. Are your women permitted to have as many husbands as you have wives?

*T.* No; they are not.

*S.* Why?

*T.* Because we think it is not best; besides, they do not desire to have more than one man, and feel and know that our system is better calculated to maintain a sound, healthy physical and mental condition than yours. Your women are prematurely old, and die early in life. Again, fœticides are rife in fashionable society, but never with us.

*S.* Suppose one of your wives should be taken in adultery, what would be the results to her? what her punishment?

*T.* She would be dealt with according to law, and punished for her offense.

*S.* And the man, if taken in the act of adultery; what of him?

*T.* Punished by a swift and sure punishment. We have no such cases, however.

*S.* Have you given woman any voice in this matter of plurality of wives, or polygamy?

*T.* We compel no woman to become sealed to us.

*S.* What do you mean by "sealed to us"?

*T.* When a woman is set apart, by the authority of our Government, as the wife of any one man.

*S.* In such cases, do you consult the friends, guardian, or parents, if a minor?

*T.* Yes; always. No woman is taken to our homes against her will, or just opposition of friends.

*S.* I have been informed to the contrary, by those who have left your ranks.

*T.* That may be. But, sir, you must remember that those who informed you are renegades. Traitors are always bitter in your own ranks. Who are so bitter as those who go over to the enemy.

*S.* Suppose Brigham Young should receive a revelation to do away with polygamy; what would be the result?

*T.* There is no supposition about it. Polygamy will continue; it is one of the fixed institutions of Mormonism, and we shall come into the Union of the States with polygamy.

*S.* Did Joseph Smith endorse polygamy?

*T.* Yes; and received a revelation to that effect.

*S.* His sons deny it.

*T.* It makes no difference what they deny. I knew Joseph Smith well, and know that he endorsed polygamy.

*S.* How long have you been a Mormon?

*T.* Since Mormonism was a year and five months organized. I was with them in Kirtland, Ohio, Missouri, Illinois, and went with them to the plains.

*S.* And you are firm in your conviction that you are right; that Mormonism is a fixture in America, and will continue?

*T.* I am; and I know that we are right!

*S.* I frankly say to you, sir, that from all I have read and heard of Mormonism, and from what you have said to-day, that I am an unbeliever in the doctrines, teachings, and practices, of polygamy; and, further, that it is a system of oppression, on the part of man, against woman. Now, sir, I am a Spiritualist, and frankly say to you, I do not believe in your system, and, at the same time, confess that I know nothing about your system, or the social workings of polygamy; and, with this frank statement, will you, as an Elder, and in authority, permit me to teach my views, criticise yours, examine into its system and workings, as I examine and criticise other denominations in this part of the country? What say you, for I may cross the plains next summer?

*T.* I will guarantee you perfect freedom of speech; you shall speak in our halls, or tabernacles; you shall be my guest, and a welcome one; and I wish you to come.

Thus ended our conversation with Elder Tanner. It was in the presence of several witnesses — men and women. The Elder was under a sharp, running cross-fire, and he stood it well — perfectly cool, all through the conversation, manifesting that calm, gentlemanly conduct that said, in so many words, "I am master of my position." We dare not attack him from the Bible standpoint, for the Bible sustains polygamy; but we do not, though he does.

The conversation lasted full two hours. We have endeavored to follow the conversation between us, not touching the side fires. We wish, however, we had a verbatim report of all that was said, by all the parties that were present.

For instance: One lady, of culture and brains, came in from another room, and, in great excitement, and with a vim, said: "I have come into this room to see a man that has four wives, and dares to say so."

Said the Mormon, very calmly, "I am the man; you now see me."

"It's well for you that I ain't one of your wives, I can tell you that; for, if I were, I would make it too warm for you," said the woman.

"We would have no trouble; and I would win you over to respect and love me, by kindness," said the Mormon.

"Not with your affections divided with others," said the woman.

We turned our eyes toward an open door, and there we witnessed that which would have made Hogarth shout for joy, for there we saw a young miss, with mind intent on vengeance dire, in defiant attitude, standing; her eyes sparkling with resentment; lips firm, compressed, white and thin; with strong resolve to resent this monstrous sin, her tiny fingers working with vengeance deep into the palms of her snow-white hands; she stood erect, a gentle Amazon, ready to meet, in domestic strife, the oppressor of her sex. It was a beautiful sight — this human, living and breathing statuary, that spoke louder than words, "Mortal man, beware; for, with undivided love, I am gentle as a lamb, but if betrayed, take care."

After the Elder had left, we asked our young friend

what she thought of the man with four wives, and her answer was: "If I were one of them, there would be a funeral!"

From all we saw and heard, on both sides, we agree with our fair, young friend.

Surely, readers, we are approaching a crisis on this question of polygamy. The demands of ninety thousand people are not to be winked at, or treated lightly. In ten years from this time, there will be a fearful tragedy enacted on the plains of Utah, and Mormonism will be crushed out in blood, or become a fixture in the land. Which shall it be?

## *A TALK WITH A MINISTER.*

The following conversation took place in 1869, at B——, Wisconsin, between the Rev. Mr. H. and the writer:

*W.* Mr. H., we would like to ask a few questions of you, in regard to your religious views. Will you permit us to do so?

*H.* Most certainly; and will give you candid answers.

*W.* Thank you. What is your guide in religious matters; reason, faith, or the Bible?

*H.* The Bible is our only guide; by it we must walk.

*W.* Are we not to exercise our reason on these things? Have we no right to think?

*H.* I cannot exercise my reasoning powers. I

must accept the Bible, through faith, as the revealed word of God and his Christ.

*W.* But I am so constituted that I have no faith; I never had. God has given me reason; shall I exercise it?

*H.* No; not in things pertaining to God.

*W.* But how am I to know what pertains to God, unless I exercise my reasoning faculties?

*H.* We must take the Bible and abide by it.

*W.* But here are the Catholics — no mean power; they condemn the Protestants, as well as the King James version of the Bible. You, as a Protestant, condemn the Catholics and their version of the Holy Scriptures. Here is an exercise of reason. Which of you are right?

*H.* We are not so far apart as you think. We believe in one thing, and that is the divinity of Christ, and in the atonement — the power of the blood of the Lamb to save.

*W.* Then why not harmonize, and worship under one system of theology?

*H.* For the reason that we do not agree on church government, and the manner of the communion of the Lord's supper.

*W.* Then you do exercise your reason in regard to the meaning of the Bible?

*H.* No; not in regard to the authenticity of the Bible, but in the meaning of the Bible.

*W.* Is not that reason? and are you not reasoning when you differ with others in regard to the import of the Bible?

*H.* O, well! so far as the rules of church government may be concerned, we exercise our reason, and no further.

*W.* Is your house the house of God, and the only house of God?

*H.* Yes; our house is dedicated to God, and we use it as such, and for no other purpose.

*W.* Is the Catholic house the house of God?

*H.* Y-e-s; as they understand the Bible.

*W.* Is not your position an exercise of your reason?

*H.* Only in accordance with the Bible, harmonizing with God's revelations.

*W.* Where, in the Bible, do you find authority for the teachings of Protestantism?

*H.* We find it in the teachings of the Old, and more especially the New Testament.

*W.* And then Protestantism, and especially your church doctrines, are the results of human conclusions. Is not this the reasoning of man?

*H.* Yes; but it is the reasonings of revelation also.

*W.* Through you, or some one else?

*H.* Through the apostles and the prophets, who were just men, inspired of God.

*W.* So declared by the councils of the past.

*H.* We consider that we are right.

*W.* And so do the Catholics; but they condemn your views, even to the extent of burning your Bibles, and you condemn them.

*H.* And yet, they believe as we do; that is, in the

divine authenticity of the Bible, and the power of the blood of Jesus to save.

*W.* That brings us back again to the original starting point — reason. Is it finite or infinite reason?

*H.* We accept the infinite reason.

*W.* The Catholics, being evangelical in their teachings, will you let them use your church for worship, or preach from your pulpit?

*H.* No; and if asked to do so, should frankly say to them, "No; you cannot use my pulpit!"

*W.* But they believe in the evangelical idea of atonement, and salvation through the blood of Jesus Christ, as the only means of grace.

*H.* True; but they do not agree with us.

*W.* So they say of you. Here, again, we find you in the full exercise of your reasoning faculties. Plainly, Mr. H., what denominations are you willing to let into your pulpit, or permit to worship in your house?

*H.* The evangelical churches only.

*W.* Who are evangelical?

*H.* The Old and New School Presbyterians, Congregationalists, Methodists, Baptists, and their branches, only.

*W.* Are not the Swedenborgians believers in Christ?

*H.* Yes.

*W.* Would you exclude them from your pulpit?

*H.* Most certainly.

*W.* Then you would exclude every denomination except those mentioned a short time ago?

*H.* Yes, sir; I certainly would.

*W.* What of the Christian, or Campbellite church? Would you let them use your pulpit?

*H.* I should frankly say to them, as I would to you, "You cannot use our church; I cannot, in conscience, permit you to worship God, after your way, in my church."

*W.* Here you are, acting from reason again.

*H.* No; I am only carrying out the teaching of my Master, and his word — the Bible.

*W.* Then your faith in the power of the blood of Jesus to save is your only rule of action?

*H.* Most certainly.

*W.* Let me make a case. The father of A. and J. is an Old School Baptist; their mother, a very liberal Methodist; on Sundays, they attend their respective churches; the father orders A. and J. to accompany him to the Baptist Church; the mother countermands the order, and bids them go with her. Which should the boys go with?

*H.* The father, of course, he being the head of the house.

*W.* Is not the mother's wish to be considered of any value, in regard to her children's religious education? Has she no voice in the matter?

*H.* The father's will is law in this case.

*W.* Well, supposing A. elects to go with the mother, and J. with the father — both children being minors — what then?

*H.* Again the father's will should be the law, and the mother, as well as the children, be guided by him.

*W.* Is the mother, in this case, exercising her faith, or reason, or either? Is she not, in fact, through your decision, deprived of faith, reason, and the right to worship God after the dictates of her own heart, or soul?

*H.* N-o-t a-l-t-o-g-e-t-h-e-r.

*W.* Well, let us carry the case a little further. A. says: "Father, I elect to go with mother, and do not believe with you, and prefer to go to the Methodist Church; I do not believe in election and fore-ordination." The father says: "My boy, you have no voice in this matter; you shall go to church with me." And the boy is compelled to leave his mother, and go with his father. Is this right?

*H.* Yes; the father is responsible to God and society for the present character and future welfare of the soul of A., and is justified in coercing the lad into obeying him.

*W.* Again we ask, where was the mother's rights? or had she none?

*H.* The mother has rights, but not to the extent of supplanting the father and husband, in his right to control the religious training of his children.

*W.* Let us look at the results through this compulsion. A year later, A. left his home — fled from paternal oppression, though loved by his father — and is to-day a man of power and influence in the land, while J., who was elected, and remained at home, died, a few years ago, at Panama, South America, a confirmed drunkard. Who was the elected one?

*H.* (With marked surprise.) This is a very rare case, and only one in a thousand.

*W.* You are mistaken; it is of frequent occurrence. "For the children of this world are, in their generation, wiser than the children of light." But, candidly, Mr. H., if, as a man, you could refuse honest men and women the right to worship in the house of God, under your control, here on earth, would you? And would you, if you were God, exclude all these denominations from Heaven, as you exclude them from your church?

*H.* (Much embarrassed.) What do you mean?

*W.* I mean this: If you were God, instead of man, would you, as God, expel from Heaven, or refuse to save, any one, or all, of the denominations rejected by you as a human being, man, and minister of the Gospel?

*H.* I understand you, and decline to answer the question; but you may rest assured of one thing, and that is, I would be just in either case.

*W.* Is it just, to exclude those denominations from worshiping in your God's house here on earth?

*H.* Yes; from my standpoint. The bells are ringing, and I must go.

*W.* And the bells of Heaven are ringing for volunteers to put down this damnable theology, for what this man would do on earth he will do in Heaven; and, as we need not expect mercy at his hands here, or hereafter, we must "fight it out on this line, if it takes all eternity." And now let us to the battle of God, and the victory is ours. Let the bells ring!

# CHAPTER XIV.

The Parting with Mary — The Prayer for Farmer Mary's Sake — The Test.

## *TOUR IN MICHIGAN.*

Friday evening, November 1, 1872, we left the home of Farmer Mary and our little ones, for a tour of forty-two days in the fruitful State of Michigan, Farmer Mary accompanying us on our way as far as Chicago. Ah! my Mary, long years we have stood side by side amid the storm and sunshine of life. Sometimes the wolf has placed his huge paws on the threshhold, showing his fangs in hunger to us, and yet we have had our daily bread. Thanks be to the All Father and the dear old Mother God, whose children we are, we live, are well, and are prospered. We have a home, and darling boys and girls to comfort and cheer us as we walk down the hill of life toward the vale of the Summer Land. At eight o'clock we bade each other good-bye — Farmer Mary to our home returned — we to the work of the Gods.

At half-past nine, P. M., we were in our berth in the sleeping car, thinking of one who, eighteen hundred and thirty-nine years ago, was shivering in the cold, going on foot from one town of Judea to another, at the rate of twenty or thirty miles in twenty-four hours, teaching the Infidel Jews Spiritualism. And then we thought of the cruel murder of this man by the priests of the age, and of the fearful death of his disciples; and then we thought of our own work and the disciples and apostles of Spiritualism as it is in our time, and the enmity of all the priests of our day. And thus comparing, we wondered if Jesus had ever dreamed of a time in the future when the medium could lie down at night in a comfortable bed, and the next morning find himself two or three hundred miles from his starting place, or that he could send his word around the world in forty minutes. While we were thus communing, we heard a voice in prayer, and thus it said: "O God, I pray Thee to watch over this train of cars, and these precious souls, in their swift flight over the iron rail to-night; and I pray Thee, oh! my Savior, to accompany Thy servant on his journey, and at its end to bless him by seeing him safely there. Strengthen me, O God, to do my duty and to do it well — all of which favors we ask for Christ's sake. Amen." Well, my Gentle Wilson, where are your prayers? we asked. Then we prayed: "Oh! Pullman, we thank thee for this magnificent sleeping car. Oh! Michigan Central Railroad Company, we thank thee for this well-ordered and well-balanced railway, trusting our precious body in the hands of — first, the engineer; second, the conductor; third, the brakesmen, and lastly we commit ourselves into thy hands, oh! Michigan Central Railroad Company, for the next forty-two days, and beseech thee to employ only such servants as will keep a sharp look-out, remain sober, and land us safely at last in our home. One favor more we ask, oh! Michigan Central Railroad, that you may be moved to send the Gentle Wilson a half-fare ticket over all the railways you own or control — all of which favors we ask for Farmer Mary's sake. Amen?" And as we finished our praying, the praying man inquired, "I say, stranger, are you a Christian?"

"No, sir!"

"Christian or no Christian," said a farmer in the berth opposite us, "we on this side second that prayer."

"All those in favor of the prayer for Farmer Mary's sake, will manifest it by saying 'I,'" exclaimed a voice in the berth next to us, and "I, I, I," came down the aisle of the car. "The I's have it!" exclaimed our burly friend, and we went to sleep.

Saturday, November 2, found us at Jackson at 4.30 A. M., waiting for the train for Bay City via Jackson, Lansing and Saginaw Railroad. While sitting in the depot, we heard the following conversation:

"Who was that fellow who prayed to Pullman and the Michigan Central Railroad Company last night?" asked one man of another.

"I don't know; but one thing is certain — he ought to be prosecuted for blasphemy."

"What did he say?" we asked.

"Oh, he thanked Pullman and the Michigan Central Railroad Company for good sleeping cars, and then asked for half-fare tickets — all for Farmer Mary's sake."

"Well, my friend, had he not a right to ask such

favors? and does not the Bible teach us that whatsoever we desire believing, we shall receive?"

"All aboard for Lansing, Saginaw and Bay City!" shouted the conductor; and in a few moments we were once more rolling on our way over the iron rail to our point of destination, Bay City.

We delivered eight lectures there — held three afternoon meetings on Sundays, and four Monday evening seances, and attended one social. Our meetings were well attended, the audiences giving marked attention, and for the first time the society has not had to draw on private funds to any extent to pay their speaker, the collections and benefits reaching one hundred and twelve dollars all told. This is well, and as it should be. We gave many fine tests of spirit-life while in Bay City, as well as readings of character — among which we think the following worthy of record:

*First.* To a lady, a Mrs. H——: "There is with you a spirit girl who died as a child, and she is your sister Mary." This statement was corroborated to the letter.

*Second.* Turning to a man, we said: "Sir, we see you at fourteen years of age stepping forth into life, your own master. At twenty, we find you taking upon yourself responsibilities of an onerous character. At twenty-seven we see you in a storm of excitement — your life is in danger and you barely escape. What say you?"

"You are right, sir. At fourteen years of age I ran away from home and became my own master. At twenty-seven I was in the army, and in that year I was in several battle storms."

*Third.* To a lady: "We see you in sorrow and grief eleven years ago. This is in July. In September a light goes out from you. It is the spirit life of a woman — your mother and child."

"Yes, eleven years ago I buried my mother and child."

*Fourth.* To a man who sat in the rear part of the house: "We see with this man a woman. She is his sister, and she gives me the following fact: 'We see him in a struggle with a horse — he is thrown and severely hurt. He is eleven years old.'" We fully described the horse. "At fifteen years of age we see him struggling in the water with another whom he rescues from drowning. At twenty years, he cuts loose from all control and changes every surrounding in life. At twenty-four he takes upon him new relations that affect him socially, locally and pecuniarily. At thirty-two, sickness, sorrow and grief are with him. At thirty-eight we see a change locally that culminates in what and where he now is." We then read his character as a man, described his father and mother. "What say you, sir, to this reading — are we right or wrong?"

Slowly the man rose up, asking, "Do you mean me, sir?"

"Yes; and we do not want you to favor us."

"Well, sir, I shall not. I don't know how you do these things, for I am not a Spiritualist, nor have I ever seen you before, and yet every word you have spoken is true. The incident as being with the horse is remarkably true. The scar is here on my head to-night; in fact, it is wonderfully true!'

"How about the sister?"

"That is true."

The people were very much surprised at these verifications.

## *MICHIGAN CITY, INDIANA.*

E. V. Wilson has just delivered a course of three lectures at Union Hall in this city, a full description of which would be more of a task than my pen is able to give. Our large hall was completely crowded, jammed full, every vacant place, sitting and standing, with the intelligent, thinking portion of the people. Many were turned away in consequence of there not being room inside of the building to contain them.

We have had many very eloquent speakers here during the last political campaign, among whom were our honored statesmen, O. P. Morton and Schuyler Colfax, and I believe that everybody will agree with me that neither one of them have excelled Brother Wilson in eloquence and logic. He is nature's own orator, and his subject was "Modern Spiritualism." The effect of the grand truths delivered, and the tremendous power with which they were driven home, will last until many generations shall have passed away. We could hardly restrain our tears when we took Brother Wilson by the hand to bid him good-bye, remembering his words of truth and love, and that we should perhaps never meet him again on this side of the river.

He gave upwards of one hundred tests, all but a very few of which were correct beyond a doubt. We can say truly, that in Michigan City, never before did "man speak as this man spake."

L. S. Hart.

*Michigan City, Ind., Dec.* 11, 1872.

---

## CHAPTER XV.

The Visit to Saugatuck—The Inquisitive Man—The Fire Fiend—The Minister, his Wrath—The Return Home.

### *THE VISIT TO SAUGATUCK.*

Friday, July 12th, 1872, we left for Saugatuck, Mich., speaking Friday and Saturday evenings to a numerous audience, giving many fine tests, and creating a marked interest. There are many earnest inquirers after immortality in this city and vicinity, and some as true workers as there are in the world. The Cooks, father and son, Mr. Morrison and others, are up and ready to work, every time. Brothers J. M. Peebles and C. E. Dunn were in hot water here a few years ago, passing through the ordeal of mob law, instigated by the officers and leaders of society. How changed to-day! Our speakers come and go at will; are heard and paid in some cases by those who mobbed them the year before.

Sunday, July 14th, we spoke at Fennville, to good audiences, having a right good time. Truly, the Spiritualists of Saugatuck, Plummersville, Ganges and Fennville, are a host in more senses than one. They are numerous, honest, generous, truthful and ready to do. We love them, and always have a good time when with them.

Monday morning, July 15th, at four o'clock, we were on the rail and away to Muskegon. We spoke here to full houses for three evenings, and one evening at Port Sherman, at the mouth of the river. Brothers Rogers, Ingalls and others, are honest and earnest workers in our cause.

Friday, July 19th, we left Muskegon for Pentwater and Hart, Mich., speaking in these places four times, having large audiences and giving many fine tests. At Hart we had a joyous time, and many were aroused to think deeply of their future. We found many inquirers in all of these places, and really an earnest desire for the truth as it is in Spiritualism.

The following incident occured on the day we left Chicago, and when near Michigan City. A young man very abruptly asked us:

"Are you a second Jesus?"

"No, sir! we never play second fiddle. Why did you ask that question?"

"Are you not a Spiritualist?"

"Yes, sir; we are."

"I thought so."

"Why did you think so?"

"Because you Spiritualists always look happy, and seem to have no fear of death, hell and the judgment; in fact, you have no God, no future punishment."

"Where did you learn all this of Spiritualism?"

"Well, I have known many, read of more, and heard from others."

"Well, sir," we replied, "we are happy, believe in one God, a spirit, and worship him in spirit. We have no hell-fire to cast our enemies into, but punishment for every offense, and yet give the offender an opportunity to improve, and live a better life. We know that we are immortal and progressive, and that our soul's rights to progress are not based on Gods, churches, devils nor hell, hence we are happy."

"Well, sir, I can do nothing of myself. My future depends not on me, but on my Savior; he alone can save me. He will bear the burden of my offense; his blood will make me white as snow; in him my salvation is sure."

"Well, my friend, we prefer reason to faith; work to prayer; practice to profession; love to hate, and responsibility to the want thereof. We shall save ourselves, and Jesus will not bear the burden of our offense."

Standing with his eyes open, his mouth ajar, and his nose expanded, he exclaimed:

"You are lost! lost!! lost!!!"

"We are not," we replied. "We know just where

we are, where we are going, and when we will return."

"Michigan City!" shouted the brakesman, and we parted; he in sadness, following Jesus; we in joy, following our nose.

At New Buffalo we were detained several hours on the platform of the station. We asked of a stranger if he knew a Mr. J. O. Smith, or a Mrs. Beson.

"Do you know 'em?"

"We ask you if you know these people," we replied.

"Wall, I reckon you're an old friend of Mrs. Beson's?"

"That is not our question, sir."

"Do they owe you anything?"

"We asked you, sir, if you knew these people; will you answer, yes or no?"

"You're from the East, I think, ain't you?"

"No, sir; we are from the West. Will you tell us whether you know these people?"

"Are you a lawyer?"

"No."

"Maybe you're a doctor?"

"No."

"Out collecting?"

"No."

"What church do you belong to?"

"The church of humanity."

"Then you're a minister?"

"No."

"Well, you're a Christian?"

"No."

"What in thunder are you?"

"We are a speaker and teacher in Spiritualism. Do you know J. O. Smith, or Mrs. Beson? Yes or no."

"Wall, yes; Smith lives out here about four miles, and Miss Beson has gone away, I believe. I say, Mister, kin you find an ile well? for if you kin, I'll give you five dollars to find one for me."

"Yes, sir; we can find an 'ile well' for you, and tell you just where it is, and warrant it to flow two hundred barrels a day, for five dollars."

In a moment there were a half dozen men ready with their five dollars, to take a share in the oil well, and among them a young man looking every inch the minister.

"Are you a minister?" we asked.

"Yes, sir."

"Well, let us form an 'ile company' here, and make you the President."

"I must first know where it is, sir, before I take any interest in it."

"Well," we replied, "when we get the five dollars we will locate the well."

"Wall, stranger, I must know the country where it is before I invest."

"Will you organize and invest when we name the country?"

"Yes; if it is possible."

"It is perfectly possible," we replied, "and our friend, the minister, will testify to the correctness of our statement.

"Name the place," cried all present.

We replied, "The well is hell; the oil, the fat of sinners, and there is a world of it."

Our minister turned red; our friend, the questioner, turned pale; all looked blue, and the project was abandoned; but we did not find Smith or Beson.

At Grand Junction the fire king swept everything before it last fall. Observing to a stranger:

"You suffered terribly here from the fire last fall."

"Yes; God in his mercy scourged us with fire fearfully."

"Are you a Christian, sir?"

"Yes; I trust I am."

"Do you love God?"

"Yes; with all my heart."

"And have served him faithfully?"

"Yes; to the best of my ability."

"And this is the way you are paid off for your loyalty, love and service!"

Turning sharply upon us, with a frown on his face, his fingers clenched, his hand menacingly extended, he asked:

"Do you mean to insult me?" and he spoke with a hiss.

"No; we do not mean to insult you, and yet, if the coat fits you, put it on, for they who charge God with scourging his own people — women and children — are guilty of grossly insulting Deity."

"Who are you, sir, that dare insult me, and the people of this section of the country?"

"I am the voice of one crying in the wilderness. Get out of the way of the Lord, for his chariot is coming, and his name is Spiritualism. I am E. V. Wilson, 'the gentle,' and am going to Saugatuck to speak and give tests, and now tender you half of our time. Come, and raise your altar, and kindle your fire, and consume us."

"I will have nothing to do with you, sir."

"Good-bye," and we moved on.

At Muskegon, we had a stirring time with one whose great trouble was, he was not certain whether he made God, or God made him, but will learn when the fool-catcher comes along next Spring.

We returned home by steamboat from Muskegon, having a very pleasant trip, making many friends, speaking fifteen times. Pentwater, Muskegon, and Saugatuck, are lumbering towns, doing a fine trade, and are live places. Hart is a nice little place, only wanting a railroad to make it become a great place. We like our Michigan friends; they are all good.

---

## CHAPTER XVI.

### *A REMARKABLE COINCIDENT.*

On Sunday, at half past three o'clock, P. M., June 16, 1872, at a seance given in the Old School House, at West Mitchell, Mitchell county, Iowa, we saw two ladies, sitting side by side, dressed in black — in fact, in deep mourning. We felt a strong influence from spirit-life drawing us toward them. Walking to their seats, under influence, and stretching out our right hand toward them, we spoke very nearly as follows:

"Greetings, friends — sisters of mine — from my home in the Summer Land; joyous greetings we bring you, on the shores of time."

Then, stepping to our place, we turned to the people, saying: "Do not think we have chosen these two ladies because they are in mourning, for that of which we speak is from a brother of these ladies, who died seven years ago, and says, 'that if just treatment had been extended toward me, to-day I would not be a spirit, but a mortal, sensate man, loving and loved in return.'"

At this point, one of the ladies fainted away, becoming unconscious, and causing the influence to lose its hold — it was gone.

During the afternoon and evening there was much comment in reference to the statement, and the general opinion was, that we had made a great blunder — first, in addressing them as "friends — sisters mine," for they were not sisters, and only knowing each other less than a year — one an English woman, and the other an American — one a wife, and the other single; second — the opinion gained ground that we, seeing them in black, guessed the cause, but had lost the case. Our reply to our friend — we never make any to our enemies, save in hard blows — was: "Wait and see the glory of God."

And now for the glory. At ten o'clock P. M., October 9, 1872, on our way from our lecture, in the Town House, of West Mitchell, Iowa, a gentleman accosted us, thus:

"A cool evening, Mr. Wilson."

"Yes, sir; and it is the time of year for cool evenings," we replied.

"You don't know me," said our man.

"No, sir," we replied.

"Do you remember the young woman, in black, who fainted, last summer, when you were here?"

"Very well, sir; what do you know about her?"

"Before I answer your question, can you tell me why you addressed those ladies — admitting, as you claim, speaking as the spirit — 'Friends — sisters mine,' for they were in no way related, and had known each other only a year, or a little over?"

"We can't answer that question. We remember the fact, however."

"Well," said our friend of the evening, "one of those ladies is my wife; the other — the one who fainted — only a friend on a visit to our house, who came over from London a little over a year ago. On reaching home, she told us that, seven years and three months ago, she lost a brother, under very peculiar circumstances, and that the address, and the mentioning that the spirit was a brother, caused the fainting. But, said I, the spirit addressed both of you; why this? Here we were in a mystery, and we considered the testimony blocked. A night or two after, we were again canvassing the matter, and I remembered that my wife had lost a brother. Turning to her, I asked how long since her brother died. She replied, five or six years ago. Said, I let us get at the exact time; and when we had reached the fact, we found that my wife's brother had been in the spirit world seven years less three months. A remarkable coincident!"

Yes, reader, a remarkable coincident! and we venture the assertion that there is not another such a case in Mitchell county, if there is in the State of Iowa, for these immortal brothers to unite as one mind and address their sisters as "friends — sisters mine," and yet these women were far apart when the brothers were born again. Neither the sisters nor brothers had ever known each other. Remarkable coincident! These inspirations from life in the Summer Land, carrying glad tidings from beyond the River of Death, that flows between the Christian and his God — flashes of light from the soul's future — are our attractions, and they have left "The Gates Ajar," and watchers are waiting for us to come; some, more anxious, come down to us.

How beautifully Sister Emma Tuttle touches the soul, in her "Lights and Shadows":

"Ah, she comes! Love light is streaming
From her eyes, with beauty gleaming,
Brighter far than Memory's dreaming
Of their earnest, faded light."

"Like wan Grief to Gladness kneeling,
Come sweet feeling, o'er me stealing,
With the beauteous revealing
Of the angel pure and bright."

### *ANOTHER REMARKABLE COINCIDENCE.*

At the same meeting in which we gave the previous remarkable coincident, we stated that there was the spirit of a woman here, who says she took the law into her own hands, committing suicide by poison, nine years ago. We then described her minutely, but got no name. Again our enemies were jubilant, and our friends uneasy, but we, leaning on our staff, replied, "Wait, and see the glory of God."

Last night, October 9, the glory came, and the victory was ours.

At the conclusion of our lecture and test-giving, a gentleman in the audience arose, saying, "The medium sitting by my side saw the spirit of a woman in the aisle of the house, who told her that, nine years ago, she committed suicide by taking poison, and that she left a written statement of the fact."

A gentleman present stated that it was a fact, and that it was nine years ago this summer, and her name was Owen.

Again our vision was verified, and the truth prevailed, and our seers agreed that each saw alike. Thus, in the mouths of two or three witnesses the truths of Spiritualism are verified. Truly, our religion is a religion of knowledge, and not a religion of faith.

# CHAPTER XVII.

The Steam Engine and Its Eccentricities — No. 30 — Jim Smith's Advice.

*THE STEAM ENGINE AND ITS ECCENTRICITIES.*

"Engine 61, on the Erie Railway, at one time became so erratic that no engineer would run her. She invariably ran off the track before her trips were completed, and caused continual delays and annoyance on the road, and yet our best men could detect no fault in the machinery. Afterward, of her own accord, she did her work up properly."

We copy the above from the "Banner of Light," No. 9, Vol. 24. In addition, give a story we heard an old engineer tell:

Once upon a time, when I was running an engine between London and Liverpool, England, my engine got ugly, and would not work. I made a careful examination of her machinery, but found nothing the matter. Sometimes she would not make steam; again would make too much; and that, too, when everything was equal. One night — I remember it well; I was then running into Liverpool; it was a cloudy, damp night — we had a heavy train, and had on a heavy head of steam; I put my hand upon the throttle lever, and felt a sharp, magnetic shock. Says I to Jim — you see, Jim was my fireman — "the old engine is going to talk again."

Says Jim: "How do you know?"

"Cause," says I, "she says so."

"How does she speak?" says Jim.

"With lightning," says I. "Just you touch that 'ere lever, and you will hear her speak."

And Jim did so, and you 'd have laughed to see him take his hand off.

"D—n the thing," says Jim; "she 's full of lightning."

Well, soon my pet was mad, and refused to work. I had been used to these tricks of hers, and always knew they were coming whenever I felt these electric currents. So I says to Jim, "We will wait a little, and may be she will conclude to go on."

Soon Old 30 began to back up, and at this moment I saw the hand of a man on the reverse lever. I raised my eyes and looked again, but the hand was gone. At this moment, the bell was struck once, and I looked forward, and there stood a man as large as life. Jim and I both saw him very plain.

Says I, "What are you doing there?"

Then there was a strange laugh, and the man was gone; and the old engine went on about her business, as usual.

Jim and I concluded we would say nothing about the man we had seen. So, when it was time for our engine to go out again, we concluded to keep a sharp look out for our man, and the lightning warning. Well, it came—the lightning—and soon I saw my man, and this time by my side, as natural as life; but Jim did not see him.

Says I, "What, in hell, do you want?"

Says he, "Take care, Bob; do not use such words. Don't you know me?"

And then I looked at him, sharply, and says I, "My God! you are Jack Smith, that was killed by a smash-up fifteen miles this side of Y——."

"Yes," says Jack; "but I am not dead; and I take this method of impressing and informing you of my presence; and whenever you feel this electric current, you may know that I am near you, and you must be on your guard, for there is danger ahead."

Well, this continued four or five years, and then I left England for America, but I have not seen or heard from Jim since I came to this country.

I give this story as I heard it, and in connection with the one quoted from the "Banner of Light." It suggests to me the facts of an engine I once examined, in Milwaukee, in 1861-2, that, at times, was so heavily charged with electricity, it could not be used; and yet the conductor, engineer, and others of the M. M. P. R. R., could not account for the phenomena. On one occasion, when examining the engine, I put my hand on one of the levers, and felt the electric current at once; instantly I saw a spirit; it was the spirit of an engineer that had been killed on the road west of Wakesha, sometime before, and was identified by my description.

My friend, Dr. Roberts, directs me to give the following theory to the world. It is this:

Magnetism, so called, is the human agent, and electricity the spiritual agent, through which mortals and immortals commune with each other. Friction produces electricity. The great amount of friction required for draft, or power to hold on and draw at the same time, rapidly generates electricity; and the engine, being a magnet of great attractive power, in rapid motion becomes surcharged with electric fluids, and when in motion, generates faster than it discharges; hence, electric explosions take place, sometimes strong enough to lift the engine, make it jump up, and occasionally flounder and bounce off of the track. The Doctor suggests copper rods, attached to the engines, and so arranged as to trail on the ground. Reason: Copper rods are not attractors of magnetism, or electricity, but are good conductors of either. He also says, that when an engine is fully charged with electricity, it becomes a good battery for spirits to manifest through, and that whenever the magnetism of the conductor, engineer, or fireman, will warrant phenomena, then the spirits can and will communicate.

Will some railroad engineer try the copper rods, when his engine gets balky, and refuses to work? Can any one give a better reason for these freaks of the engine?

# CHAPTER XVIII.

Spiritualism in Syracuse, New York — Dr. Jared B. Parker — The School Teacher — Lieutenant Charles George.

## *SPIRITUALISM IN SYRACUSE, NEW YORK.*

We lectured in Syracuse on Tuesday, Wednesday, Thursday and Friday afternoon and evening, January, 1869. Our audiences averaged from four to five hundred. There have been very few lectures on this subject in Syracuse, and to very small audiences. Many of the friends in the city were afraid that the lectures would be a failure; but knowing no such thing as failure in our Spiritualism, we visited Syracuse, and we think that we gained a great victory.

Our meetings were held in the court house, and resulted in a grand success for free lectures. Our audiences averaged five hundred. We gave over one hundred approved tests and communications, among which are the following:

While lecturing Tuesday evening, January 5, there came upon the platform the spirit of a tall, spare man, dark complexion, over fifty, gray hair, very much attenuated, and said:

"I am Jacob Hulin. I used to live in this city, on Pearl street, and died twenty-six years ago. There are many in the house I know."

"Does any one identify this man?" we asked.

"We do," many answered.

Next came a spirit, or immortal man, small of form, dark complexion, face broad and full of wrinkles, forehead large and receding, hair thin, dark and mingled with gray; and he said, "I am an old citizen of this place, and died here a few years ago. I know many here. I am Doctor Jared B. Parker."

Many exclaimed, "We knew him."

We then gave many minor tests, and concluded by reading the life-history of Mr. Van Tassel, once a Methodist minister, now an honored and true apostle of the gospel of truth. The reading of his life-history was pronounced exceedingly accurate.

Wednesday. Private conversation. Present, four persons.

"Mrs. ——, I see you at nineteen years of age, in costume, on some public occasion. You are standing with a group of ladies. Suddenly there is wild confusion, and there lies at your feet a dead man, describing him. The diamond ring on your finger has a sad history. There is blood on it; it is associated with a death — a suicide. There is a dagger, small and of exquisite workmanship; it rests in an open hand over the ring, and with the point to you."

She answered, "It is strictly true — too true."

In the presence of a full house, the brothers H—— came from the spirit land, gave their names, told how they were killed, and when. A second group came; one was Mr. G. Brayton; the other gave his name as Elisha Ladd. He told when he was killed, where, and how. These two spirits were fully described, and at once identified.

We delineated the character of Mr. S., a well known citizen, and the reading was pronounced exceedingly correct.

While lecturing, Thursday evening, January 7, there came upon the platform the spirit of a fine looking, tall man, who was carefully described. He bowed to the people, and gave his name as Mr. Russell. This spirit was fully identified by many persons present.

Then came forward a spirit full of sorrow, and was fully described. He had been a school teacher; had fallen from his high estate through the influence of whisky; had not got rid of the curse. He gave his name as Bennett. He was fully identified by several.

The next was a very marked case of spirit identity. There sat a man, thirty feet from us, Mr. J. S. After pointing him out, we said, there stands by this man the spirit of a soldier, in uniform, describing him very carefully. He says he was killed in 1863, in the army of the Potomac. He says that you are his uncle Ira, and wishes to be remembered to you; all of which was approved, and the multitude was very much surprised.

After that we went home with Mr. W. Kelsey, on Lodi Hill. After some conversation, we went into the spirit state, saw and described many spirits, among whom came the spirit of Seth Kelsey; he talked sometime with his brothers, and of his dear old wife, and his daughter, and sent them words of cheer; and then gave place to the Rev. Mr. Adams, formerly a Presbyterian minister, who preached in Syracuse many years ago. He fully identified himself, and spoke of his change from time to eternity, and of his views here and in the spirit world. This was a remarkable case of spirit identity.

Then came Lieutenant Charles George, who claimed to be the husband of a lady in the room, calling her Sarah. He told of a walk he had with her long ago, described the place, spoke very feelingly of his little son, and gave good advice to his wife, and bade us good night.

Then came the spirit of a black man. He gave his name as Jim Wagoner, the blacksmith, and identified himself to a young man who was in the room.

We gave a seance on Friday, January 8, to a full house, and many fine tests of spirit life.

Dr. W., of Baldwinsville, was sitting on his seat; I saw by him a spirit, and stepping up to him, said, "Sir, there stands by you the spirit of a dear, good woman, who calls you husband, and says, 'Cheer up, for I am with you; do not weep, for I am not dead, but have been in the spirit life but a little while, and here is our baby darling, just followed me into the spirit world. Do not weep.'"

This man came from B., on purpose to attend these meetings. He had never seen me before; had buried his wife but a few days ago, and the child three or four days before, and the description of them were fully identified. And he wept.

Dear readers, are we not surrounded by a great cloud of witnesses, and shall he not give us in charge of his angels.

At night we lectured to fully seven hundred people. We gave many fine tests, and received the congratulations of the audience, and was invited to return at an early day. We left our friends rejoicing; and Spiritualism, triumphant!

---

## CHAPTER XIX.

### *A TALK WITH THE SPIRITS.*

May I have room to relate what I saw and heard on Monday evening, at Lyceum Hall, Cleveland, May 15th, 1869? Passing along Superior street in front of Case Hall, I saw a light in Lyceum Hall. Crossing over and ascending the stairs, I inquired of one I met on the way, "What is going on up here?"

His reply was, "Wilson gives a seance to the Spiritualists."

So, moving forward I came to a door, and there I found a cluster of men standing around a stout, plain-looking, gray-haired man, of some fifty summer's sunshine. I notice that some dropped a quarter stamp in his hand, and some did not.

"What," said I, "spirits take money?"

"Yes," said the gray haired man; "the little fish is looking for coin to pay the tribute with."

Well, we paid our quarter and went forward, taking our seat in the midst of over one hundred persons.

At eight o'clock, our friend of the gray hairs came forward, and said:

"Ladies and Gentlemen: When our friends go to California or Australia, we are most anxious to hear from them, and when a stranger from the land of gold and silver comes into our midst, how eagerly we ply him with questions, asking information of the absent one, and on mail days how we throng to the postoffice, anxiously asking: 'Any letter for me to-day?' and when the clerk says, 'None,' how the eyes fill with moisture and the lips tremble as we turn away in sorrow; and when we bury our dead, how we weep and are not comforted, and refuse any information in regard to them. We believe they are immortal and are happy, and yet we refuse to hear of or from them. They are no more dead to us than the relative or friend is, in California or Australia. We are anxious to hear from the latter and refuse to hear from the former. Why? Because they are dead; and may we ask, 'What dies, the mind or the matter?' We answer: 'Matter dies; mind never.' And then we may ask, 'Is man immortal?' Certainly. The road he travels on into immortality he can return by. To illustrate (turning to an old man): There stands by this old man, a soldier; five feet ten inches in height; weight, one hundred and fifty pounds; dark brown hair, light complexion, eyes full, nose large and firm mouth; belonged to the army and was killed, and says you are his father."

"It is my son," said the old man, and his voice trembled as he spoke.

*Second*. Turning to Mr. W., he said: "There stands by you a spirit woman, who says she is your spirit wife, and places her right hand on your shoulder, and her left on the head of the lady by your side. She was a little younger than you, and you formed her acquaintance at eighteen. He then gave a very minute description of the spirit woman. What do you know of her? Have you lost a wife?"

"No, sir; I have never lost a wife," said Mr. W.

Nothing disturbed, the medium said: "She continues by you. Says, I know you, but not this woman. I was engaged to you when I was seventeen. You went from me. The engagement was broken up, and at twenty years of age I died. I was pledged to be your wife. Came to you in love and truth, and what I have said is true. Sir," said the medium, "what do you know of this?"

Said Mr. W.: "It is true, and the description of the woman is correct."

*Third*. A man in the middle of the house was next pointed out, the medium saying: "Seventeen years ago you were associated with two men in a business transaction. You entertained a long journey and large outlays. It was an important undertaking. The second man was not reliable, the third man was; you are the first man. You became dissatisfied with the second man; the undertaking was broken up and the matter a failure. The second man is living; the third man is dead. This took place in 1852, beginning in March and concluding in August. What do you know of this matter?"

"It is true, sir," said the man, "in every particular."

*Fourth.* Crossing the hall, he said to a man: "There stands by you one who was with you very often in 1859, 1860 and 1861. He entered the army in 1862; held a first lieutenant's commission, and was killed. He and you were firm friends, and he is with you often." The medium then gave a detailed description of the spirit Lieutenant, asking the stranger if he recognized him.

The answer was, "I do, indeed."

*Fifth.* The medium here approached a man, and touched his hand, or asked him to lay his hand on his, which was done. Then walking leisurely from him, gave a minute delineation of the man's habits, character, and manner of thinking, etc. This was one of the most minute readings that I ever listened to, and I have heard many of the best phrenologists in the land. When through, the medium asked: "Is there any one here who knows this man?"

Several answered, "Yes," and one said, "I know him better than he knows himself."

Said the medium: "Had you been called on to read this man's character, in what would you differ from me?"

"In nothing; save I could not tell it as well as you have."

"What do you say, sir?" turning to the man.

"It is true; but you have spread it on pretty thick."

*Sixth.* The medium walked slowly through the

hall, to a man and woman at the rear of the audience. Walking behind the parties, he said: "There is with this man and woman, two spirits; one a woman, the other a little child. The child is in the woman's arms. She holds the child over the head of the woman, and the child peeps over into the lady's face in a playful mood. The spirit woman is either this woman's sister or aunt; I believe her sister, and if her sister, she was a little older than the woman, and suffered intensely before and when dying. The child is under two years of age, and is the woman's child. I do not recognize the sex of the child. What do you know of this?" said the medium.

The woman answered and said: "I have lost a sister who was a little older than myself, who suffered intensely before she died; and I lost a child seventeen months old, and you have described them very well."

In this case there was a slight discrepancy between the medium's view of the age of the child and the woman's knowledge of the age.

*Seventh.* The medium went from these parties to a man and said: "Four years ago this man suffered terribly with nervous sick-headache. Eleven years ago, he came near dying from an attack of inflammation of the lungs, and at eleven years of age, he was thrown from a bay colt and hurt in the back — pointing out the spot — by a kick from the colt or from the fall, and it troubles him yet. Will you tell us if this be true."

The man answered: "I am from Richfield, Ohio, and all this man has told me is true. At eleven years of age, I was thrown from a bay colt, and hurt in the manner specified."

*Eighth.* He went to a gray-haired man and said: "There is a peculiar spirit with you who knew you when a boy, and was a boy with you;" giving a minute description of the spirit when a boy, and then said, "this fellow was a half-witted fellow, a butt for the boys in the neighborhood to plague and fool with, and, sir, he now stands in a most ridiculous position, crying, 'Why did you do that,' and, sir, you and others had pushed him in the mud. Will you tell us what you know of this matter?"

The man answered: "I remember such a boy, a half-witted fellow, and remember the incident of the mud-hole referred to, very well; but I do not know whether the fellow is dead or alive. It was many years ago."

These are but few of the wonderful tests, communications and readings that this medium gave, and out of nineteen persons read and forty-five tests given, the medium proved all but two to be true, and that, too, by the parties pointed out, and all through the evening he illustrated and demonstrated that it was spirits that gave him his information.

Now, as ministers and newspaper men are supposed to know all things in heaven and on earth, from Moses of Judea, to Jeff. Davis of Mississippi, from the old red sandstone to the alluvial, and from the alluvial to the far off comet in space, I ask you to tell me what this phenomena is, and how the medium does these things; and is it not wise to understand their nature?

D. A. EDDY.

# CHAPTER XX.

Farmington, Ohio — The Badger Graham — Mr. Hashmord's Statement — The Trap — The Faction — The Victory.

## *FARMINGTON, OHIO.*

Where is Farmington? you may ask. We answer, it is in Trumbull county, Ohio, ten miles north of the Cleveland and Mahoning Railroad; and a nice little country place it is; and contains many liberal souls, and some of the truest Spiritualists in the world. From this pleasant country town, came our intellectual inspirational brother, A. B. French; and none better qualified than he, to do our Master's work. Long may he live and prosper; and as I look up to his picture in oil, that hangs on the wall at my left (for I am stopping with his parents,) I cannot help saying, God speed thee, dear brother, and good angels guard thee in the good work before thee.

I have been here four days and nights; found here, Brothers Wheelock, Sutliff, Kellogg, and many others, from afar; all drawn together, to attend a discussion, and a very animated one, going on between our Brother Wheelock, Ohio State Missionary, and Prof. A. M. Craft, of the Western Reserve Seminary, under the control of the Methodist church. Both are young men of fine ability, and good debaters. Wheelock is very excitable and nervous, but a good reasoner and clear thinker, and holds his opponent well to his work.

Prof. Craft, is steadier of nerve, better posted on his subject, evidently having given it a great deal of attention. Uses exhortation for effect, rather than argument, and frequently, very personal; in fact, both parties are. On the whole, from what I have heard, Brother Wheelock has held his own remarkably well.

We were called here to give four lectures and readings, as well as tests, and when it was understood that we were to be on hand, the church people clubbed together, and imported the Rev. Mr. Graham, a genuine Methodist Badger, from Pennsylvania, to meet us.

On reaching Farmington, on April 9, 1869, we found Union Hall full to overflowing, and Brother Wheelock speaking. Soon it was Prof. Craft's turn. On arising, and after learning that we were in the house, under our magnetic presence, he, Prof. Craft, was made to cry with a loud voice, "Wilson! Wilson!! whale! whale!!" This man's cry reminded us of the days of Jesus, and the man among the tombs, and evidently the Professor was as badly affected by our presence on this occasion, as the evil spirits were at the presence of Jesus.

In the evening, we met our Badger, but received no bites or scratches of any account from him.

During the evening, we referred to a man near the desk: "You are a bundle of fish hooks done up in a package of sand paper," and then gave our explanation of the symbol, which was accepted as true by all present.

During the next day, this man called on us for an explanation of what we meant, which was readily given, and after this, we said: "Sir, to-day, when in your seat there," pointing to the place, "we saw with you a young woman about eighteen or twenty years of age, holding in her arms a child about three months old. She held it out to you and said, not yours, but your wife's. What do you know of this?"

He answered, "I have never lost a wife nor a child."

"We did not say that you had lost either. Now, sir, we will describe this woman," and did so, and then the child, adding, it is a boy.

Again, he repeated, "I never lost either."

"We did not say you did; but, sir, we now ask you, are you not living with a woman who buried her first husband, and a little boy three months old?"

"I am," he answered.

Again, we asked, "Have you not buried a sister?"

He answered, "Yes, I have, but your description does not answer for her."

"Will you describe her?"

He did so, and agreed with us in every particular; after which, he went over to the enemy, and told them that he had been told by Wilson, that his spirit wife had appeared to him, standing by his side, holding in her arms a little boy three months old, saying, "Your boy, yours," and that, too, in the face of the fact, as all his neighbors knew he had not lost a wife nor child.

In the evening, when Father Graham came to reply, he used our statement in this wise: "This world-renowned medium from Chicago, this man greater than Christ, gives us a spiritual test. Here it is, and I have it from the man he gave it to, who is a respected citizen and a Christian man, well known to you all, and there is not a word of truth in it. It is this: 'I see by you, your wife, and she holds in her arms a little child, and says it is yours, and they died long ago.' This like every other Spiritual test, is a humbug, and there is no truth in it, and our friend has never lost a wife," which was followed by a great laugh.

Our turn came soon, and we asked, "Who is your authority for this statement, Mr. Graham?"

He answered, "Mr. Hashmord."

"Is Mr. Hashmord in the house?"

He answered, "Yes, sir, I am here; what do you want?"

"Did you make this statement, Mr. Graham has read this evening?"

"Yes, sir, I did."

"Did I tell you thus?"

"Yes, sir, you did."

We then turned to the audience and repeated what we told the man, and asked him if this was not what we told him, and he answered, "No."

We then turned to the audience and asked, "Is there any one in the house who heard us make this statement to Mr. Hashmord?" and there stood up fifteen men, and all stated that which we said was true, and that which Graham, the minister, had said, was false.

"Well," said Graham, "Hashmord told me so;" after which Mr. Hashmord very imprudently called us to account before the audience, stating: "You said that

I had lost a wife, and everybody knows I have not."

We answered, "You have lost a wife, and your spirit sister says you abused your first wife to such an extent that she was compelled to obtain a divorce from you; hence, you have lost a wife; and, sir, your spirit sister tells me much more about you." And then Mr. H. drew his head into his shell.

The discussion was an able one, and we are told by good judges that Brother Wheelock came off with honors well earned.

On Tuesday evening following, the friends of Spiritualism made a donation visit to Brother Wheelock, from which he realized fifty-two dollars. Altogether, it has done good, and our cause has lost nothing, but gained grandly.

---

## CHAPTER XXI.

### *AN EVENING WITH E. V. WILSON AND THE SPIRITS.*

The lecturer, whose name is at the head of this correct history of an evening spent in communion with the spirit world, Mr. Wilson, claims to see, hear and describe spirits — to give correct life histories, as well as important events and incidents in the life of individuals who come before him. And certainly, so far as our experience goes, he has maintained his claims, and proved himself a medium of no mean capacity. He came to our place on Monday, the 27th ult., ostensibly to rest. But at once, without invitation or pay, he began to give remarkable facts and tests in the lives of whomsoever he met. He lectured to large and intelligent audiences on the evenings of the 28th, 29th and 30th, giving on each occasion wonderful tests, as well as most correct readings of character. On Friday evening, December 1, he offered to give a seance at my house in order to demonstrate his powers as a medium, as well as his power of control over the human will, under spirit influence. There were sixteen persons present— many of them influential families of our town, and members in *good standing in our popular churches.* Amongst them were two or three of our best physicians, and what is more to the point, only two or three of those present could be called Spiritualists. The only conditions required by Mr. Wilson were cheerfulness, pleasant and lively conversation, and entire freedom from reference to any one present. His only request was, "Sit promiscuously around the room—let me take my own course;" or, to use Balaam's language, "And he took up his parable, and said, Balaam the son of Beor, hath said, and the man whose eyes are open hath said, He hath said which heard the word of God, and knew the knowledge of the Most High, which saw the vision of the Almighty, falling into a trance, but having his eyes open."

After some more comments, Mr. Wilson said, "I see a boy by the side of that young lady. He is about twelve or fourteen years old, of medium size, light complexion, and has been dead about two years, and says he is her brother;" a truth, and all recognized the fact. Then he continued, "I hear the cars running very rapidly — there is a crash, and many are hurt; here comes one who was killed by this accident." He then minutely described him, saying, "he belongs to this place," another fact, and we recognized him. In the meantime, a lady and gentleman came quietly into the room and took their seats. These persons are members of the church, and Mr. Wilson had never seen them. When seated, Mr. Wilson turned to the man and said, "A boy from spirit land came into the room between you and the lady, and said, 'My father and mother.'" Turning to the audience he said, "It is the boy I saw with the young lady a short time ago." Correct again.

Turning to Drs. T. and L. he said, "I see by you a stout, thick-set man, five feet eight or nine inches in height, dark complexion, dark brown hair, heavy brows, large mouth and coarse features. He stands by the side of Dr. T., and looks at Dr. L. and then at Dr. T., and then across the room to Capt. B. He knows the doctors, and looks at them with a heavy ugly frown on his face, full of temper and hatred, and his arms folded across his breast. He changes his position, and shows me his person. He was killed three years ago, in a row. He was shot — shot three times; first, here, in the right breast; second, here, in the right side, just above the hip; third, here, through the head; either of the shots through the breast or head were fatal. Gentlemen, you were both present at the autopsy." "Correct," said the doctors, "and your communication is true to the letter." "Yes," said Capt. B., "I knew him well, and he served in my regiment. I gave him leave of absence, during which he was shot, and his name was Frank Adkins." Mr. Wilson resumed, "Here is the boy Henry, the stepson of Dr. S., whom I saw last night at the lecture; and here is the young girl, from spirit land, whom I described as being with Henry last night, and Dr. L. She is your daughter Almira. She thought a great deal of this boy Henry, and it was her that I saw Dr. S. stand by the bedside of, when sick or dying, eight years ago. Doctor, she died of milk sickness." He then described the house, room, furniture, even the bedstead on which she died. He then described the cow from whom the milk was taken. When asked how the boy Henry died, he replied promptly, "He was drowned." Now, all this communication is true to the letter, and proved so by most of the parties present, and especially by the parent, with the exception of the cow, there being no knowledge of such a cow to any one present, save that the cow might have belonged to a neighbor, and gave the milk that caused the death of Dr. L.'s daughter. Again Mr. Wilson said, "Dr. L., three years ago there came a man, a physician, up to you in a great passion, and accused you of doing him a great wrong, of which you was not guilty; it was about a patient, a soldier." Here Mr. W. described both the doctor and the soldier, all of which Dr. L. identified.

To Mrs. Dr. T., Mr. Wilson said, "Sixteen years ago, Madam, you were seized here in the right side, with a terrible pain, and you suffered intensely. What have you to say—is it true or not?" "I shall answer no questions," said Mrs. T. "I don't care a snap of my finger, whether you do or not," said Mr. W. "It is, however, due to those present that you acknowledge or deny the fact." "I shall do neither," said the lady. "Ah!" said Dr. T., "I am honest enough to own up, if Mr. W. tells me the *truth;* now is it true that such a thing occurred with you at the time specified? If so, own up." "Well, yes," said the lady, "there was." To a blind man he said, "From your boyhood, say from six years old, up to the present time, you have been under the control of spiritual powers, and have frequently been guided by these invisibles." Mr. W. then gave a succinct history of this man's life, as well as incidents in the lives of many others, with wonderful and startling accuracy. He then described many spirits whom we recognized beyond a doubt, amongst whom was the father of Capt. B., as well as two wives that Capt. B. had buried.

Truly we could say with the woman of Samaria, "I have met a man that told me all that I ever did. Come and see; is not this the Christ?" And truly did we feel that we were "surrounded by ministering angels."

Thus passed a pleasant and happy evening with E. V. Wilson and the spirits, and were we to repeat all the facts and communications given by him while with us, it would be a volume of facts more strange than fiction. Our people are very much roused upon the subject, and anxiously look forward to another visit from Mr. Wilson and the spirits.

One more fact is worthy a place in this record. It occurred here, in this place. In the midst of his lecture on Thursday evening, Mr. Wilson said, "There just came into the room two spirits, (he described them most accurately,) and they were killed here by the citizens, shot for supposed or real complicity with a rebel raid made some time ago into this neighborhood." This was as true as truth itself. Where does the power come from? A good Methodist brother answers this question correctly, when he says, "This is of a surety from the spirit world, and these are they who have preceded us into the land of the hereafter."

Fraternally thine for Truth,

T. F. B.

*Newburg, Ind., Dec.* 3, 1865.

# CHAPTER XXII.

## *A FEW FACTS FROM SPIRIT LIFE.*

Lecturing in Danville, N. Y., on Monday evening, January 25, 1860, we saw and described, as follows:

*First.* We see, by the side of this man, a spirit. In life, he was a soldier [describing him fully]; he is your cousin, or nephew, and was killed in 1863.

*Answer.* I had a nephew who was killed, as you described.

*Second.* By this woman was a spirit lady, very beautiful indeed — a cultivated and refined soul. [We described her very minutely.] She calls you sister, but we do not think she is your sister, but a friend and playmate of your girlhood days. She died very suddenly, at seventeen years of age.

After a little thought, she answered: "No; I can call nothing to mind, and have no idea of any such person."

"A failure," we promptly replied; "let it pass."

"No," said the spirit, "it is not a failure; she will remember me; I am Emma Francis."

This we did not repeat, but went on with our facts.

The next evening, the lady to whom the communication was given, called on us, at the pleasant home of Mrs. Little, and voluntarily said: "I have called to correct the statement made by me last night, at the hall. I have identified the spirit you described, and your description of her was very correct indeed. She died when she was seventeen years old, and we were as dear to each other as sisters could be, and her name was Francis."

"Emma Francis," we heard a voice say.

"It may have been," said the lady.

"Why did you deny this last night?" said Mrs. Little.

"Because I was sure that she was nineteen and past, when she died; and Mr. W. was so positive that she was but seventeen, that I concluded that it was not my friend and sister Francis; but, on reaching home, I found, from her biography, that he was right."

Here is but one of the many cases of spirit tests, independent of the mind of the party to whom it is given — a clear case of spirit history, corroborated by written evidence, and outside of the memory of either medium or party to whom the communication comes.

They that have ears to hear, let them hear, and eyes to see, let them see and understand.

*Third.* After the lecture, and before the audience had left the house, there came the spirit of a sweet, pretty little girl of three or four years of age, and touched me, in her innocent, child-like way, and said, only as little angels can say, "Tell my papa that I am here," and then left me, and stood by the side of an old, gray-haired man; and as she took her place by his side, she was changed, in the twinkling of an eye, to a magnificent angel woman, wrapped in Heaven's mantle of white, and with love beaming from her eyes, she laid her white hand on the shoulder of the old man, and said: "My father, I welcome thee, and in joy greet thee from my spirit home." And then, bowing her spirit form to the wrinkled brow of the old man, kissed him and disappeared.

We called the old man's attention to the fact, and he turned, looked at the place where the angel daughter had stood, and said: "She is my daughter, and died when four years old."

*Fourth.* On Friday evening, January 29, 1869, after the discussion had closed, several friends followed us to the house of Mrs. Little, with whom we stopped, for a social chat; and, among others, came Dr. and Mrs. P., who, by the way, are not Spiritualists. While in conversation with them, we heard the voice of a woman say, "Dr. P.; I want Dr. P."

We turned toward Dr. P., and we saw, as follows: First, a splendid female form — one of the finest we ever saw; then we saw a room and its contents — among other things, a low-posted bedstead, with the woman on it that we had seen standing by the side of the Doctor; she was in a night-dress, open in front, with frill border reaching from pit of stomach up to, and around, her neck, and same kind of border around the wrists; her face was full, flushed, and indicative of good health. She was handsome, and lay in unrest, with eyes closed; her hair was loose, and lay in masses over the white pillows, and its lustrous brown black was in marked contrast with the whiteness of the pillows; the bedstead stood out from the walls; and I saw her lips move, and heard her moan, "Why don't you call Dr. P.?"

I then saw, by the bed, an old man of seventy years, hair white and thin on the top of his head. [Described him minutely, even to his cane, and observed that he was a conceited, strong-willed man.] By him stands a much younger man, stout, thick-set, dark hair, dark complexion, and, apparently, about thirty-five years of age. These men are doctors; and now, Dr. P., I see you by the side of the bed, in consultation over the woman; you each make a diagnosis; yours is rejected; theirs is acted on. The woman died, and now her spirit stands by you, and says, "Dr. P., could I have had you in the beginning of my troubles, I should have been in the form to-day."

Doctor, this was twenty-two years ago, and you were twenty-six years old, and the woman about twenty-two or three. Answer; yes or no.

Says the Doctor: "Twenty-two years ago, I was opening up a practice in the town of ——, and was called the 'new doctor,' and there occurred just what you have related. I was twenty-six years old, and I differed with the two doctors you have described, and, on the death of the lady in question, demanded a *post mortem* examination, which was conducted by two disinterested physicians, who sustained my diagnosis, thus sustaining my professional reputation. Your communication is wonderfully correct."

"Yes," said Mrs. P., in a sad voice, "I knew the woman well; she died in child-birth, and her form was pronounced, by the doctors who made the *post mortem* examination to have been the finest they ever saw."

"All of these things ye may do, and much more, if ye have faith as large as a grain of mustard seed."

O, ye Advents! who believe in Jesus as the Son of God, why do n't you do these things, or else expel the demons that do them? Ye are of the Sadducees — blind leaders, leading the blind.

"Woe unto you, Sadducees, hypocrites, liars."— *Jesus.*

---

## CHAPTER XXIII.

Skaneateles — The Lake — The Village — The Reading of Captain M. — The Four Wives.

### *SKANEATELES.*

Skaneateles! Who is he, what is he, where does he live, and what does he do?

Be patient, dear readers, and we will tell you all we know about him, and that is not much.

Skaneateles was once an Indian Chief, of the Onondaga tribe, and was drowned in Skaneateles Lake, New York, many years ago, while under the influence of King Alcohol, the Prime Minister of Civilization, and is now a spirit, acting through mediums, to counsel the children of those who robbed him and his tribe of their homes and birth-right; to cure the lame and the sick — coming, with peace and love in his nature, to those who despitefully used him — and is an angel of mercy, clothed in love, seeking to do good unto his enemies.

And is it not a wonderful fact, that the savage nature of the Indian, on becoming a spiritual being, is lost. He is changed to an angel of mercy, and, in our experience with spirits and Spiritualists, during fifteen years, we do not remember of ever meeting a bitter, revengeful Indian spirit. We wish we could say as much of the spirits of white men and women. This much for the Indian.

Skaneateles Lake is a beautiful body of water, some sixteen miles in length, narrow and deep, clear and pure, situated in Onondaga county, New York, south-west of Syracuse some eighteen miles, and is resorted to, during the heat of summer, by the rich, the gay, and the sick, from every part of the Union The sloping shores are noted for their American rural character and pleasant scenery, and, in the future, must become the "Como," or "Windermere," of America. The country is well improved around it, and on its banks are many fine mansions, and its waters are used for mechanical purposes.

Skaneateles Village is a flourishing little town of some fifteen hundred inhabitants, situated at the foot of the lake, and known, far and wide, for its conservative element. Hitherto, Spiritualism has had but little foothold here, being kept under by a system of religious lies and phrases, such as, "It is the work of the Devil," "It is free love," "It breaks up families," as well as "What good will it do?"

The last question is the language of folly; the others, the language of theology, bigotry, and superstition.

And now that we have told you all about Skaneateles — Indian, lake and village — let us tell you something of Spiritualism, for there are Spiritualists here, and more than the churches are aware of. Hearing of the great revival work going on in Buffalo, Syracuse, and many other places, under our ministration, a call was extended for us to come and help, and for four days we have been teaching, explaining, and demonstrating the precepts, practices, and facts, of immortality.

Our first lecture, on "The Bible," was clearly demonstrative of the fact that this book belongs to the Spiritualists.

Our second lecture, on "The Law of Spirit Control," all declared to be one of the ablest lectures ever delivered in this village.

Our third lecture, "Diabolism, or the Devil," carried the place by storm.

Our fourth and last lecture, "God in the Past, Present, and Future, Theologically and Spiritually considered and contrasted," swept everything before it; and, what is best of all, as well as approval of the speaker's position and ability, is in the fact that the meetings were self-sustaining, the receipts being more than the expenses.

Aside from our lectures, we gave one public and

one private seance, giving many fine tests, from which we select the following:

"Captain M. First, I see by you a fine-looking little girl, about six years old," describing her carefully. "Second, there is with you a spirit by the name of Antoine Baptise, a Portugese sailor, who says he was with you, in a terrible storm, off the coast of Spain, in 1836, and was subsequently lost off the Cape of Good Hope. Third, there is with you a man — an Irishman — a sailor; you are at sea off the coast of Ireland, when the man mutinies; you are called forward; the man seizes a handspike from the capstan stocks, and makes a blow at you, just missing you and nearly killing a man near you; this man is now a spirit. Fourth, there is a man with you," describing him, "who gives me the name of Edward Wilson, and says he was the first officer of the ship 'John Adams,' that he knew you well, and that you and he were together in Liverpool, England, in 1832. Fifth, there is with you a very stout old sea captain, who gives his name as Stubbs, of Maine, and says that you and he sailed out of New York together, in 1828, he in the ship 'Caledonia,' and you in a merchantman, for the East Indies. And now, sir, do not be offended at what I am going to say. There is here, on your right, a woman; just behind you, and over your head, a second woman; on your left, a third woman." Here we entered into a very minute and graphic description of the women; after which, we said: "There are two others here, one of them I believe to be your daughter; the others say they are your wives; and yet, sir, I see a fifth wife in the form, by your side."

*Response.* All you have told me is true. The little girl is mine, and died at five. Antoine Baptise I knew well, and a famous good man he was; I learned, subsequently, that he was lost by shipwreck. I recollect the storm off the coast of Spain, in 1836, very well. The Irishman and the mutiny I also remember, and that he came very near killing me; it was off the coast of Ireland. First Officer Edward Wilson, of the ship "John Adams," was an intimate friend of mine, and I remember the meeting in Liverpool very well. I remember the ship "Caledonia," and of my sailing for the East Indies, in 1828, but cannot bring to mind Captain Stubbs, and friends. In regard to the spirits of these women, that have been described, it is minutely true. He has described my second, third, and fourth wives in every particular. I am now living with my fifth wife. I have always doubted Spiritualism, and have never been a Spiritualist, but I cannot deny these things. I am a stranger to Mr. Wilson, and this is his first visit to our town. He could not have been told of these things, for there is no one here that knew of them.

We gave very many other fine tests during our visit, in all about seventy-five, and many of them as marked as those connected with Captain M.

Here we have repeated the scene that occurred at the well of Samaria, only that this time it is a man and five wives; then it was a woman with five husbands. These things were not done in a corner, nor are they based upon our testimony alone. They were witnessed by many persons, and those, too, unbelievers. And we may say, in the language of Captain M.: "I cannot deny; I must believe; I have no longer any doubt."

We are in possession of the names of many who witnessed these things, and are prepared to prove them.

---

## CHAPTER XXIV.

### *BELIEF IN IMMORTALITY.*

*First.* May 4th, at Bonaparte, Iowa, before a full house, we turned to a stranger, and said, "We see by you a man," fully describing him. "He holds out to you the left hand, and on the index finger there is an irritation, angry and swollen. The hand and arm are immense. We now see him on his bed; you and five others are around the bed. He is terribly swollen. It is a fearful sight, and at his death and some time before, he was a living mass of putrid matter. He died twenty-six years ago this summer, and we get the name of Webster. What do you know of this statement?"

He answered: "Twenty-six years ago this spring

and summer, I was practicing medicine in Southern Illinois, and was called to see just such a man, and in every particular it is wonderfully correct. His name was Webster. The cause of his death was malignant erysipelas, or what was then known as the black tongue, but in this man's case it began on the forefinger of the left hand."

We asked, "Is there any collusion in this matter between us?"

He answered, somewhat tartly, "I am Dr. George, and never saw this man, Wilson, before."

*Second.* May 9th, at Ottumwa, when lecturing, the spirit man or form of the late Major Fulton came and stood by his brother-in-law, and was fully identified. This good Methodist passed on not long ago, and at the time of his departure for the Summer Land, was surrounded by a great many immortals, many of whom he fully recognized as relatives, friends and old acquaintances, besides many he did not know.

We here append an article in favor of Spiritualism, clipped from the "Des Moines Valley Gazette," published at Eddyville, May 5, 1870. We are informed that John Wilcox, the editor, is a Methodist.

"Be always ready to give an answer to every man that asketh you a reason of the hope that is in you." 1st Peter, iii: 15.

"Do you believe the statement of 'Amicus,' in his delineation of the remarkable death of Major C. E. Fulton, and if so, was it not a mere phantom hallucination of his diseased brain?"

"This and similar questions have been asked us since our publication of the 'Amicus' Courier article. We answer that we do believe emphatically, *the statement*, and give as a reason for our belief, the fact that its truth is vouched for by the newspapers, with many of the good citizens of Ottumwa, who were personally cognizant with the (to some) strange phenomenon. To admit the facts, as stated by 'Amicus,' and doubt the reality of the manifestations to Major Fulton, would be to doubt the veracity of that Christian gentleman in his last assertions upon a dying bed, and virtually denounce the Bible, with all history, written, oral and traditional, to say nothing of the testimony of millions of good and truthful men and women now living, who bear testimony to constantly recurring incidents, no less strange in their developments than was the case in question. In furtherance of the 'reason for the hope within,' we need not advert to the world of corroborative testimony outside the Bible, but a few of the many quotations that might be adduced from its sacred pages, will suffice. See the following Scriptural passages:

"'And there came two angels to Sodom at even, and Lot, seeing them, rose up to meet them.' Genesis xxix: 1.

"'And he lifted up his eyes and looked, and lo! three men stood beside him.' Genesis xviii: 1, 2.

"'And the angel of the Lord found her (Hagar) by a fountain of water in the wilderness * * and said, whence camest thou?' Genesis xvi: 7.

"'This Moses whom they refused * * did God

send to be a ruler and a deliverer by the hand of the angel which appeared to him in the bush.' Acts vii: 35.

"'And Jacob went on his way, and the angels of God met him.' Genesis xxxii: 1.

"'And as he (Elijah) lay and slept under a juniper tree, behold then an angel touched him, and said unto him, 'Arise and eat.'' 1st Kings xix: 5.

"'Then the Lord opened the eyes of Balaam and he saw the angel of the Lord standing in the way.' Numbers xxii: 31.

"'While I was speaking in prayer, even the man Gabriel, whom I had seen in the vision at the beginning * * touched me about the time of the evening oblation.' Daniel ix: 21.

"'And she said, an old man cometh up, and he is covered with a mantle. And Saul perceived that it was Samuel, and he stooped with his face to the ground, and bowed himself.' 1st Samuel xxviii: 14.

"'Fear came upon me and trembling, which made all my bones to shake. Then the spirit passed before my face. * * It stood still, but I could not discern the form thereof. * * I heard a voice saying, shall mortal man appear more just than God?' Job iv: 14, 15, 16.

"Speaking of the rolling away the stone and the raising of Christ, Matthew says, 'The angel of the Lord descended from heaven and rolled back the stone from the door. * * His countenance was like lightning, and his raiment white as snow.'

"Luke says, 'The stone was rolled away. * * And entering into the sepulchre, they saw a young man sitting on the right side, clothed in a long white garment.'

"Mark says, 'They entered into the sepulchre and found not the body of the Lord Jesus, * * and much perplexed thereabout, behold two men stood by them in shining garments. * * And they said unto them, why seek ye the living among the dead?' Matthew xxviii: 2, 3; Mark xvi: 4, 5; Luke xxiv: 3, 4.

"'And behold, there talked with him two men, which were Moses and Elias.' Luke ix: 30.

"'And there arose a great cry, and the scribes strove, saying, we find no evil in this man; but if a spirit or an angel hath spoken to him, let us not fight against God.' Acts xxiii: 9.

"'After this I looked, and behold a door was opened in heaven; * * and I heard a voice as it were of a trumpet talking with me, which said, come up hither.' Revelations iv: 1.

"'And I John saw these things and heard them; and when I had heard and seen, I fell down to worship before the feet of the angel which showed me these things. Then saith he unto me, see thou do it not; for I am thy fellow-servant, and of thy brethren, the prophets; * * worship God.' Revelations xxii: 8, 9.

"In the above quotations, the terms, 'angels,' 'angels from heaven,' 'angels of the Lord,' 'men in shining garments,' 'men in long white garments,' 'men of God,' 'man,' 'the man Gabriel,' 'thy fellow servant,' etc., are used interchangeably, and thus necessarily signify the same spiritual beings. This is clearly set forth in the account of the 'angels of the Lord,' that appeared to Manoah's wife. In the history of this spiritual appearing, he is once called the 'man of God,' and three times a 'man.' So the Evangelists, speaking of the Marys coming to the tomb, Matthew says the stone was rolled away by 'the angel of the Lord from heaven,' while Mark, in referring to the same matter, calls this angel of the Lord a 'young man,' and describes him as clothed 'in a long white garment.' These men of God, or angels from heaven, were once mortals — the fathers, the mothers, the sisters and the brothers of earthly friends; and hence their abiding interest in, and deep sympathy for, the loved of earth. Pure love is immortal, and cannot die. It merely buds below to blossom in paradise. With a soul alive to this love and sympathy between the physical and the immortal world, Jesus beautifully said, 'There is joy in the presence of the angels of God over one sinner that repenteth.'

"The preceding Scriptural passages, with numerous others, declare in the most positive manner possible that an 'angel' touched Elijah, under a juniper tree; that the 'man Gabriel' touched the prophet David; that Samuel, in spirit-life, 'perceived' and held converse with Saul; that a spirit passed before Job's face, and he heard a voice; that a spirit or angel spoke to Paul; that such rolled the stone away from the tomb, opened the iron gate, and unloosed Peter's chains; that an angel conversed with John on Patmos, that proved to be his 'fellow servant'; and that the two men, Moses and Elias, long in spirit-life, appeared and talked with Jesus on the mount, in the presence of Peter, James and John. Now, then, if these things transpired in the past, why not now? Has God changed? Have the heavens over us become brass? Have angel powers become palsied? Have divine laws changed? Does a blade of grass grow different now from what it did in Moses' and the Savior's time? Will not an alkali and an acid unite now, and by the same law as in the Bible ages? Do not the same laws that governed matter and mind, angels and spirits, in the prophetic and apostolic ages, govern them now? Admitting the unchangeability of God and His laws, nothing can be more evident! Then the logical inference is indisputable, that angels and spirits can and do manifest themselves to mortals now as in the past; thus verifying the Scripture promises:

"'These signs shall follow them that believe.'

"And 'Lo I am with you alway, even unto the end of the world.'

"Yes, we believe that the Great Captain, with his angel crew, manifested themselves to Major Fulton as his enfranchised spirit was embarking on 'the old ship Zion,' which was then shoved off from the mundane shore, to sail for climes Elysian. Were we to believe otherwise, we should doubt the soul's immortality, and be wretched indeed. Yes, 'Lord I believe, help thou mine unbelief.'"

*Third.* May 12th, at Ottumwa, Iowa, we held a seance. Gave fourteen readings, and many tests. We turned to an old man, saying, "There are three children with you, two boys and a girl," describing them, and giving the time of their death. The man was Mr. Millisach, and in every particular the statement was true and confirmed.

Below we append the criticism of Editor Wilcox, on "Modestus." It is good and full of point. Why, Brother Wilcox, don't you know that "Modestus" is true to his nature, and only waits an opportunity to enter his own kingdom and bray through Balaam's ass.

"Modestus," ostensibly a Sadducee, in adverting to the "Amicus" article in the "Ottumwa Courier," feigns to think Major Fulton a great dupe, jester, or deceiver in the hour of death. His sophistry, if adhered to, would undermine the faith of nine-tenths of all believers and destroy their tangible hopes of immortality; leaving mankind to grope in darkness, without a ray of heaven's sunlight, in a world overshadowed and obscured by atheism. To prop his sophistry he places the Creator in the category with His creatures, who, when compared to the Infinite, would not bear the relation of a mote to a continent, and quotes, "No man hath seen God at any time," a fact which though in and of itself is undisputed by all, yet in the abstract has nothing to do with the question at issue. The fact that no man ever saw God, is no evidence that no man ever saw his fellow man. Such "reason" may do for atheists, but it does not argue well for a believer in immortality.

# CHAPTER XXV.

## *MEDIUMSHIP DEFINED.*

Dr. T. J. Lewis, of Chicago, writes me, asking, "What are the physical, or spiritual, requisites by which mediumship is made to exhibit itself through the human body?"

The Doctor writes, "I have asked many times, and of various parties, and yet the question is unanswered. Will you answer?"

I answer, that I can only give my views from spirit teachings, and a long and practical experience.

*First*—Mediumship depends not on mind, but on matter. Every mind in the animal kingdom is subjective to spirit influences, be it man or beast, when the skin, or outer covering, of the animal will warrant it. The quality of the mind will always determine the character of the phenomena. If you want the physical phenomena only, you need not pay much attention to the quality of the mind, or quantity of the medium's brains, or culture thereof. A flea can draw three times its own weight; so can a man; this is a phenomena of muscular strength only, and common to life everywhere. Spirit phenomena depends on the conditions of the physical man, not his mind; the cuticle and nerve, not the brains.

*Second*—Phenomena is two-fold—physical and mental; the physical may be divided into classes: the first, having motion, without intelligence; the second, intelligent physical action. The purely mental, that which draws word pictures — the teacher, poet, and thinker.

*Third* — Man has three physical peculiarities not found in any other animal. We will class them, as follows: First — the cold clammy, or sticky, skin — all persons having this peculiar cuticle — are good subjects for spirit influence, the mesmerizer, revivalist, penitentiary, lunatic asylum, and prostitution; not in that they are more exposed. They are subjective alike to good and evil influences. From this class of the human family, comes all of our physical mediums: the Davenport Brothers, the Ferries, the Misses Lord, and others. All of these have brains enough to keep to their physical mediumships. H. Melville Fay, Von Vleck, Bly, McQueen, and others, are good mediums, but lack standupativeness — cannot stand temptation — hence, fall into the hands of the Philistines, and betray their Master. All of these have cold, viscous, sticky skins. This condition of the system being a good conductor, hence, accessible to spirit influence, and are easily affected by animal magnetism, or spirit electricity. Hence, any man or woman possessing this viscous outer skin, a spirit can influence, to a greater or less extent, for physical phenomena.

*Second.* Persons having warm, viscous skins, are also subject to influences of a mental character as a rule, perspire freely; of this class, come our poets, philosophers, sweet singers, and seers. And out of five hundred mediums that I have met, all the physical mediums have the cold, clammy cuticle, and the mental ones, the warm, viscous cuticle.

*Third.* All persons having a dry, warm, silky cuticle, free from viscous conditions, are not mediums — cannot be influenced by man, or spirit, through animal magnetism, or spirit electricity. With this class of the human family we find our tyrants and bigots — men and women, wanting in soul sympathy; here are found our misers, and crueltry reigns triumphant; the Borgias, Catharine of Russia, Nero, and Jeffries of England, and others, are of this class, or conditions of nature.

Under these conditions of insulation and non-insulation, lies the nervous system, always ready to conduct any imponderable element to the brain, that can penetrate through the skin, or natural covering of the nervous system. Hence, through animal magnetism, we send our thoughts and history over the nervous system to the brain of the medium, and, according to his or her insulation, the history will be correct, or incorrect. And when we get that which is not known to the medium, or in the mind of the applicant for spirit information, then we are *en rapport* with the spirit world. The properties used for this purpose are: first, animal magnetism, generated entirely in and of the human system — the odd force in our natures; second, electricity, under the control of spirit intelligence, is the imponderable property through which they reach us, acting directly on the brain, through the nervous man.

Regarding my own mediumistic powers, I feel, first, the continuous flow of animal magnetism, until my nervous system is ready for a communication. Then comes the signal, "Are you ready?" I flash back from the brain, "All ready." Then, in quick succession, comes thought; each thought accompanied with an electric concussion, or beat; and, sometimes, so rapidly that I cannot speak them as fast as they are given; hence, confusion frequently takes place. Hence, my conclusions are, that mediumship depends on matter — the physical man — for its phenomena, and not the mind; and the imponderable properties used are: first, animal magnetism; second, electricity; the one of the human system, and the other of the spiritual system.

*Proof.* Writing has been done without human contact, and yet the presence of the medium required; ponderable matter moved; the ring-feat accomplished; musical instruments played on; water produced in a dry room; the formation of a physical body of human shape; the formation of flowers, as well as picture-drawing; and yet, not one of these phenomena has ever taken place outside of the joint action of mortal and immortal beings, and the confluence of animal magnetism and spiritual electricity — the one of man, and the other of spirit. Healing of the sick is accomplished by spirits ejecting from the patient the diseased fluids of his nature, and the injection of a healthy, electrified animal magnetic current of and from the healer.

Revivals are produced through the same laws, and

the mediumship of the minister is a necessity for their God to send the Holy Spirit (?) through; and it is a fact, that the best revivalists most frequently have but little, if any, brains; and the converts, instead of getting the spirit of God, get the magnetism of the minister, and are as he is, until they are in confluence with an electrical current and spirit control; and then comes the Holy Ghost, so called, and they pass from under the minister's control; and whenever this condition is reached, in the revival, the convert sees spirits, and talks with them, as we Spiritualists are in the habit of doing.

These views are ours, in regard to the laws of mediumship.

---

## CHAPTER XXVI.

A Remarkable Spirit Phenomena — A Spiritual Incident — Remarkable Phenomena — Came at Last.

### *A REMARKABLE SPIRIT PHENOMENA.*

William P. Parker, of Yates City, Knox county, Illinois, says:

About twelve years ago, my wife, Julia, was attacked with inflammatory rheumatism of a malignant type, and for twelve weeks was entirely helpless, being under the care of Dr. John Gregory, of Farmington, Illinois; he had given her up, and publicly stated that she could not get well. On a certain day, the Rev. Mr. McGee, a Methodist, then carrying on a revival meeting in Livola Center, Illinois, called at my house, saw my wife, examined her (he having studied medicine), and said: "She will not live beyond three o'clock this afternoon, for mortification has already taken place, and she is now dying," and in public made a statement to that effect. This examination, by the Rev. Mr. McGee, was made on Monday morning, at ten o'clock.

My wife said: "If spirits could come back and assist those who suffer, I would be much pleased if they could, or would, come and help me."

At this time, her limbs were very much swollen, and, of herself, she could not move them, and, when moved by others, suffered terribly. She had but finished the words, when she was seized by some invisible power, and, without the help of others — no one being within five feet of her — was lifted off of the bed some four feet, and then let down, turned over and back, exercised in every possible way and manner, for the space of thirty minutes, when, to our great surprise, the swollen condition disappeared, her limbs became natural and limber, and all pain was gone. Soon after this phenomena, Dr. Gregory called. We told him what had taken place. He was very much surprised — examined his patient very carefully, asked us many questions, but left no medicine, simply saying, when he left: "You will request the phenomena to take place again to-morrow, at the same time it did to-day."

On the next day, a little before the time for the phenomena to repeat itself, Dr. G. came, and the same thing occurred again, in his presence. The Doctor was not fully satisfied of the cause, but very much surprised at the results, as well as the phenomena; it came again, and we saw it for the third time. My wife was cured, and that, too, without any medicine being given.

Dr. Gregory wrote out an account of the whole transaction, making a clear statement of the case, and sent it to the medical faculty, at Chicago, with whom it remained for some time, and then was returned to him with this reply: "It is beyond our knowledge, and we have no precedent to which we can refer you."

NOTE. How strange it is that so wonderful a phenomena should take place, and known to the medical faculty, and not have publicity. Are not the blind leading the blind? And yet the case of Mrs. Wm. Parker is as well established as the fact that U. S. Grant is President of the United States, and, no doubt, by and by, when another such case occurs, and it is placed in the hands of the medical faculty, they will shake their heads very wisely, and return it to the writer with, "We have no precedent, hence it is not worthy of our notice." But how different it would have been had this occurred to the wife of Abraham, Isaac, Jacob, or Solomon. We are, as Christians, willing to believe the story of Samson and his foxes; of Elisha and his ax-pole; of Jonah and his great fish; but doubt this phenomena at our door, and with any number of witnesses living who saw it and are willing to testify thereto.

## *A SPIRITUALISTIC INCIDENT.*

We clip the following rich incident from an old California paper. It is worth reading:

The male and female media, who make a business or pleasure of holding consultation with disembodied spirits, for those who are not similarly gifted, but whose curiosity leads them to seek a glimpse "beyond the veil," have some curious experiences occasionally, and meet now and then very eccentric clients. There is a medium of the gentle sex, who does business, we believe, on Howard street; to her there came, inspired by the universal curiosity, a reverend divine, of this city, skilled in theology, and at home in the Asiatic languages. It was his firm determination to expose this humbug, and destroy, as Paul did of old, at Ephesus, the profits and emoluments of all who minister to "strange gods." The simple preparations were made; the little plain, lacquered table was placed in position, and the customary scraps of paper laid before the visitor, on which to write his questions. The medium did not seem much discomposed by the sanctified appearance of the gentleman, nor did her nerves tremble when she became aware that he was testing her "familiars" in what was to her an unknown language. She had confidence in her "spirits." The questions were put in Hindostanee, Sanscrit, Arabic, Persian, and all sorts of strange languages. The reverend scholiast was airing his learning admirably, and, as he thought, to the complete discomfiture of the poor little medium. But he was mistaken; for back from the spirit world, or somewhere else, came, in the same languages in which the questions were put, full and most satisfactory answers.

The questioner stared. He was sorely puzzled, while the medium sat calm and unmoved, with a stray sunbeam, from the partially-curtained window, glistening in her rich blonde tresses.

The divine tried her powers again and again, until his mind was in a state of bewilderment; and he was fain to acknowledge, to himself, that he had signally failed in his attempted exposure. He arose to leave, but could not retreat without a parting word.

"Madam," said he, turning to the medium, who had risen with him, and was standing demurely by his side, "your art is from the Devil; abandon it, for the sake of humanity and your own peace of mind."

Then there came a new light into the eyes of the hitherto quiet medium — the light that shines when the temper is aroused.

"Doctor," said she, in calm, but decided, tones, "you, I presume, are a minister of some church in this city, and you make a living by the practice of your profession. I simply do the same thing by the exercise of my peculiar gift. It may be right, or it may be wrong; I do not presume to argue that point. Let it rest. But I may say this: If, as you assert, the gift is from the Father of Evil, does it not follow, from the promptness and correctness with which your answers came, that your friends must have a very near relation to that much-abused individual?"

This was too much for the Doctor. He was beaten at all points. With a muttered "Good day," he passed out into the street, and the medium saw him no more.

Are we wrong in supposing that the little golden-haired lady had a quiet laugh to herself after the remarkable interview was over?

## *REMARKABLE PHENOMENA.*

The following remarkable test and communication was given to the writer in 1854, at the house of John Swain, Esq., in the city of Toronto, C. W. There were present, Mr. and Mrs. Caulkens, Thos. Anderson, Richard Arnold, Mr. and Mrs. Swain, and others. It was on a winter evening. The circle came to order at eight o'clock. After a little, there were raps, and the voluntary movement of matter; then we were ordered to darken the room; then came lights—some red, some blue, and some yellow; after which, there were vivid flashes of light frequently illuminating the room, to such an extent that we could read large primer print on the wall, anywhere in the room. We were then ordered to sit in a circle and join our hands; we did so; after which, the air began to move as if the room was full of fans, all in motion; soon there came something, in the form of a great bird, and alighted on the head of each — that is, each in turn — moving its wings like unto a great bird. This continued for some minutes, when the circle was ordered to kneel; we did so, and the room was full of light — sometimes quite steady, and then in flashes — after which, one of our number was ordered to kneel in the center of the circle; then came a crown of light — that is, a series of circles of light — and rested on his brow; resting there a moment, it then assumed the form of a wreath, a trifle less than his head, and again rested on his head. During all this time the utmost quiet was maintained, for all were absorbed in wonder and surprise. This condition continued for about five minutes, and then came the baptism. Water fell, or was sprinkled, on and over each one in the room, and that, too, when there was no water in the room. Silence continued yet a little longer, and then one of our number (Sister M. Swain), under an excellent influence, spoke, to the following effect:

"Brother: The winged angel of ancient wisdom hath joined the ranks of modern progression, and these twain now call on thee to take up thy parable and work for humanity. Be brave and fearless; be faithful and true; your work is for eternity."

Then speaking to all, she said: "Brothers and sisters, join hands, and form the circle of peace and love around our brother."

After a little, she again said: "Angels of Peace, Angels of Light, Angels of Health, Angels of Truth,

Angels of Strength, Angels of Courage, Angels of Life, around our brother gather, and impart to him, each in turn, that which thou hast for him, that he may be endowed to do the work before him in truth and love."

Then came the baptism once more; after which, came that wonderful influence which makes our circle a heaven on earth, and, with one mind, we felt that it was good for us to be there. And then our brother responded:

"Father in Heaven, brothers and sisters on earth, I promise to work for thee and humanity, and faithfully do the right."

After this, came three grand flashes of light, and the angels left us. For a few minutes, we were silent, then arose, shook hands with each other, and, in love with our glorious gospel, we went to our homes, feeling that we were a little nearer God and the Summer Land.

NOTE. The above is the only instance in our experience that we have had dealings with spirits having wings, and feet like birds. If others have met with similar incidents, we would like to hear from them.

## *CAME AT LAST.*

In 1860 and 1861, we were itinerating through Northern Wisconsin, and, when lecturing in Watertown, there came to us a spirit, saying:

"I was a peddler, and was murdered in this place

—— years ago, by a woman and her companion, the woman being the principal actor."

At the time, there was no confirmation of the communication, save a vague rumor of a peddler who had disappeared suddenly, and that was but a rumor, and we put the communication on the list of failures.

Subsequently, while at Madison, there came to us a man, asking if we remembered lecturing in Watertown. We replied that we did.

"Do you remember the communication regarding the murdered peddler?"

We replied that we did, but that it was a failure.

"By no means," he said. "Some time ago a woman died, in Michigan, and on her death-bed confessed to the murder of a peddler, in Watertown, Wisconsin, and that she buried him in a cellar under the house she lived in. On receipt of the news from Michigan, the people remembered your communication."

Here is another proof of the truthfulness of spiritual communication, and an independent one. How strange that the churches will reject the fundamental truth of eternity—the fact of a hereafter—a life to come. Everywhere the priesthood are making vigorous efforts to crush out Spiritualism and install theology; yet, but for Spiritualism and the spiritual facts of the Bible, there is no evidence of man's immortality.

## CHAPTER XXVII.

Electricity and Religion — Christian Generosity — Brick Bats and Theology — Baptized into Glory.

### *ELECTRICITY AND RELIGION.*

The Rev. Aaron Bickley, late of Ohio, now of Salem, Illinois, relates of a revival: "That a young woman became rigid and fixed in position, standing erect, during a revival meeting he once attended in Ohio; after standing thus for some time, her hand was suddenly raised to a position on a level with her shoulder. At the time this took place, there was a young man on the anxious seat under conviction of sins; he was suffering mentally. On his kneeling down to pray, this young woman suddenly turned toward him, pointing her finger directly at him. At this he cried out with a loud voice, as if hurt, sprang to his feet — ran out of the house in seeming great alarm. After which occurrence, no persuasion of relatives, friends, or ministers could induce him to return again to the church. He stated that it seemed as though he had been hit with an electric current. This woman would turn and point at A., B. or C., and they were at once under her power, and would leave the anxious seat from under our (the minister's) control. All whom she pointed at instantly received an electric shock. We had to separate these persons from the religious portion of the house, placing them in a house by themselves, and when separated, she, or those under her influence, could tell readily who was converted, who was under her control, and who would next be converted. It was a strange electrical phenomena, and beyond our comprehension and control. We deemed it evil, because it laughed at our power, as well as took away from us our converts."

The above is in substance a story told us at Salem, Illinois, not long ago.

In the meantime we will give our views of the matter. In all revival meetings there are three physical conditions with the people:

1. That texture and condition of the cuticle, that is dry and silk-like, is positive, in fact non-conductors of odd forces, mesmeric influences, animal magnetism, or electricity. Such as these are never revival subjects.

2. The warm, clammy cuticle, which are natural conditions, can be affected by either or all of the above influences, are never very rabid or loud-mouthed in their religious experiences; they are the conservatives in religious revivals, and are seldom excitably affected, usually calm under conversion.

3. The cold, clammy cuticle: Such as these are the best revival subjects; first on the anxious seat, loudest in their shouts, full of glory, get sanctified very easily, and lose all their gettings as readily as they receive it. All such are good subjects for good or evil influences; subjects alike for the penitentiary, the lunatic asylum, prostitution, intemperance, and the revival meeting. They are magnetic conditions, hence

easily affected by any of the influences referred to above; the subtle force of which permeates the whole system of the being, bringing him or her into sin, or virtue, and so long as the evil or good producing the influence is present with the victim, the victim is a prisoner.

In the case referred to by the Rev. Aaron Bickley, the young man was only under a partial animal magnetic influence, and had a warm clammy cuticle, and his influence was entirely of and from the minister, and had never been nearer heaven than the brain of the tallest minister at the meeting. Hence, he was under their control, magnetically.

The young lady was non-insulated, had the cold, clammy cuticle, was fully and thoroughly magnetized by the minister, and arising for the purpose of coming forward for prayer, she came in contact with a spirit electrician, who took her out of the hands of the minister and all on whom this spirit could concentrate his electric battery, through her magnetism. The same were subjective to her and the spirit, or, to the spirit through her. It does not follow that the spirit or the influence was evil, but, on the contrary, good. And that it was of God is patent, inasmuch as it was superior to, and independent of, the minister, or the revival. If ministers would study the law of influences a little more, and theology a little less — if they knew a little more of man and less of metaphysics — they would know more of God.

If they were well posted in electrical laws, they would not talk of electricity as they do, for whenever they make an electric current intelligent, they place an operator at each end of the electric chain, and if the receiver is in sight the giver must be beyond.

If any clergyman or other person can give a better solution of Mr. Bickley's story, we should like to receive it.

### *CHRISTIAN GENEROSITY ILLUSTRATED.*

Dr. Tyng, Jr., preaches the gospel to the poor in New Jersey, and is tried for a misdemeanor for violation of a canon of *the Church*, and is suspended from his holy profession. Are the following words from Jesus found in the canons of Dr. Tyng's church? "And the gospel is preached to the poor." Matthew xi: 4.

Mr. Stuart, of Philadelphia, introduces instrumental music into the services of his church, and the church authorities expel him. Dr. Stuart's church evidently have little confidence in the musical proclivities of the inspired Psalmist, David the King, for he says, "Let them praise his name in the dance; let them praise his name on the timbrel and harp." Psalms cxlix: 3. Again, "Praise ye the Lord; praise him with the sound of the trumpet; praise him with the psalter and harp; with the timbrel and dance; with the stringed instruments and organs; upon the loud cymbals." Psalms cl.

The Methodists of London, Nebraska, turn the members of the Christian Church out of doors, and that, too, after the Christian people had contributed of their means to build the church. Question. Which of these denominations will God side with?

The Presbyterians of Salem, Illinois, are holding meetings in the Baptist church. The church takes fire during the revival and burns up. The Presbyterian folks then built themselves a nice church, and dedicated it to the Lord, and bless the Lord that they have a house of their own. The Baptist people rejoice with them, and come to worship in their Presbyterian brethrens' house.

"No, no," say the Presbyterians, "we cannot let you into our church. It would not be right for us to thus desecrate the Lord's house."

"But look here," say the Baptist folks, "we let you into our house, and you burned it up, and we do not want you to pay for the house, but only to let us in out of the cold."

"But, my Baptist friends, we did not burn your house; God, in his merciful Providence, done it, that you might see the foolishness of your ways, and repent you of your plunging follies. It is now a warning, and you should heed it, and leave your cold water baths, and come under our sprinkling pot, and then there is no danger of your getting cold, or getting drowned. But, so far as your preaching or holding meetings in our house, that is out of the question."

The Presbyterians of Salem evidently do not believe in Jesus or his golden rule.

And we advise the Baptists hereafter to accept of the gospel of Spiritualism, and worship in public halls, and then they will have no churches to be burned up by the Lord, because they let Presbyterians hold revival meetings in them.

### *BRICKBATS AND THEOLOGY VS. SPIRITUAL FACTS AND ARGUMENTS.*

In the spring of 1868, we lectured in Clarence, Missouri, a thriving little town on the Hannibal and St. Joseph Railroad. The people have built a nice little church for Sunday meetings, and after our engagement, they called on the minister for the use of the house, the trustees being willing.

"No sir," said the Reverend Steal, "cannot let you in."

"But," said the applicants, "we are citizens here, and help support preaching."

"That does not alter the case. You cannot have the Lord's house for the devil to teach in." Well, this ended the matter, so far as the house was concerned. But when we came, we had to go into a small hall not half large enough for the audience. Some of the trustees proposed to take the church, will ye, nil ye. As a Spiritualist, believing in the golden rule? (for we would not like any one to break into our house.) Hence we declined to speak in the church.

Well, the Rev. Mr. Steal opposed our meetings, advised the people to keep away, for it was the work of the devil. But the people came, they saw, and heard, and believed, and called for more lectures.

On Monday, the second of November, we lectured again in Clarence, with increased audiences, in a new hall. And not satisfied with refusing us the church, they treated us to a dose of brickbats and stones. When in the midst of our discourse, with all the brain of Clarence with us, there was a crash. Many thought it a pistol. Glass was scattered in every direction. The fine, large window was, in short, ruined. The missile was thrown by some one outside of the house. Who threw it? Echo does not answer — reason and logic does.

Let us see facts. The Radicals and Spiritualists were all in the hall. The minister was not in the hall, nor were the faithful few of his church. He had refused us the church. He had advised the people to keep away from our meetings. He had pronounced our teachings of the devil. He believes the devil should be surprised, and accepts the logic of Moses. Who threw the brickbat?

Echo does not answer. Logic does. It is all right, my religious friend. Continue to do thus. You only lack the power to crucify. You are willing to do anything in the name of your Christ, for you believe him capable of and willing to forgive your every offense done in his name. Give us a few more brickbats, for every one you give us makes converts to our side, and the one you threw in Clarence added a dozen to our cause. Refuse us the house of God to lecture in, and let it to a political rabble, or a negro minstrel company. How true the adage that "Birds of a feather flock together."

*BAPTIZED INTO GLORY.*

We clip the following from an Atchison (Kansas) paper, of October, 1868:

"A man named Stephenson was drowned in the Platt river, last Sunday, at Savannah, Missouri, while being baptized."

Will the minister who officiated at this awful tragedy explain how it came about? Why did you drop him, Mr. Minister? And why did you go into such deep water? Oh holy man! what will his wife and children say (if he has any)? But his friends and the public. How do you clear your skirts of the crime of manslaughter? You may answer that it was his wish to be baptized. Granted, but he did not ask you to drown him. Far from it.

Again: You coaxed him, plead with him, prayed with him; yea, verily, frightened him into letting you baptize him, and you took the poor fellow down into the water and drowned him. Suppose we, the Spiritualists, had done this, would you let us off? Not a bit of it. You would have given us fits, and then dosed us on hell-fire for a full eternity to cure the fits. All your papers would have had a double-leaded editorial, of four columns' length, on the evils of Spiritualism, and every soul of your church, and all other churches, would have been clamorous for the trial and execution of the villain who drowned a man baptizing him spiritually. But it is a horse of another color when it takes place in your church; and no doubt you will console his friends with the holy thought that in ducking your brother under the water you ducked him into heaven. Well, well, we hope you did. But look out, Mr. Minister, and take a light with you whenever you go to bed, or you may meet a wet sheet one of these nights, and they are cold and unpleasant things to sleep with.

---

## CHAPTER XXVIII.

The Cause in Philadelphia—The Prayer Gauge.

### *THE CAUSE IN PHILADELPHIA.*

We have had Wheeler and Wilson with us during February, 1870—not they of sewing-machine notoriety—but, as some of our theological friends think, they belong to the Ripping Machine Company. Old theology suffered some by the scathing words of these noble men. It was their first appearance in the City of Brotherly Love. Brother Wheeler lectured for our society, and has earned for himself the reputation of being not only a clear, bold, and logical thinker, but, what is still more important, in this practical age, a very able and practical lecturer. The complaint which we heard against him was, that he crowded too many thoughts into his lecture.

The spirits who use him seem determined to do all

they can, to scatter broadcast the truths that are to redeem the world. We think Brother Wheeler should be kept at the work; and the friends who desire to have a great amount of thought compressed into a small space, cannot do better than to engage him. He will stir the pool of Siloam, that the sick may enter in and be healed while the waters are troubled. A very interesting feature, in connection with Mr. Wheeler's mediumship, is the improvisation of poems of real merit.

We need not say anything to the public of our colaborer, E. V. Wilson, who has been all over the land, wielding his sledge-hammer. He has given four lectures and seances here. From a large number of striking tests, we will select two or three. A gentleman from Camden was present, who had been attending spiritual meetings and visiting mediums for more than thirteen years, and had never received any tests. Mr. Wilson stepped up to him, and said:

"I see by your side a little girl, about three years old; she stands there in a playful manner, passing her hand through your hair; she was not your daughter nor your sister, but a child to whom you were much attached; she died five years ago last August."

He then gave a minute description of her. The gentleman said:

"I was living in a family where there was a little girl of that description. She died at the very time you speak of. I consider the identity entirely satisfactory. This is the first test I have ever received."

Again Brother Wilson said:

"I now see standing beside you a tall, slim girl, who is your sister; she died at the age of sixteen."

The gentleman was a stout man. Mr. Wilson continued;

"She is very unlike you — takes after her mother, and you from your father."

He then gave a minute description, which was fully recognized, and pronounced satisfactory.

A gentleman, about fifty years of age, asked Mr. Wilson if he did not think he could account for all these things by reading the minds of the people?

"Well," replied Mr. W., "If you could, that would be a spiritual phenomenon in itself, but I do not think you can. But I saw, while we were talking, an incident in your life, which, if you have no objection, I will tell the audience about."

"Not the least," said he.

"When you were a boy, about eleven years old, you were butted by a sheep, knocked down and rolled over; he struck you in the back, and hurt you considerably."

"That is all very true. I went into the barn-yard, when I was just turned of eleven years old, and was knocked down, just as you say, and rolled over by a sheep."

This reminds us of an incident that occurred in our own experience, some years ago, showing that spirits are cognizant of the conditions of animals, either directly, or through human beings. We were writing a letter to Hannah Brown, just after we had published the narrative of Dr. Ackley. Samuel Paist, a blind medium, was sitting by our side. We asked if the doctor was present, and, receiving an affirmative answer, inquired whether he had anything to say to Mrs. Brown. The medium, smiling, said: "Why; it is very strange; he says:"

"Tell her I am glad she has got over her dog fever."

In a few days, we had a response from her, in which she remarked that this was a very remarkable test. There had been a number of robberies in Cleveland, and they were desirous of having a watch-dog. She had spent considerable time in hunting for one, and her milk man had brought one in not an hour before the time alluded to by the Doctor, and the animal was lying on the rug, asleep, when he made the remark to us, at a distance of five hundred miles from the place.

Many of the old Spiritualists are devoted to the alphabet of our philosophy, and seek tests with all the eagerness of new converts. We have no controversy with this, for the sensuous physical manifestations are, in reality, the basis on which all of our philosophy and religion must rest; and we hail with pleasure the abundant evidences which are abroad in the land to-day, that the Spirit World is in earnest in presenting these most valuable evidences to humanity.

Let us sustain and encourage our mediums everywhere; defend them from the poisonous breath of slander, and thus enable them to become more perfect instruments, through which the angel world may shower down blessings on humanity.

## "THE PRAYER GAUGE."

Professor Tyndall seems to have shocked Christianity in a fearful manner, by his proposal to "measure prayer." Everywhere, in churches, conventions, and conferences, Christians are disturbed, and are denouncing the proposition of the Professor as "atheistic and blasphemous," hence it is rejected.

Will Professor Tyndall make this proposition to the world? First, let a hospital in London, or Paris, be set apart for the church; let the Catholics have full charge of one-half the patients, and the Protestants of the other half; let the subjects in the Protestant wards be Catholics, and those in the Catholic wards Protestants; and let nothing but prayer and faith be exercised in these wards, and, at the end of the year, weigh results. Second, let science, through her doctors, have the full charge of a hospital in the same city with our Christians, where there shall not be a prayer made during the year, and only such treatment as science may determine, and let the number of patients be the same, and, at the end of the year, count results. Third, give the Spiritualists a hospital in the same city; let us have an equal number of patients, taking our chances; let us come in with our magnetizers, healers, seers, and clairvoyant physicians, and, at the end of the year, weigh results.

We will not declare the proposition to be "atheistic or blasphemous," for we believe in God, science, and the power of spirits to heal the sick, and we believe in our mediums.

Christians, in rejecting Professor Tyndall's proposal,

you refuse to test the power you claim to receive from Jesus; you deny the teachings of the Old and New Testaments, and concede that you are not called of Christ, and that you have not the power he gave his disciples.

We, the Spiritualists, have that power — the power from God, through spirits who were once men and women, who, in the language of John's angel, on Patmos, can say, "I am he that liveth, and was dead; and, behold, I am alive forevermore."

O, ministers of Jesus Christ! O, Christianity! how are ye fallen! The Rev. Professor Braden said to us, in Cleveland, Ohio, in March, 1871, when discussing Bible Spiritualism: "Sir, there is the rock of ages — the word of God, the Bible — sustained by logic, science, history, and God." Profesor Braden is a Christian minister, and believes in Jesus Christ. Professor Braden said to us: "When science sustains Spiritualism, I shall accept it." Science has and does sustain Spiritualism; and we say to all ministers of Christ: Gentlemen, when you have fully accepted the "prayer gauge," laid down by Professor Tyndall, and are fully sustained, we will believe in you, and not before.

# CHAPTER XXIX.

Lexington, Ky.—A Startling Test—I am in your Hands—J. B. Sandusky Testifies—The Doubting Tom Marshall.

*FROM LEXINGTON, KENTUCKY.*

In this chapter we present you with the following account of our debut in the ancient and conservative city of Lexington, Kentucky.

From what we have seen of Lexington and its people, we are favorably impressed with their kindly natures, generous hospitality and intelligence.

Our audience last night was a thinking one, and such an one as we love to speak before. The field here is a rich one, and open to the acceptance of the truths of Spiritualism. There must, however, be no nonsense, cant or hypocrisy preached here. The speaker and medium must be prepared to do battle with intellectual giants.

Last night, January 16, 1873, we gave nine tests of marked and startling character. To Mr. H. we delineated his character, and then mentioned four dates in his life history, giving incident and details, all of which were approved save one. We then stated, "Ladies and Gentlemen: we frankly confess to you, that we have been posted in regard to this man's history. The parties posting us are two spirits now with him—one a female who died long ago when a little girl—she is now a full grown woman, clothed in a loose garment down to the feet. She is a brunette in complexion, dark eyes, very dark glossy hair, features oval, hair full and hanging loose over her shoulders. This woman is your sister. The other spirit is a man, and we believe he is your father, or belongs to your father's family. He is tall, of commanding appearance, and unlike you in every respect — he is fair, has gray hair, is clean shaved, forehead high and full, and was seventy-five or eighty years old when he left the form.

"I am in your hands, sir, and you are to prove or disprove this statement. We close the door behind us, cutting off every avenue of retreat. What we have stated is true or false. What say you?"

Mr. H. replied: "So far as my character as a man may be concerned, I shall leave the people that know me to decide. In regard to historical events in my life, you have reported them very correctly — save in this statement of eight years ago — that I do not identify."

Mr. J. B. Sandusky arose and said, "I have known this man from his boyhood up to the present time, and I could not have read him as correctly as Mr. Wilson has done this evening."

We then asked him, "What about your sister?"

"I had a sister, a young girl, who died in 1833. I was quite young at the time, and only remember her as a little girl, hence could not testify of her clearly from memory. I do not identify the man."

"Will you describe your father?"

"Yes; my father was six feet one in height, of a commanding appearance, and fair of complexion —

had gray hair, and at his death wore a long full gray beard. He died between seventy and eighty years of age, and has been dead about eight years."

"Had your father worn this beard all his life?"

"No; only a few years before his death."

Several gentlemen confirmed the accuracy of our description of the father of Mr. H., minus the beard.

We then turned to Mr. W., saying, "We see by you, and between you and the gentleman sitting on your right, a young woman," fully describing her. "It is our opinion she is your daughter. She does not say so. It is only our opinion—have you buried a daughter?"

"No; I have never buried a daughter."

"Do you identify this spirit woman as one that you know?"

"No; I do not."

Turning to the other man on his right, "Do you identify this spirit woman?"

"Yes; you have described my daughter, who died some four years ago, as correctly as I could have done."

To Mrs. Dr. S. we said, "When fifteen years old, in your sixteenth year, in October, you resolved on a conclusion—that conclusion has affected your whole life, and it was—'If I cannot have the whole confidence of every friend, relative or companion, I want none of it;' further, that conclusion then at the age referred to, not only affected you, but another, causing you to throw overboard the acquaintance and friendship of one, a man every way your equal in life, you detecting this trait of withholding his confidence from you." The lady answered, "You are correct, exceedingly so; and I was thinking of the time, the party and conclusion as you spoke them."

We then stated, "Ladies and Gentlemen: there is here to-night a man from spirit-life — he is tall and of commanding appearance; he was a professional man of extraordinary ability, an attorney by profession, and stood here in this position — the thumb of his left hand in his waistcoat, thus balancing his weight on his right foot, the left slightly advanced, his right hand hanging at ease, his chest slightly thrown forward, head a little to the left and thrown back, age about fifty, his hair dark gray, has side whiskers, his face and form evidences dissipation of which we believe he died some fourteen years ago. He was an able and eloquent man. He identifies these two men on my left, and knew those parties setting before me, and then steps over to this old man, lays his right hand on his shoulder familiarly, saying, 'Old friend, does this shake your skepticism in regard to Spiritualism?'"

"Yes, it does," said the man.

"Did you know the man?" we asked.

"Yes, I did."

Then many said it is Tom. Marshall; and all were exceedingly surprised. Thus we have opened the ball and intend to keep it rolling on and on until the victory is won.

## CHAPTER XXX.

### *TESTS AT GREENVILLE, ILLINOIS.*

Greenville, Bond county, Illinois, forty-nine miles southeast of St. Louis, is comparatively a new field for Spiritualism, and yet there is material in this locality for the harvest. All that they require now is "the test." It is a thriving place of some 1,000 inhabitants, with several churches, and any amount of infidelity; and why should there not be, where Christians will pay seventy-five dollars a night for a New Yorker to make faces for them to look at, and grumble at ten or fifteen dollars a night for the Gospel, that cheers the soul and points out the way to life eternal; and yet, such is the fact, not only at Greenville, but all over the country.

We gave four lectures and a matinee at this place, commencing with ninety souls, and concluding with a house packed to overflowing; and the cry still echoes in our ears, "Come again! come again!"

In Greenville, we gave many tests of character, life incidents, diagnoses of disease, and descriptions of spirits, nine out of ten of which were fully recognized.

To Wm. M. Evans, merchant. "We see with you a woman," fully describing her; "she is your wife."

Mr. Evans said: "This is the first correct description of my wife that has ever been given by a spirit medium, and is strictly correct."

Mr. M., a skeptic, unknown to us — we read his character, and gave the important incidents in his life. We then read the antecedents of his family — the father and mother — and stated to the people, "This statement we have received is given us by the spirit of a woman, who says she is his sister."

Mr. M., as well as those who knew him, said, in the main, "You are correct."

"What about the sister?"

"I have buried a sister that answers well to the description given by the speaker."

To an old man, after reading his character, describing his parents, and telling him which one of his family he resembled, we said: "There is with you five spirits — an old man and woman; the man on your right, and the woman on your left; the woman is stout, fair, and very much like yourself; she is your mother; the other is spare, not stout, five feet nine inches in height, very dark, dark hair and eyes; he is your father, and is unlike you. Between these are two or three others — one a youth when he left the form — he is your son; the third is a woman; [fully described her;] she does not say she is your wife, and yet her interest in you is equivalent to that a wife would have in one she had loved as a husband; it is our opinion that she is your wife. The next, a girl of twenty years when she left the form, is now an immortal woman by your side, only waiting to welcome you to her home in spirit life. What say you; are we right, or wrong?"

"Well, about half and half, as any one might guess."

Ha-ha-ha, and an accompanied laugh from all over the house followed.

Wait, ladies and gentlemen; be sure you have something to laugh at, and then laugh to your heart's content. Now, sir, I want you to answer me correctly. What part of the statement made by us is not correct?

"Well, you have not described my father, for one thing."

"Will you describe him?"

"Well, he was not as tall, nor as heavy, as I am; besides, he had dark complexion, with dark eyes and hair."

"Very well, sir. In what does that differ from our statement?"

"You said I was like him."

"No, sir; we said no such thing; we said you were unlike him, and like your mother."

"Well, you are right there. But I have never lost a wife, unless she has died, or run off, since I left home."

"But, sir, we did not say she was your wife. Do you identify this woman as a relative of yours?"

"Well, you tell."

"No, sir; we have had our say; we are now after what you say."

"Well, I don't know; I will talk with you some other time."

"No, sir; at no other time, but now. Do you recognize this young man and woman? Have you lost a son and daughter?"

"Well, yes; I have."

"How, sir, about the incidents and life-history given by these spirits; is it false, or true? We insist on an answer."

A gentleman rose up, saying: "I will answer. He is my father-in-law; and you are strictly right in all you have said."

"Yes, you are about right," said the old man.

We subsequently saw his daughter, who affirmed all that was said, and "the woman you took for his wife was his sister, who died at twenty-five," she said.

To a lady (Mrs. W.), on the breaking up of the meeting that night, we said: "There is a sweet little one — a child in long clothes — held out in the air before you; it is yours, and it entered spirit life a child."

"Yes," said the mother, "it is my darling," and the soft, mellow voice of the woman spoke the soul of the mother.

To Mrs. E. "I find with you a spirit, who lost his life by an accident — from the fall of some ponderous matter. He is a young man. [We fully described him.] He is your brother."

"Yes."

"We see by us a boy. If living to-day, he would be about fourteen years old. He was drowned when a child, and some eleven or twelve years ago."

This child was recognized by many, who knew him. The mother and son were both drowned on the same day.

Thus the work goes bravely on, making many to think of, if not to believe, the facts of immortality, as made plain by Spiritualism. In fact, the evidence of immortality is now demonstrated, and no longer are we left to doubt, and compelled to rest our hopes of immortal, or continued, life on the testimony of the few. The science of Spiritualism is fast sweeping from our way, to the Summer Land, the superstitions of the past—one by one they disappear: First, an angry God gives place to one of love; second, the City of New Jerusalem becomes the beautiful Summer Land, with flowers, trees, green fields interspersed with streams, rivers, lakes, seas, and oceans, all settled with islands. Then the Devil, that old horned, hoofed, and long-tailed fellow, with his fiery breath, freighted with the smell of sulphur, saltpetre, kerosene, and blue lightning, has changed, through the teachings of Spiritualism, into a very gentlemanly Diakka, living in the beautiful Wilderness of Mischief, whose chief delight is to impose on the credulity of the Bostonians and New Yorkers.

---

## CHAPTER XXXI.

### *THE OLD SPIRIT OF BITTERNESS STILL LIVES.*

We spoke in West Chester, Pennsylvania, on the evenings of February 13 and 14, 1873, to small, but intelligent, audiences.

On our way to Philadelphia, Saturday morning, the 15th, we happened to be seated in front of a lady and gentleman of Quaker extraction, who were canvassing matters and things in general, in a very animated manner. We were reading the "Philadelphia Press," and, at first, did not note what they were talking about. Soon, however, we heard thus:

"Were you at the Spiritual meeting last night?"

"No! were you?"

"Assuredly not. I do not believe in their teachings. Father, mother, and my brother went, and wanted me to go, but I told them, very decidedly, that I did not sanction the meeting, nor would I countenance it by my presence."

"What did your friends think of the meeting?"

"Oh! they said the man was an able speaker, and taught from the Bible. But I do n't believe these Spiritual meetings ought to be sanctioned. What will the world come to, if they continue to increase? There ought to be a stop put to it! Yes, there had."

At this point of their conversation, we stepped in, saying:

"My good woman, that is precisely what our Puritan fathers, in New England, said of you Quakers, and they carried their say into effect; they arrested your people, fined, whipped, and imprisoned them, and, we believe, they hung some of them by the neck until they were dead. They did not believe in tolerating Quaker meetings, any more than you do these Spiritual meetings. And, Madam, are you not now just where these old Puritans were? Did you ever hear a Spiritualist say that Quaker meetings ought not to be tolerated?"

"Oh! but, sir, those things are of the past. Times have changed, and their bitterness toward us has passed away."

"Yes, Madam, those things are of the past, and their descendants have changed the spleen and hatred of the Pilgrim fathers from the Quakers to the Spiritualists, and the children of those persecuted Quakers have joined hands with the enemies of their fathers, and hate the common foe, Spiritualism."

"Oh, no! not that! We do not hate them, or persecute them, as those Puritans did the Quakers."

"No! not exactly. You do not stone the Spiritualists, but you manifest the spirit to do so. You have exhibited that old bitter spirit in this conversation, in a marked degree. You said, 'I will not countenance, or tolerate, these meetings, and they ought to be stopped.' You do not deal the blow, but you exhibit the spirit to do it, and only lack the opportunity to do so."

"But, my dear sir," said her friend, "the Spiritualists tear the Bible all to pieces; they do not believe in God, and are free-lovers; they throw down all barriers between right and wrong; they have nothing for us to pin to whatever."

As he closed his speech, he looked as though he had silenced all opposition, but we replied:

"First, how do you know they tear the Bible to pieces? Do you read the Spiritual papers?"

"No; I do not."

"Have you attended their meetings?"

"No; I have not."

"Then how do you know they do these things?"

"Well, it is common report."

"But, my dear sir, 'common report' is a great liar. And now, as to the free-love question, the only legitimate free-lovers in the United States, found their principles on Jesus Christ and him crucified—they deny Spiritualism."

"But," he asked, "what shall we have to lean upon, if you take away the Bible, and have no God?"

"My dear sir, you may have just as many Bibles and Gods to lean on as you please. We do not accept your Bible or your God. Conscience, our guide, never fails us when we obey it; and you and this lady have nothing else to lean on. You accept God, the Bible, and your religion from your internal knowledge of right, and then undertake to enforce your views—not God's."

"But, sir," said he, "conscience is not reliable. We must have something more to lean upon than the selfish expression of conscience; we must have God, the Bible, and his Christ."

"Do you endorse the Bible and the Hebraic God?"

"Yes, sir, I do," said he.

"So do I, sir," said the lady; "and I never trust my conscience."

"No; it will not do," said he.

"Let us see if you pin to the Bible. Do you eat swine flesh?"

"Yes; but we are not living in those days."

"But you are worshiping the God of those days, and have 'pinned' to the Bible of those days. Do you wear garments of mixed materials?"

"Yes; but what has that to do with it?"

"It is Bible, sir, and a commandment from God. He has never revoked those laws; how dare you do it? Are you circumcised?"

"No; nor do not mean to be."

"Well, you must be, if you 'pin' to the Bible, for it is the command of God, and Jesus did not revoke the law. Are you willing to go in unto your brother's wife, you having a wife, and raise up to your brother seed, in case your brother dies without seed?"

"No; I will not."

"Then you only 'pin' to such parts of the Bible as your conscience, or internal knowledge, will warrant you to do?"

"Well, we certainly mean to exercise our judgment in these things."

"We believe, sir, that this is all the Spiritualists demand."

"Is our conscience an infallible guide?" asked the lady.

"Most decidedly! we have no other."

"Then you reject the advice of Jesus?" said he.

"No; we accept it on its merit, for just what our conscience is willing to pay for it."

"Who, then, will be leader?"

"He that knows the most and is nearest right."

"Then you reject God and his Christ?"

"That very much depends on whose God I am

called on to accept. If you mean the Hebraic God, and his Christ, in the sense they are taught, I certainly reject them both."

"What God do you accept, sir?"

"The God of nature, who never died, who measures all space in a thought, holds all matter on the tip of his finger, whose soul is fire, and electricity his nerve force — a law in which we live, move, and have our being. Man is his mouth-piece."

"I am sorry to hear you say that, for you cut yourself off from his mercies."

"Whose mercies do we lose?"

"God's mercy."

"What God?"

"The God of the Bible."

"But, sir, when did he ever show us any mercy? Has he been merciful to these black men, with us? Did he exhibit mercy to the poor of Chicago, or the French? Has he not sent us delusions, lying spirits, earthquakes, deluges, scourges, wars, and pestilence?"

"Yes; but we deserved it."

"But, sir, if we deserve it, did he not make us deserve it?"

"But we have no right to question him."

"Who?"

"God."

"But, sir, you question him every day, and every hour. You tell him what to do, and what not to do. You, in your prayers, beg him come, and bid him bless, at your wish."

"Philadelphia!" cried the brakeman, and we parted.

# CHAPTER XXXII.

The Death Scene of Phineas Eames — Under Spirit Control.

*APOTHEOSIS.*

To our friends who rendered us help on the occasion of the terrible calamity that overtook our brother-in-law and his family, on the eighth of October, 1871, we wish to say, that the work of the fire-king so fearfully began at that time, closed up in the birth of Phineas Eames into spirit-life from our farm-house, Lombard, Illinois, on Saturday morning, June 7, 1873, at 10½ o'clock — the anniversary of his fifty-fifth birthday.

Our readers will remember the account of his terrible suffering in the Peshtigo and Menominee fires, related in Chapter VII., whereby he lost his wife and two children, an only son and baby daughter, and himself nearly burned to death — his wonderful preservation with his two surviving daughters of twelve and fourteen years of age — how in his hour of distress, suffering the most excruciating pain and agony, ablaze with fire from head to foot, praying that he might die and be freed from his sufferings, the angels came (as of old) and ministered unto him, he both seeing them and feeling their touch — from that hour his pain left him, never more to return, and during the days and weeks he lay helpless in the Fire-hospital, no pain was felt from his burns, and he was a living demonstration of spirit power. When able to be removed we sent for him to come with his motherless girls and make our home theirs. They came, and for many months Mr. Eames was quite helpless.

In September, 1872, with the assistance rendered us by generous friends, we placed the girls (Nettie and Mary) in school at Rockford, Illinois, under the motherly care and teaching of Mrs. S. W. Holem's non sectarian school. In the meantime, Mr. Eames continued to improve in health all through the summer, besides making himself useful on our farm, as far as he was able to do so.

In November last, he felt a strong desire to return to the scenes of his misfortune, and see what could be done with the wreck of his once happy home. As the State assisted old settlers who wished to rebuild, with the assistance thus attained he commenced the work of rebuilding, but could not finish. Visiting the scenes of his misfortune, recalling the terrible death of his wife and children, his exposure to the unusual cold weather of last winter, all combined, proved more than he could bear, and he sank beneath the pressure. Again, we were informed of his very dangerous condition, friends writing us that he was sick unto death, and desired to see his daughters once more, and wishing to return to our home. On the twenty-third of May, Mary went for him, found him better than she expected. His physician advising the change; all thought it would do him good. On the morning of the twenty-ninth of May, Mary returned with him to our home, and for a few days he seemed much better, walked abroad and expressed himself as being very happy in being at home again.

We called in our family physician, Dr. Pratt, of Wheaton, who informed us that his stay with us was short indeed. We sent for his daughters to return home from their school, and be with their father the few days he was to remain with us in earth-life. They came on the third of June, and their presence cheered and comforted him. He fully realizing his condition, talked with the girls, Nettie and Mary, as if going on a journey, making every preparation, giving them counsel and advice in regard to the future, earnestly impressing upon them his desire for them to continue their studies, and to prove by their application and deportment their appreciation of all the love and kindness bestowed on them by teachers and friends. Then with heart overflowing with love he commended his (soon to be orphans) girls to our continued care, and that of their aunt, Mrs. Gould, who willingly assumes with us the responsibility of their education. To their teachers, at Rockford, together with the ladies of Dr. Kerr's congregation, who have so nobly assisted us the past year in their education, he sent a father's dying blessing and thanks, and felt (with us) that they, in their good work, have truly lived and carried out the Christ principle of our beautiful Spiritualism. God and the angels be with them.

Each day and hour, he impressed upon us all, his firm belief in spirit power to sustain by their presence, and cheer him in his birth into spirit-life, and as the end drew near, told us what he saw and heard.

Thursday evening, he saw a vision of two boats; in one was his wife, her mother and sister, and his son who was burned. In the other boat was the father of his wife, her brother, and brother-in-law, the late Ingraham Gould, Esq., of Beaver Dam. They talked with him sometime, and on leaving said, "We will come again, and the third time will take you with us to our spirit home." On Friday, June 6th, he saw the boats again, and the friends from Spirit Land, and their visit made him very happy, and for some time they held sweet converse with him on facts and scenes in Spirit Life. On Saturday morning, about sunrise, June 7th, his fifty-fifth birthday, he said:

"Mary, the boat has come for me. It is large, and very dear ones are in it." Then quietly, with perfect peace in his soul, he stepped into the ferry that carries us over the river to our home in the Summer Land, patiently waiting for the summons to cross the river. He then called the family around him together with the move of the hand, and taking each one by the hand, bid them good-bye, and after resting a few moments said, "Friends, I am aware that my time here is short, and that soon I shall leave you. I wish you all to know that I am a Spiritualist, and trust that the time will come when you will all think as I do. I am perfectly resigned to the will of God, and have not a shadow of fear, and am ready and willing to go, only waiting for the summons. I wish it distinctly understood, I want no orthodox minister to preach my funeral sermon, but a Spiritualist, if one can be obtained. I am too weak to say more. I ask you all to so live that you may meet me over the river. Good-bye."

This was before six o'clock on the morning of June 7th, Saturday, during the hours of transition, he requested music, and some of the family was at the piano every moment, cheering him with music till all was over. He retained his faculties to the last moment of earth-life, reviving every few moments to speak a word of cheering love to us, and many times, during the hours of transition, he would kiss the lips of his daughters, who occupied a place by him, Nettie on one side and Mary on the other. Long will they remember, as well as all present, the grand sublimity of this birth into spirit life. A little before his last earth moment the doctor called, and as he came into the calm and quiet room where the spirit-birth was taking place, Mrs. Gould said, "Brother Eames, Dr. Kippax is here." He revived and gave him his hand, saying, "It is all over. Good-bye." Then he asked for music again, as it had ceased while the doctor was talking; who also testified to the soothing power of music in this trying hour that comes to all. Thus gently he was born into spirit life, entering upon his journey over the river without a struggle or a groan, and while we were singing a favorite piece of his:

> "Joyfully, joyfully onward I move,
> Bound for the land of bright spirits above."

The angel friends who stood around him, joined in with us, and we heard their voices of praise distinctly, and while singing, the last breath here was drawn, and his spirit was born into the higher life beyond the river, at half-past ten o'clock, A. M.

Was this death? Call it not death! but life continued. We obtained the services of Dr. Julia H. Severance, of Milwaukee, to speak words of cheer to the living, on the occasion of laying the casket that once contained the germ of life, known to men as Phineas Eames, away in the ground, on Monday, at the hour of evening twilight, June 9th, 1873.

Many kind friends came together on this occasion, listening for the first time to a Spiritualist burial service. Wreaths of white flowers were lovingly laid upon the casket by his children and our family as we tenderly lowered it to its last resting-place — all realizing fully that he was not in the casket we were placing in the ground, but standing with us, our spirit brother, and henceforth would become the angel guardian of his children, assisting us in their culture and development into womanhood.

# CHAPTER XXXIII.

A Miracle, or Something Like It — The Lottery and Church Gambling — The Death of Ingraham Gould, Esq. — His Home in the Spirit Land.

*A MIRACLE, OR SOMETHING VERY NEAR ONE.*

We present our readers with the following letter. It is but one of many, in our possession, of kindred character. Oh! the blessed joy that sometimes steals over us, when reading these proofs of our labor, in its effects on our race, and we feel that we have lived not in vain. Please read the old man's letter:

E. V. Wilson —*Dear Sir and Brother:* It is with gratitude to God, that I remember your labors in Wheeling, West Virginia, although my age and state of health forbid my attendance but twice. That, in respect to your labors, for which I feel the most thankful, is the curing of a beloved kinsman of the use of tobacco, and all cravings for it. I was present when you performed this miracle, for all that we call miracles are performances of a similar kind. At the moment that you came down with such power on the use of the poisonous weed, all desire for the further use of tobacco left him, and a resolution never to use it more, took its place, and has continued with him to this time.

When habitual tobacco-users enter spirit-life, where

tobacco grows not, do they seek the haunts of those in earth-life who are in the use of this poisonous weed, in order to gratify tastes formed in earth-life, thus increasing in their mediums a desire for the use of tobacco? May not this account for the difficulty many have to disabuse themselves of its use, as well as the beginning of an appetite for? Is it not even so in the use of whisky, as well as of all other intoxicating drinks? Does not this account for the difficulty men have in breaking off any fixed habit? Does not this same principle operate on all sensitive natures, thus preventing their cure?

In my nephew's case, his mind was impressed with such force and power as to expel the demon quite out of his taste; and now he needs spiritual aid to keep him to his resolution until such time, that, through his growth into a healthier state, he may be able to be master of himself. Truly yours,

JOHN S. WILLIAMS.

*Bridgeport, Ohio, February* 8, 1873.

We well remember our aged brother and his kinsman, and may the resolution of the latter continue through all time.

We have frequently witnessed the spirits of drunkards and tobacco-chewers, absorbing from the brain of drinkers and chewers the eliminations of that which they were consuming; and there is no safety for the man or woman who indulges in the use of those terrible poisons. That human beings are possessed of spirits of kindred natures, who delight in their intoxicating habits, we know to be a fact, and our only safety is in abstaining from their use.

A second letter, lying before us, identifies a test which we deem worthy of record :

Dear Brother Wilson: I want to say to you that I never have been satisfied with my interview with you, and my spirit friends. Those tests that you gave me had gone so far from my memory that I could not get things together right, until I had time to study it up. I now can say that you were right, in every particular. In regard to the spirit woman you saw and described so carefully, those that were well acquainted with her say you were right. The test is a fact, and a good one.

I hope you may drop around again before long. Next time, I want to have the pleasure of hearing you one night, at least.

Truly, your brother, G. F.

*Long Lake, Minn., January* 22, 1873.

## *APOTHEOSIS.*

Gone on to the gardens of the Summer Land, from Beaver Dam, Wisconsin, in company with the angels, Ingraham Gould, in the sixty-first year of his earth-life.

My brother was born into this life at Leeds, Kennebec county, Maine, on the 19th of January, 1811; born into the superior life on the 16th of July, 1871.

In his exchange from this, to a higher, life, he has gained; we have lost a friend and a brother; Beaver

Dam has lost a citizen that cannot be replaced. His genius, enterprise, and ambition, led him to do what few men will undertake — that is, to adorn the homes of the many, as well as his own. His nursery was the pride of the city, and will long remain a green and beautiful monument to his memory. Everywhere throughout the West, may be found the weeping willow, the mountain ash, and other ornamental trees, from "Gould's Nursery."

Fruit trees, bearing rich and luscious fruits, now testify to his earnest nature — "We are the works of thy hands." Vines, bearing choice flowers and fruit, are found throughout the West — enduring monuments uttering his praise through nature's eternal laws — beautiful and silent witnesses. "Oakwood Cemetery," a beautiful, shady place, where his ashes may rest undisturbed, where the living may wander, in spirit holding sweet communion with the past, present, and future — the creation of his brain and the fruit of his toil — is a nobler monument to his memory than all that art could create out of all the granite and marble ever produced from the hills of his native New England.

The gardener of Beaver Dam, the nurseryman of Wisconsin, has been promoted to the gardens and nurseries of the Summer Land. The trees of his nursery, in the pale starlight, bowed to the silent flowers and wept, as he left for the gardens of Eden; and the flowers and trees of the Summer Land rejoiced when he came to their blooming paths and evergreen glades. "Welcome," the angels cried, "to our bowers of love!" Turning, with a loving look, toward his beautiful home, in the Summer Land, then backward gazing, he saw behind him his own sweet home — his home, his flowers, his trees — the fruit of his life-toil — and, in their midst, his sons, daughters, and wife, all blending their sorrows in the shadowy evening hour of their loss. Weep on, dear ones; it is well that you should weep, for tears are avenues of relief to our over-tasked natures. Then, turning his gaze toward "Oakwood," he beheld fifteen hundred friends standing, in silence and profound grief, around his grave, through the long and imposing service of the brotherhood to which he belonged. Then he beheld the house in which he had so long dwelt lowered to its last-resting place — himself enfranchised an immortal, and knew that he lived to be remembered on the shores of time, and in the Summer Land, thus fully realizing the gracious gospel of our Christ, Modern Spiritualism; for he was a Spiritualist, pure and true, and tender in soul.

To the dear ones left behind, he sends greetings from his home divine.

"My sons and daughters — children mine — I greet you from the gardens of Eden — from beyond the shores of time. I charge you all, my works continue. The nursery keep, and Oakwood, where my ashes rest, develop into full fruition, as I designed.

"My companion, wife, and mate of mine, I thank thee for thy devotion and care through the long nights and days of watching, while my form burned with fever, wasting away. 'T is past, Hannah. With a sudden shock, nature's wheels stood still, and I knew but this: that time had ceased, and eternity began.

"To all who around my narrow grave gathered, weeping, in spirit I send you greetings. Weep no more for me, for 'I am he that liveth and was dead; and, behold, I am alive evermore. Amen!'"

---

## CHAPTER XXXIV.

### *QUESTIONS AND ANSWERS.*

On the afternoon of Sunday, September 24th, 1871, the following questions were handed us by one of our friends. They were written by a clergyman, and required an answer. We copy *verbatim:*

"Read all these questions before answering any."

*First.* Assume that the earth was formed in the manner claimed by geologists; were there laws governing that formation? Had they any origin?

*Second.* Could those laws have had an origin without a forming power?

*Third.* Could forming power have existed without an originating or forming mind?

*Fourth.* Could mind have existed without a being in which such mind was contained?

*Fifth.* Could a being with a mind having power to originate such laws, have been other than a personal being, having definite form, size, and location?

Complying with the request, we answered in detail as follows:

*First.* Assume that the earth was formed in the manner claimed by geologists. We answer, granted. There were laws governing that formation, and they had an origin in, first, electricity, or that force or principle, which quickens into action; second, heat, caloric force, producing motion; third, magnetism, or properties of attraction; fourth, gravitation, or that which tends to the center, holding all things in place; hence these are the laws governing the earth's formation. This formation, held in its present position through atmospheric pressure, once removed, and matter would dissolve its relations, flying off from the center into infinitesimal particles; hence these four laws combined produce the phenomena — worlds.

*Second.* Could these laws have had an origin without a forming power? We answer, that each and every one of these principles are but parts of one stupendous whole. Combined, they produce the phenomena, worlds; hence electricity, a subtle fluid, purifies; magnetism is attractive; gravitation holds together; heat quickens into motion; air sustains, gives life. The world, the body and head of these combinations, and all animated things the language, and inanimate things the supporting properties on which animated things depend for life; the world forming a basis for all life.

*Third.* Could forming power have existed without an originating or forming mind? We answer, mind is power; hence when the west wind blows, it is intelligent to the extent of direction and motion. It says to the careful observer, "I am traveling slowly or swiftly to the east." It further says, "The east wind has retired." Now, we can only understand this by the law of resistance. The trees, the houses and animals are witnesses; but it is left for man to write the fact and define its action. Magnetism and the magnetic needle tell what contains iron or steel, or points the way to the north, but it is left for man to interpret the language of the wind and magnetic needle. Is man God?

Gravitation, one more of the great or God attributes, although a part of God, was not known antedating Sir Isaac Newton; hence he has the distinguished honor of telling the world, and God, through the world, that he possessed this attribute. We very naturally ask the question, had Deity any knowledge of this one part of Himself until made manifest through Sir Isaac Newton; or was there no man in all the world fully capable of mastering this principle in nature prior to the time of Sir Isaac Newton? Again we ask, was Newton God? For he discovered the law of gravitation.

*Fourth.* Could mind have existed without a being in which such mind was contained? We answer no! We now lay down the following proposition: There is a revival meeting here in St. Paul, one in St. Louis, one in London, one in Chicago, one in San Francisco, one in New Orleans, and one in Central Georgia, among the plantation negroes, and God is visibly present in spirit and in works; and we will further suppose that at a given moment God is in mind and deed here in St. Paul, to convert A., and at this precise moment he is present in these other six places, converting B., C., D., E., F. and G. Now, has God seven bodies to one mind, and if so, what is the connecting link between these bodies and that one mind?

We answer, "God is a spirit, and must be worshiped in spirit"; hence when this spirit power is equally developed in all of these places at one and the same time, through the proper mediums, the ministers, then A., B., C., D., E., F. and G. will feel the power simultaneously — each in his respective city or place; hence we see at a glance that one body of matter cannot be in several places at one and the same time; but on the other hand, we see that spirit can be present as one mind, acting on many bodies at one and the same time. To illustrate: In June last, Professor Morse appointed a time in which he would bid the telegraph operators throughout the world farewell. The time came, and the click, click, click of the instrument in New York city was simultaneously heard here in St. Paul where you are; yonder in Fort Scott, Kansas, where I was; as well as in many, many hundreds of other places. Was the body of Professor Morse in each of these places, or the mind of the grand old man acting through electro-magnetic laws, at one and the same time on many bodies? So God, a spirit, can be in many places at one and the same time, acting on and through many bodies and minds.

*Fifth.* Could a being with a mind having power to originate such laws, be other than a personal being; having definite form, size, and location? We answer, no! but ask in return the question, was a personal being necessary to the formation of such laws?

Take, for instance, electricity, such as is used by the telegraph. Does man make it? Or, is he simply the agent bringing certain properties together, from which the electric current is eliminated? Zinc, copper, and acids will produce what neither will do alone.

Science tells us how the whirlwinds are formed. Has the wind a personality, or body? Has electricity a body?

Fire exists everywhere — is in you, the iceberg — water — and water will burn, but God must take the form and shape of a scientific man, through whom his mind acts, as the mind of the man may determine before the water will burn.

Question, and a very serious one: Did God make man, or man make God? Which? Has man any God that did not originate in and through the brain of man? "In the beginning God created the heaven and the earth." Who says so? Moses. How did Moses know? The Jews had no such idea. Why did not God give Abraham this idea? Why wait three hundred and fifty years for an Egyptian scholar to discover and write what might have been told Abraham in an hour? Who made the African's Obi, the Chinese Josh, or the Indian Manitou? The Hebrew God is jealous of Obi and Josh, and wishes Americans to legislate against their coming into America. Can't you keep Josh or Obi out?

---

## CHAPTER XXXV.

### *A WONDERFUL TEST AT DES MOINES.*

In the fall of 1871, we were reading character and giving tests, through the nervo-magnetic law of spirit control, in Spiritual Hall. After reading a skeptic very correctly, he asked:

"Will you read a man of my selection?"

"Yes," we replied.

"Then read this man, on my left."

"We will, in good time."

After reading the life lines of several strangers, we stepped to the man pointed out, and asked him to lay the fingers of his right hand on the fingers of our left hand, not touching our hand with his thumb. This was done. The man was tall, spare, dark in face and hair, and was nervous, bilious, sanguine, in temperament. His touch, to us, was cold and viscous.

He was about thirty-three years of age, and outwardly appeared to be a man of medium understanding. The reading was as follows:

From twelve to sixteen years of age, this man was under strong and powerful religious influences; at seventeen there is a change — he becomes a thinker; from then till now, he has been religious in the observance of truth, law, nature, and science, valuing the speculations of men only as they are sustained by law and nature's truth. He cannot sit under the speaking of any powerful mind without being much affected by the argument and energy of the speaker. He is more than an ordinary thinker; and, while he is religious in his observance of nature and nature's law, he is skeptical in reference to human testimony. I find with him at seventeen years of age, a man — stout, thick set, full features, dark complexion, dark hair, about forty, or five and forty, years old; he is a preacher of the Gospel — a pretentious man, very positive, and a revivalist; the action of this man has much to do with your present status of thought and manhood; he was a bad man, and his actions had much to do with forming your present position in regard to religious matters; he was not an honest man, and did not believe what he taught. This all took place far from here. What do you know of this; am I right, or wrong?

"Repeat what you have said, carefully," he said.

We did so.

"In part you are right; in part you are wrong," he answered.

"In what part are we wrong?"

"You have made me a Christian, while I am an Infidel, and believe nothing, whatever, of a future existence."

"You are wrong, sir; I have not made a Christian of you, but a 'skeptic, in reference to human testimony — religious only in the observation and worship of nature.'"

"Then you are right, sir, so far as that part of my character is concerned. I am the son of a Baptist clergyman, and, as you said, 'I was under strong and marked religious influences from twelve to sixteen years of age, and in my seventeenth year began to doubt, and became an Infidel,' but you are wrong in regard to the honesty of the man you described as a minister. I knew him. You have described well, but he was honest and earnest in all he taught; hence, you see, that you are wrong in your premises."

At once, we felt an influence of a most marked and unpleasant character. We said:

"Sir, we are right. Let us refresh your memory. There lived in your neighborhood, when you were sixteen years old, a girl eighteen years of age; she was very fair — almost a full blonde — large blue eyes, full and very expressive; her hair was a light brown, tinted with auburn, long and flowing; her features were oval, regular, and well defined. There was a playful vein of mirthfulness ever present in her face; she was full of life, and was the life of the company that she might be in; she was good and confiding. I see her in company with the minister I have described. He took her away from your place, and never brought her back. She is a spirit, and is here with you to-night, and gives me this history of herself, her wrongs, of him that wronged her, and all I have said of you. What know you of this?"

Then, turning to the audience, we said:

"Ladies and Gentlemen: We rest our case here. On this statement we stand or fall; and the only witness under heaven we have to offer in corroboration of what we have said is this Infidel. Is it true, or false? what say you, sir?"

For a moment, a wild unrest of excitement thrilled the audience—men began to stand up; the Spiritualists were exceedingly anxious. Our witness sat as immovable as a rock, his head downcast, and his face resting on his right hand. We turned an anxious look toward our witness; there he sat, in silence. The excitement was becoming painful, when, of a sudden, there echoed down the hall:

"Stand up, man! Let the audience see you! Speak! what know you of this. Is it true?" demanded Dr. Connelly.

Slowly our witness arose, and, turning to the audience, said:

"When sixteen, in my seventeenth year, I was living in Kentucky. When the speaker first described the minister, I had another man in view, that answered his description in all things, save that he was an honest man, and believed what he taught. Of course, this man I had in view does not answer to the man the speaker claims to see. I have now before me another man, that fills the description to the letter. I knew the girl Mr. W. has described well; I could not describe her better. She eloped with the minister described by the speaker. The minister came back, in about a month, without her. The girl's father called on the minister, demanding the whereabouts of the girl. The minister replied that 'she was well, and at her uncle's, in Indiana.' The friends of the girl at once wrote to the uncle, making inquiries in regard to her. The uncle wrote, by return mail, that the girl was not at his house, nor had she been there. This aroused suspicions of foul play, and the neighbors demanded an explanation, but the minister refused to give it. In the meantime, the young people, and relatives of the young woman, determined to search the minister. He, getting wind of the affair, shut himself up in his house, and, when they came to search him, he attacked them, defeating them, cutting some in a terrible manner, and then fled the country. He was a bad man. The girl is dead. This man has given a correct history of the affair, and I know there is not a man in this place that knows anything of this affair, save myself. It is true."

The audience were very much surprised.

I am he that liveth, and was dead; and, behold, I am alive forevermore. Amen. Rev. i: 18.

Be not forgetful to entertain strangers, for thereby some have entertained angels unawares. Hebrews xiii: 2.

Beloved, believe not every spirit, but try the spirits,

whether they be of God; because many false prophets are gone out into the world. 1 John iv: 1.

And the spirits of the prophets are subject to the prophets. 1 Cor. xiv: 6, 32.

And thus are the secrets of his heart made manifest. 1 Cor. xiv: 25.

---

## CHAPTER XXXVI.

The Circle for Spiritual Phenomena — How to Form It.

### *THE CIRCLE FOR SPIRITUAL PHENOMENA.*

By request we give our views on this subject.

We hold that the circle is to Spiritualism what the class meetings are to Methodism, the prayer meetings are to the Baptists or Presbyterians, or what masses are to the Catholics. Where there are two or three families of Spiritualists in a neighborhood, they should meet at least once in two weeks for circle meetings. It would be well for them to have a room in the upper story of the house, dedicated to this special purpose, well lighted, well ventilated, with furniture adapted to the uses of the room. The papering of the room to be in pale blue, violet, peach blossom, or pink, as a back-ground, studded with stars of gold and silver. There should be musical instruments belonging to the room, such as are fully adapted to the use of spiritual fingers, rather than lungs — such as the harp, guitar, organ, violin, or pianoforte. These instruments should not be allowed to be taken out of the room. There should be bells of different tones, made of fine metal — one or two of pure flint glass. The room should be furnished with writing materials, pencils, quills, pens, drawing materials — in fact, everything requisite for the soul-culture and the development of the mind.

The place of meeting thus prepared, we would advise those intending to meet in the room, to come together one morning once a month, listening to:

*First.* Invocations or prayer.

*Second.* Select readings, either in prose or poetry, on subjects eminently calculated to inspire us unto good.

*Third.* Thirty minutes' conversation on spiritual subjects.

Finale, in music or singing, or both.

This meeting should be called the "Monthly Conversatione for Spiritual Worship," and it would be well to hold it on the first Sunday morning of each month. We would advise the circle proper to adopt the following rules for their government, viz.:

*First.* To choose one of their number to preside as head of the circle, whose duty it shall be to see that the business of the circle be properly conducted, and to hold his place six months, acting as secretary to the circle, keeping a correct record of every meeting, of those who were present, who not, as well as what transpired.

*Second.* The circle to meet promptly at, say 9 o'clock, A. M.; that is, each member to be in his or her place in the circle at this time — the sitting to continue one hour at least, and never to exceed one hour and a half.

*Third.* The circle to form around an oblong table, in cane seated chairs, numbering from ten to thirteen, more or less in numbers as the circle may require. The table should be made out of clear lumber, free from sap or knot or shake, and should be also free from paint, varnish, or stain. The members should attend carefully to the cleanliness of their persons, studiously avoiding all cosmetics whatever, the use of tobacco, whisky, or intoxicating drinks, or food calculated to excite the nervous system or the passions. They should enter this sanctuary of the angels quietly, in order, and as nearly at the same time as may be.

*Fourth.* Taking their places orderly, as follows: The most positive in temperament to sit at the head of the table as number one; then number two, the next positive, and so on until all are seated. We would advise the members of the circle to sit a few minutes in profound and silent meditation, each asking the angel of truth to aid, direct, and counsel them in this their circle. After which place the hands on the table, letting them rest lightly and easily upon it, the little finger of the right hand of number one resting on the little finger of the left hand of number two, and so on until the circle is completed.

*Fifth.* Open with selected reading, singing and music, or invocation. Let this part of the service be brief, after which sit in patience, waiting for visitors from the Summer Land.

*Sixth.* This phase and portion of time should not exceed thirty-five minutes in duration, and the circle should close up in the strictest order, by invoking the good angels through the law, to be with us. Close with singing and music.

SYMPTOMS TO BE OBSERVED DURING THESE SITTINGS.

*First.* Perspiration of the palms of the hands sufficient to wet the table under the hands.

*Second.* Cold, clammy, or viscous cuticle, extending well up the arm, and frequently affecting all the person. Second stage or symptoms may be noted as the warm, viscous condition of the system. The third stage, the dry, husky skin of a silky texture, seldom, if ever, moist.

*Third.* Lifting of the palm of the hand, under the hand, or pressure upward. We opine that during this stage of the development the table is being charged with the nerve property or force of the human system, from the bodies of those who make up the circle.

*Fourth.* We will next notice a tremulous motion or quivering of the fibre of the wood, or table, sometimes so powerful as to be tangible to every member of the circle. This motion is continuous, beginning in the table and extending to the most negative member of the circle, sometimes accompanied with a somniferous tendency, and occasionally producing a sound and healthy sleep. During this stage of the development members of the circle thus affected will frequently be impressed with the ailments of those who are diseased, sometimes with the very thoughts of some one or more of the members of the circle; sometimes clear spirit intuition will develop. We should, however, be very careful how we accept communications thus given as from spirits, for very frequently these impressions are but the reflections of or from the mind of one or more of the members of the circle, hence are to be carefully dissected in order to determine whether they be of the spirit out of the form or of the spirit in the form.

*Fifth.* The next development will be a violent spasmodic action — such as violent pounding on the table with the open hand or closed fist; stamping of the feet; shaking of the body; the head in spasmodic action; violent shaking of the whole body, with great effort to speak. Again the subject will grip the hand of the next member to them in a firm, vise-like grip, then suddenly spring to their feet, breaking away from the circle; frequently jumping about, sometimes dancing, sometimes uttering a wild, incoherent gibberish — an unknown tongue. During this spasmodic stage of development, and when the subject breaks away from the circle, the circle should close up and continue its sitting with singing.

*Sixth.* We will find the air under the table or around the feet of the sitters, several degrees colder than in the region of the hands or heart and head.

*Seventh.* We conclude that the phenomena of Spiritualism requires, first, the nerve-force of man — called by Ashburner "Animal Magnetism"; by Richenbaugh, "odic or od-force," and which we believe to be the property in our own natures, out of which the spirit body or force has its birth, and should be called the physics of spirits, or spirit property.

*Eighth.* The mediums form the magnetic battery; the spirits form the electric battery. This was the material out of which Jacob's vision of the ladder and angels was formed.

Finally, any number of persons, from three to twenty, cannot sit one evening in a week for three months without producing phenomena unaccounted for by science, and only accounted for as yet as spirit or an intellectual force, not dependent on the members of any one of them for its expression.

Every circle should guard against vain and idle questions. Never allow foolish things or words to occupy the time of the circle. We have foolish things enough of this life without carrying them into the sublimities of spirit life.

We believe circles may be formed for the following purposes, and with advantage to all concerned:

*First.* The divinity of the soul and the worship of God, as well as the communion of angels.

*Second.* The helps and governments of the family, of society and the State.

*Third.* For educational purposes, social, physical, and mental.

*Fourth.* For business purposes of any and all

kinds. But we conjure all Spiritualists to never ask the angels of God to help them, so long as they can get along without doing so, and then only in extreme cases.

---

## CHAPTER XXXVII.

Home Life with Farmer Mary — We Give Tests in McHenry, Illinois — The Vision, and Its Fulfillment — The Witness.

### *HOME LIFE.*

From eleven o'clock A. M., April 9, to Friday, five o'clock P. M., April 19, 1872, we enjoyed the sweet influence of home life, on the Emerson Farm, under the management of Farmer Mary. We find that, in our absence, everything has prospered at home. During these days of farm life, we have enjoyed ourselves — Mary, the children, and the "Gentle Wilson." We have feasted on fresh milk and bread, fresh eggs and fat chickens, drinking pure cold water fresh from nature's fountains. We watched the unfolding of seed-time, and saw bushels of wheat, barley, oats, and potatoes, go into the ground to die, and, in death, each kernel promised to resurrect itself in August, giving an hundredfold in increase.

Thou fool, that which thou sowest is not quickened except it die; and that which thou sowest, thou sowest not that body that shall be. 1 Cor. xv: 36, 37.

And I look forward to the harvest in knowledge for the return of the quickening of the soul of the grain, and its resurrection in spirit and life in a new body, and yet so like the old that it is at once fully identified as the improved spirit of that grain we cast away in knowledge, knowing we would receive it back again in good harvest time. So the All Father hath sown broadcast, on the face of the earth, the seeds of life, to take root and come forth in manhood and womanhood, on earth and in heaven, a quickening spirit.

Our home! how we love it, and all there are in and about it; and, by and by, we will have a new house, with plenty of room for the weary pilgrim to rest in. We — Mary and the "Gentle Wilson — have lived together twenty-nine years — September 23, 1876. How long to look ahead; how short the time when we look back; and yet, a few brief years and we will stand side by side in the Summer Land — Farmer Mary and I.

Oh, how we wish every laborer in the field had a home in the country, where they could rest, and love and be loved in return; where they could sow, and plant, and reap the fruits of their own labor.

Through April, May, and up to June 13, we have been at home four days in a week, and yet have averaged four lectures a week. Brothers and sisters, have we not been blessed? And here let us assure you that we are not forgetful of the protecting care of the All

Father and his angel helpers, in guiding us aright thus far on the journey of life. "Let us have peace."

Friday, five o'clock P. M., April 19, we are on the cars, bound for McHenry, Illinois—Mary, Dora, Bennie and I. We arrived at the good farm-house of Brother J. W. Smith, the farmer, and were welcomed by his companion and family in a manner that said, "We are glad to see you." During the evening, we held a circle for spirit communion, during which, many fine tests were given, especially one from their daughter Clara, and their old friend, Filkins. We had music, singing, and speaking in unknown tongues.

On Saturday and Sunday we held meetings in the Universalist Church, and, notwithstanding it rained a good part of the time, we had a good attendance, and enjoyed ourselves, meeting many old and tried friends. But some we missed; they had gone on, under promotion, to the Summer Land.

We gave several tests, which were fully identified. One incident we will relate. When in McHenry, in 1871, on the evening of July 23, we made the following statement:

Turning to H. Owen, Esq., we said: "Sir, we see you in the future. You seem to be entering a very dark cloud; it suddenly envelopes your whole person, and you are lost to our view; you are in the cloud a long time, during which we see a deal of commotion in it; finally, the cloud lifts, and we see you prostrate, weak, and feeble, hardly able to care for yourself. We fear, sir, that, during the fall or winter, you are to pass through an ordeal that will come near carrying you out of this life."

Mr. Owen replied: "I do not know what you can refer to. I am quite well, and everything prospers about me."

Others commented, *pro* and *con*, in regard to the statement, the unbelievers sneering, the faithful feeling that we had drawn largely upon the future, and few, if any, believing that anything would come out of it.

Eight months subsequently, we found Mr. Owen sitting in his chair, weak, feeble, and hardly able to help himself—just as we had seen him in our vision, in July, 1871—and, from Mr. Owen's own lips, we received full confirmation of the fulfilling of our vision, he being attacked last fall with congestive chills, that nearly carried him into eternity.

We wish that Dr. Child would inquire of Prof. Hare about the law controlling this phenomenon, or prophecy. Will it not form a fine text for some future communication?

# CHAPTER XXXVIII.

## *WONDERFUL PHENOMENA IN PORTAGE CO., OHIO.*

The following letter from a friend, and true Spiritualist, speaks for itself:

RAVENNA, OHIO, November 8, 1873.

MR. WILSON—*Dear Sir:* Some manifestations of interest having occurred in Deerfield, in this county, I will give you the most important incidents in the order of their development:

In the township of Deerfield, Portage county, Ohio, one-fourth of a mile from the center, stands a house, with some good acres of ground attached, that, within the last thirty years, has been bought and sold many times. No sooner would a buyer get settled, than he would be seized with a desire to sell.

About four years ago, it was bought by a Mr. Carlton. His family consisted of a wife, two daughters nearly grown, and a son, now eight years old. The Carlton family were annoyed by strange, unaccountable noises, that soon gave it the notoriety of being haunted. These sounds were often heard in one chamber, as if doors, were opening and being shut hard; also, loud raps, sometimes singing, and voices in conversation, and often groans and shrieks. Twice they saw the form of a woman walking in the garden.

Last winter, Mr. Carlton became so exasperated at

the annoyance, he thought to drive them away, by force, if possible. When the sounds were heard, he commanded them, as with authority, to quit and leave the family alone. They took no heed to orders. At this, Mr. Carlton went into a passion, enforcing his commands with oaths and curses. The sounds were as defiant as ever. Then he threw stove wood at the point whence the sound proceeded, and yet they tantantalized him. Soon after, he was taken ill, and died in a few hours.

This occurred in February last (1873). The family still live there, and these haunting sounds continued till late in summer, when Mrs. Carlton went to Paris, an adjoining town, to visit some friends. They advised her to get a medium living in Charlestown, adjoining Paris, to go to her house and learn what the spirit wanted.

The Spiritualists of Charlestown were holding circles twice a week. A Mr. Loomis, who was well known and respected there when living, controls the medium, and by him seven of the members of the circle were selected to go to the house, and they would liberate a spirit who, in a fit of insanity, had taken her own life, and had never been able to leave the locality where the deed was done. A spirit, who gives his name as John Forsyth, says he practiced medicine in Pittsburgh, and passed to spirit-life twelve years ago, is associated with Mr. Loomis in his labors.

The first week in August they went to the house. Dr. Forsyth assisted the spirit to get *en rapport* with the medium. She was very wild and shy, and afraid they were enemies. She had been attended by the spirit of John Diver, who was one of the first settlers of Deerfield, and was, in those early times, known throughout the country, but had neither the knowledge nor power to raise her out of that condition.

Since her insanity has been removed, this is the story she tells of herself:

"My name is Mary Coolie. I was born in Germany. I came to America with two brothers, who settled near Meadville, Pennsylvania, bringing their wealth with them. One brother, Cornelius Coolie, still lives there; the other died. I was seduced by a doctor (whose name had better not be given), under promise of marriage. He persuaded me to leave my home and go with him. He brought me to Deerfield, and rented this house, and, soon after, I gave birth to a still-born babe, which the doctor buried in the garden. He refused to fulfill his promise of marriage, and, in my grief, despair, and loneliness, I was bereft of my reason and became a raving maniac, and, in my frenzy, cut my throat. The doctor put my body into a rough box and buried it in the garden also, and left for parts unknown."

A few old residents remembered his coming and going, but no one there ever knew that Mary Coolie lived or died. The valuable papers that she had hid in the house, and her child, were the ties that bound her to that locality, and she had no knowledge nor power to detach herself.

In speaking of her child, she said, "her treasure was buried on the south side of the garden." Some, who heard the word treasure, thought it to be money, went to digging, with great zeal, at the point indicated, and, when they were assured that the mother called her her babe her treasure, they left.

The night following, three or four, who still thought money was buried there, returned, and, with post-augers, thought to unearth it and enrich themselves. While digging, they were startled by a strange sound, that made them pause and listen; then they went to work again with a will, when such horrible shrieks, groans, and wailings were heard that they leaped the fence and fled in the wildest terror, and dared not return. Subsequently, the earth was removed, but they found only what seemed to be human hair; thirty-two years had destroyed all other vestiges of "the treasure."

Mrs. S. F—— is the medium through whom this spirit is daily gaining strength and knowledge. Her fear and timidity have nearly left her, and she realizes more and more that all are friends, and it helps her to advance out of that hell in which she has suffered for thirty-two years.

At one time, when Mary was communicating, she was asked if the spirits killed Mr. Carlton. She said he was present, and could answer for himself. After getting hold of the medium, he (Carlton) asked to have the question repeated. He then said: "They removed me by their will-power, because I was an obstacle to the accomplishment of the results desired, and I am as much benefited by those results as Mary Coolie, and am glad to share in the blessing of being taught with her, and do not regret my removal. It is a blessing for which I shall ever be thankful."

Dear reader, we give above the contents of a letter from a friend, in whom we have the utmost confidence, and we know that she writes no uncertain report. There are points in this communication worthy of careful attention.

*First*—This kind of haunted-house phenomena is becoming more and more common throughout the country. The fact can no longer be ignored. The "Newburyport School House," the "Dunn County (Wis.) House," the "Virgil House," and many others, are proofs positive that these things are. The testimony is before us. The judgment rendered is, that this phenomena is the result of spirit, or ultramundane, life. What we now wish to understand, is the law through which this phenomena takes place. Is it the work of the Diakka?

*Second*—The lesson taught: There is no forgiveness in this life, or the after-life; every penalty must be paid; there is no escape.

*Third*—Life in the Spirit World is identical with life in this mundane world; fear, sorrow, joy, hate, spleen, and all kindred elements of passion, are parts of this great Spirit World; that we are unfolding for humanity, and, above all, that the Star of Progression hovers over that world as well as this.

*Fourth*—Not only are our media helpers to us in the present life, but they are benefactors to those unfortunate souls who are in prison in the Spirit World;

and, through the law of interblending of our natures, both spheres are benefited by spirit and mortal conditions.

*Fifth*—Certain parties, or persons, who, dying in the act of crime, or the cause of crime, or in plotting for crime, do leave a force or influence in a house, or on a spot of ground, or on any article that may be in contact with them at the time of the act, that will repeat in testimony the act in evil they commit whenever a corresponding force, or law, in another comes in contact with what they have left behind them; hence, the phenomena of the haunted house, pond, or field.

*Sixth*—Sometimes these criminals, in the very act, are bound in chains, and remain bound until relieved by the law of development, progression, or the charity of some ministering element.

*Seventh*—Can spirits remove obnoxious men and women from their path? and, if so, are we not, sojourners here, on very ticklish ground indeed? and that our continuance in this life depends on our good behavior here as well as hereafter?

Finally, is this not an age of wonder and wisdom? "Let us prove all things, and hold fast to that which is good." Let us do right, and exercise charity, and all will be well.

# CHAPTER XXXIX.

"The Mystery of Death—Where is our Little Pet?"—"I am up here, Mamma; Little Pet is Cared For."

## *"THE MYSTERY OF DEATH—WHERE IS OUR LITTLE PET?"*

"Where are you, our little Pet? Do you lie all unconscious where we weeping let you down a few days ago?. Or have you gone to the spirit world? And what is a spirit world? How can you live, feel, see, know, without that little casket, the body? And if your spirit has flown, whither has it flown? How far away have you gone, little Pet? Do you know anything that is going on here below? And if so, how much are you permitted to know, and how do you know it? Do you see yourself, or do the angels tell you? Do you know how much we grieve for you, how many sad tears we shed, how we try to sing some of those home songs, in which your little voice used to mingle, and how we suddenly cease and all weep aloud? Do you see us when we go to visit your little grave, and do you hear us as we talk of planting the flowers, and placing the green sod, and erecting the little marble block there?

"Are you happy, little Pet? You used to say that you 'would like to go to heaven, but that you would jump down again and come back.' Do you feel like jumping down now? You used to say you 'wanted to go to heaven, but you did not want wings.' Have you got wings now, little Pet? But oh, how we miss you, little Pet! You were the light and joy of our household, and we all feel very lonely without you! Yet if you are only cared for tenderly and are happy, we can wait. But we should like to more than *believe.* We should like to *know.* If we could only hear from you one clear, distinct *Yes!* to these various queries so often made, so there could be no mistake about it, it would be very consoling. But we know you cannot answer. The curtain between this and the future world is down, never to be lifted until each one makes his exit.

"'The gates are not ajar,' and if we are faithful here it will be well with us there, and we shall go and meet the good and the innocent — the dear ones gone before. Adieu then, little Pet! Ah! yes, we have said it many times before, but it comes back again upon us, and so we alternate

"'Between the calming and the weeping.'

"Farewell, little Pet, for this side of heaven. And how many like us have been afflicted! How many little coffins have been made! How many little graves have been dug, and how many sweet, pleasant homes have been darkened! But they have gone in sweet, beautiful and heavenly innocency. It must be well with them. Is it well with us? 'They will not return to us; shall we go to them?'"

We find the above reflections and questionings in the columns of the "Atchison (Kansas) Champion."

They are from the heart of a sorrowing parent, whose soul is hungry for heavenly knowledge of the dead. Christian faith fails to answer these "questionings," and only differs from Atheism in the declared mysteries of a God through faith in his blood. Atheism says to this sorrowing soul, "Your little Pet is dead — silent — forever in the grave, with no more pain, grief, sorrow or joy. You can see the place where its little casket is laid in the dust. His little voice is silent forever."

This conclusion the parent's soul rejects. The mystery of faith is equally unsatisfactory, as evidenced by the "questionings." Spiritualism answers every question, solves the hidden mystery, and declares there is no death. We have stood just where these questions now stand. We inquired after four little pets and their mother. We inquired of the minister of God — "Say, man of God, where are our pets?"

He honestly and gravely answered, "There;" pointing with the finger to their graves.

"But what of them in the judgment?"

"The mother, having been baptized, will be accepted of God; the little pets, having never been baptized, will be damned."

"But, holy man of God, Jesus said, 'Suffer little children to come unto me, and forbid them not, for of such is the kingdom of heaven.'"

"True, sir; but these pets are not of the kingdom, for they were not committed to the Father's care through the holy offices of Mother Church."

"Well, then, holy man of God, Atheism is more

merciful than you, and we trust that oblivion may wrap its dark mantle of forgetfulness around them all, and that the wife and mother, with our pets, may be silent forever, knowing not anything."

Later in life an angel came to us — the wife and mother — and carried us up to the pearly gates that stood "ajar," and pointing through them, said: "Behold our little pets, sporting in the sunshine on the beautiful play-grounds in the Summer Land."

And on reading a parent's "questionings," we thought we heard the little Pet answer, "I am up here, mamma, where flowers blossom all the year, and birds of paradise sing me to sleep. I am not 'all unconscious' in the grave where you weeping let me down a few days ago.' Only the tiny casket lies there. Mamma and papa, I am not there. Dear papa and mamma, I am up in the spirit land, with the angels — and cousin Nellie, and grandma, too, are here with me, and other little pets also. The spirit world is a beautiful place, full of flowers and shady trees, green fields and singing birds. On many a tree the bough bends freighted with luscious fruit. Murmuring streams course their way through valleys fair, by mountain side now tumbling down a rocky steep, making merry for your pet. We live on fruit plucked from trees, or berries from bushes bending beneath their weight. With fingers fair and white we feel, and with eyes bright and blue, we see as when on earth they gazed on you — all united in one little casket, far more beautiful than the body I left below. My spirit has flown, but not so far away — just up here beneath the stars; and all the time when not studying, singing or playing, we are thinking of and visiting you, my ma. We know what you are doing there below. We are with your guardian spirits; sometimes in your room; again, they leave us in our happy homes while away on a mission of love to our old home. On returning, they tell us of all that is going on below; and we are permitted to know all that you do — weeping and laughing with you in your joy and sorrow. Sometimes we see for ourselves; sometimes the angels tell us what we do not know; and what we know is given us through our senses, just as with you. And oh! my mamma and papa, we know your grief, your joy, and those sad tears you shed, we have caught again and again; and when you come up here, you will find them crystalized gems in our home — old mementos from the shores of time. And when you sing, our souls are filled with glee as in chorus we rejoice. Sometimes we go with you to visit the little grave, and hear you talk of planting flowers above where the casket is laid; but, mamma, we had rather meet you in the parlor where we played. Bring out the little shoe and cap, the whip and top, and other toys. Do not weep, mamma, but let us play with the shoe and cap, with the whip and top, as in former days. I am not in the grave, mamma. I am happy and full of joy, and only weep when you are sad. Do not weep at the grave, for your tears make me sad. Always when with you in the form, you wiped my tears away. Come, mamma, wipe my tears away once again, by smiling on your little Pet through your own. I would not have you cease your weeping, for tears are jewels worn in our crowns. I like heaven, mamma. God and all the angels are good; they strive to teach me the better way; and often I come from the Summer Land in joy, to the old earth home—not on the wings of a bird, but on the wings of love. And if you will sit in the mellow even tide, I will whisper loving words to your soul, so you will not miss your little Pet, and I will again be the light and joy of the old household home. Mamma, little Pet is cared for by loving angels; his every want is supplied. He knows no sorrow, save your own. Mamma and papa, will you leave the door 'ajar' and bid me come? You shall more than believe. You shall know that I am not dead, but live, and shall live forevermore. And, mamma, I can answer and I will tell you when: Do you remember one night the clock had just chimed nine; you opened the drawer and took up the little blue shoe, and bowed your head and wept, mamma;—and then again, you spun the top, and when it whirled all so swift, you cried aloud, 'Do you see the top, little Pet?' And, mamma, when you stood by the little grave where my casket is laid, there bowing low on bended knee, you prayed for little Pet. I was with you, mamma, and kissed your cheek, and dried your tears. We can answer to your call in a thousand ways. The curtain is lifted and the 'gates are ajar,' and all can come in; all can go out; all meet on the mutual land of our spirit home. We are not gone, but near you in innocence and joy. All is well with us; let it be well with you. We will return to you; you shall come to us."

Little Pet has solved the mystery of death, and lives forevermore. Don't take it to heart — remember the words of the Master:

"I am he that liveth, and was dead; and, behold, I am alive forevermore. Amen." Rev. i; 18.

---

## CHAPTER XL.

Church and State — A Good Example of the Power and Influence of Christianity — Sarah Ann Whitely — She then Called Mary, Husband, My Sons and Daughters.

### *CHURCH AND STATE.*

Shall we have God in the Constitution of the United States? and, if so, whose God? The ultramontane section of the Catholic Church are taking high ground, both in Europe and America. We copy the following from the pastoral recently issued by Bishop Gilmour, of the diocese of Cleveland, Ohio, in which occurs sentiments, or rather commands, that lay the ax at the root of freedom. Read it:

"There must be less petty jealousies among us; nationalities must be made subordinate to religion, and we must learn that *we are Catholics first, and citizens next.* Catholicity does not bring us in conflict with the State, yet it teaches that God is above man, and *the Church above the State.* To the Church, as the representative of God, we owe a spiritual allegiance, *yet in all that does not conflict with the law of God,* we owe an unqualified obedience to the State."

We shall not quarrel with the Bishop, or any other man, about his religious views. We shall defend ours, and when Rome, through her prelate, lays down a rule of action, that declares the Church superior to the State, and that, too, when the head of that church is a foreign prelate, we think it is time that the people awoke to a sense of the danger that threatens us.

We do not propose to go into an elaborate argument on this subject at this time. What we wish to do is call the attention of our readers to this monstrous document. Bishop Gilmour is a bold, out-spoken man, and may be considered a fair specimen of the leading minds of the Church of Rome, in the United States, and it will not be their fault if religious liberty has not an end on American soil.

The spirit of the Bishop's pastoral is this: "There is a higher law, that makes the President of these United States, Congress, and our State Governments, subject to the Roman Church, and that Church is subject to the Pope."

We can afford to laugh at that fanatic, who supposes he is doing God's will, so long as he is single-handed; but when that fanaticism becomes a leading feature in a church numbering millions, then there is danger. Directly in connection with the spirit of this pastoral, we have another danger, coupled with which there are some of the best minds in our land. We refer to the Christian Convention for the purpose of accomplishing the sixteenth amendment to our constitutional form of government, recognizing God and his Christ. The spirit of this Protestant Christian Convention is the same as that manifested in Bishop Gilmour's pastoral. The design of both parties is patent, and is this: Whoever rejects the authority of our God and his Christ, let him be damned!

We will suppose that this sixteenth amendment is accomplished, and God becomes a fact, in our Government, there must then be legislation necessary to carry out the object, to define his wants — a bureau and secretary of the Department of God.

The next point to determine will be, Whose God? This can only be determined at the ballot box, and that sectarian element having a majority of votes determines whose God shall rule.

Bishop Gilmour has spoken, in his pastoral, and there is no misunderstanding him. "We must learn that we are Catholics first, and citizens next; and the Church above the State; to the Church, as the representative of God, we owe a spiritual allegiance, yet in all that does not conflict with the laws of God, we owe an unqualified obedience to the State."

Reader, has not Rome declared, again and again, that the Protestant Churches conflict with the Church of the living God? Does not Bishop Glamour say the Pope first, then the Church, and the State last? The priesthood first, then the people.

Spiritualism declares that Church and State are two, and subjective to the will of the people.

### *A GOOD EXAMPLE OF THE POWER AND INFLUENCE OF THE TEACHINGS OF CHRISTIANITY.*

We heard this statement from a friend of ours at Dallas City, Illinois, who is, also, a friend of the party from whom the story came — Hon. R. G. Ingersoll, author of "The Gods."

Says Ingersoll: "Not long ago, I was retained to defend a murderer. On calling on him, in his cell, I demanded a full and complete account of the whole affair, for on a statement of facts would rest my defense; and then there occurred the following questions and answers;

*Ingersoll.* Did you kill the man?

*Prisoner.* Yes, I killed him.

*I.* What did you kill him for?

*P.* For his money.

*I.* You say you killed this man for his money. Had you no enmity toward him, or other cause?"

*P.* None, whatever.

*I.* How much money did you get?

*P.* Seven cents.

*I.* Is that all you got? Had he no other property or valuables?

*P.* Now, sir, I am mistaken; he had some bread and meat with him.

*I.* What did you do with the money?

*P.* I bought whisky with it.

*I.* And what did you do with the bread and meat?

*P.* I eat the bread; it being Friday, I threw the meat away.

Reader, who can read the above and not recognize the fact, that, had this man been educated to respect human life and private property, as he had the dogma of the Church, he would never have murdered him. He could fearlessly kill his brother man for his money, knowing that the crime could be washed out by the blood of Jesus; but to eat meat on Friday was an unpardonable sin, not to be reached by the atoning blood of Jesus Christ.

Does not this case teach us that the principles embodied in the atonement offer an inducement to men to do wrong?

If any man come to me, and hate not his father, and mother, and wife, and children, and brethen, and sisters, yea, and his own life also, he cannot be my disciple. Luke xiv: 26.

## *APOTHEOSIS.*

While at Bonaparte, Iowa, we were moved to speak of our immortal sister, Sarah Ann G. Whitley, who went to live in the Summer Land on the 20th of February, 1872, fully matured in truth and years. She was sick only five days. She was fully warned of her change. On the mornings of the 18th, 19th, and 20th, she was informed of her change, and told to be ready.

On Monday morning, the 19th, she called her husband to her side, saying:

"James, I have got my second token, calling me, and, before to-morrow's sun sinks behind the western sky, I shall leave you and the dear children for my home in the Spirit World."

Then, giving full instructions regarding household matters, the children, and her things, she charged her husband with the care of the little ones she was about to leave. She then said:

"Husband, please bury my body in a plain coffin, quietly laying it away in the ground. Let there be no great ado, or marked formalities, at my funeral. I wish to retire from this world as quietly as I have lived in it. You will continue our family circle twice a week, and I will be with you, guiding, cheering, and assisting our little ones in the sacred duties of life."

She then called Mary, our eldest daughter, to her, and told her to "take the two rings from her fingers; keep one, and give the other to her sister."

Then, turning to us all, she said: "Husband, my sons and daughters, I do not regret one action of my life, or anything I have done. There is nothing in my life to repent of. The only pang or regret with me is in leaving you, my children, and my husband. I would like to remain with you in the form, until you had reached man and woman's estate, but it is not to be, and I must go home. I do not fear death. I shall not die, but go to a better home, and there await your coming. I trust the transition may be easy and without pain."

The hour of her departure came on the 20th of February. The husband and children were around her. She breathed easily life's final moments away, leaving this normal world without a struggle, and became an angel mother, remembering, loving, and watching over the dear ones she has left for a season. She was a true wife, a good mother, and as true to Spiritualism as the needle to the pole. She will be missed by many friends from the earth circle of sisters, but we know that she is not *dead*.

The Whitley family continues their home circle, and their mother is with them. Some one of the children see and hear her in their family circles, and her words of advice are still heard in the household. We knew Sister Whitley in the earth-life, and know that she was true, good, and faithful, and, as an angel, she cannot be less true and good.

May her pure spirit continue to meet her family in the home circle, greeting them with the sacred words of John, the Evangelist:

I am he that liveth, and was dead; and, behold, I am alive forevermore. Amen! Rev. i: 18.

"Holy ministers of light!
Hidden from our mortal sight,
But whose presence can impart
Peace and comfort to the heart;
When we weep, or when we pray,
When we falter in the way,
Or our hearts grow faint with fear,
Let us feel your presence near."

—*Poems of Progress.*

# CHAPTER XLI.

We Close the Year 1871 in Chicago — New Year's Dinner at Home — We Speak in Wheaton — On the Wing — Arrive in Philadelphia — Give many Tests.

*CLOSE OF THE YEAR.*

Well, dear readers, we closed our work for 1871 on Sunday afternoon, December 31, in Chicago; speaking in that city for the first time in three years, and we were greeted and made welcome by a large and enthusiastic audience morning and evening; in fact, the largest audience of the season. Acting upon the principle that Spiritualists are ever willing to pay for what pleases them, and what they want, we hold that we gave general satisfaction, and our lectures were wanted in Chicago.

If the society of Spiritualists of Chicago will unite, acting in harmony and accord, they are sure to succeed. But all party spirit must be cast aside, the Christ of our hope and knowledge must be elevated, the personal pronoun dropped, and *we* take its place. Brothers and sisters, you are a power in Chicago, and if you will do wisely, may make yourself felt. We pray you to be faithful to Spiritualism, and true to the sacred trusts imparted to you. Organize on a sure financial basis, build you a hall, and take your place in the new Chicago of the future.

Our partner and mate, Farmer Mary, wrote us in

November last that our New Year's dinner would be ready at 2½ o'clock, P. M., January 1st, 1872, sharp time, and feeling that it would be good for us to accept the call, we were on hand at the appointed time. Eighteen of us were joined together in the sacred family circle around the social old black walnut table, and all will bear testimony that we did justice to the well-roasted turkeys and viands, the products of Mary's farm.

After dinner, and in social conversation passed the hours until night time came; then we formed the sacred family circle and for two hours we held holy communion with the dear ones who had gone on before. This was truly a feast of love — music from on high with invocation and praise mingled sweetly together. We of earth-life greeted those of the Summer Land who had deigned to meet us in our humble home. Fathers, mothers, brothers, sisters, husbands, wives, sons and daughters, with many an old friend, from their homes divine mingled with us, giving words of cheer and consolation. Truly it was good for us thus to meet and mingle on the shores of time. It was a joyous evening to us all, and we doubt if there existed in all this great Republic a happier New Year's party than ours. We had song and music, poetry and prose, prayer and praise, speaking and drawing, and words of advice and comfort during the session. And all retired from the New Year's circle, feeling that it was a blessed privilege to meet with those who, in the language of the angel, spoke with John on the isle called Patmos, saying: "I am he that liveth, and was dead; and, behold, I am alive forevermore. Amen." Rev. i: 18.

January 3d. We spoke in Wheaton, our county seat, to fifty very intelligent men and women — which was a good audience, considering the dark and stormy night that it was. These home lectures are donations of ours to the cause.

Thursday, January 4th. We bade adieu to our little ones, and started for Philadelphia, the city of Brotherly Love.

We reached Philadelphia Saturday morning, January 6th, at 7.25, and at 8 o'clock we were comfortably seated at the breakfast table of our friend, Dr. H. T. Child, 634 Race street. It does one's soul good to sit down in the midst of this truly happy Quaker spiritual family. For the family circle, in its happy combination, is the highest type of heaven on earth.

God bless, and good angels guard and keep all truly happy families together. Amen.

Sunday, January 7th. At 10.30 A. M., we took our place as a teacher before a Philadelphia audience. Our discourse was a review of the testimony of modern theology as on record in the suit now on trial before the people of the world, known as "Ancient and Modern Theology *vs.* Modern Spiritualism," which seemingly gave good satisfaction.

At 3 o'clock, P. M., full four hundred people came together to attend Dr. Child's spiritual circle in Institute Hall, corner of Broad street and Spring Garden.

This was truly a feast of good things, well gotten up, and ably managed. Many fine tests were given.

At 7½ P. M. we continued our review of the evidence of the prosecution, showing up their weak points, etc., before an audience of five hundred or more men and women — the best audience of the season, save one.

The following tests were given by the mediums present:

*First.* By P. Blaker, who, in trance, came to Dr. Child and whispered:

"Aunt Rebecca is here, and says Cousin Charles is very sick, and will not live long."

Dr. C. replied, "I know Aunt Rebecca well. She is a spirit. I know who Cousin Charles is, very well, but do not know that he is sick or likely to die."

Three or four hours after this we were riding in a street car, and the doctor's brother came into the car.

"Where has thee been?" asked Dr. C.

"I have been out to Cousin Charles'."

"How is he?" asked the doctor.

"Very bad, indeed! He is very low, and not expected to live."

*Second.* Mrs. A. Anthony, medium, saw with us an elderly Quaker woman (spirit), fully describing her, and giving the name of Eliza. This spirit has been seen and described as with us by several mediums, in different places, and always the same dress and name. We, however, never knew her in the earth life.

*Third.* By Mrs. A. D. Hass, a medium who spoke to us words of cheer, giving one or two minor tests.

*Fourth.* A medium — woman — whose name we

did not know, under a very humorous influence, acted and said some very funny things, causing considerable mirth. This spirit claimed to be Benjamin Franklin (?).

*Fifth.* E. V. W., medium, after several calls, stepped forward and gave the following tests:

*First.* "I see by this man, (pointing out an old white-haired man) two spirits, one a young man, who died when a very little child — now about thirty years of age. There is with him a woman," fully describing her. "We should judge her about thirty or thirty-five years old when she died. Her name is Isabella, and his name is James. He says this old man is his father, and this spirit is his mother. Now, friends, we doubt the statement of James in regard to this woman of spirit life being his mother. What does our old friend of the earth life say about this matter?"

The old man replied: "I lost a wife who answers the description given by you, many years ago. She was about forty years of age, and her name was Isabella. She and I lost a little baby boy named James, who would now be about thirty years of age, if he were living in earth life."

*Second.* We saw an old Quaker spirit standing on the platform, fully describing him, who gave us the name of Isaac Stokes. He said he was born in Salem, New Jersey, and moved to this city in 1778, and died in 1818, at the age of eighty-two years.

This spirit was identified by an old man from Salem, N. J.

*Third.* We saw by a woman, whose name we did

not learn, a beautiful vision. First, four little stars, all of which culminated in one bright light. Out of this light there stepped a fine spirit boy, about four years old when he left this earth life. We described this scene to the woman, who stated that she had lost four children, and this little boy was one of them — aged nearly four when he left her.

There was a pathos and accent in this marked reply that moved many to tears.

*Fourth.* To a gentleman, we believe Mr. Shumway. We saw a sister standing by him, who agreed, in facts, with one he had lost.

*Fifth.* By a stranger we saw a soldier in full uniform, who said:

"My name is Charlie; I worked for you in 1861; enlisted in the spring of 1862, and was killed at the battle of Gettysburg in 1863."

This test was fully identified by the man and his wife.

*Sixth.* Isabella and James, mentioned in the third test, came the second time, bringing seven other spirits with them; the second wife, five children, (sons and daughters) and the aunt who loved the old man when a boy of eight and ten as well as the mother loved him — each in turn identifying themselves to the old man, who, when the test was finished, arose in much excitement, saying:

"They are all mine. I have lost six children — sons and daughters — and two wives, and I was a great favorite with this aunt."

Later we heard the man say, "I am well paid for this day's attendance here."

It was spoken from the soul, and tears of heaven's own joy glistened in his eyes.

*Seventh.* To a young woman we said: "There stands by you a spirit woman; your sister, two years older than yourself, being some time in spirit life."

She replied: "You are right; I have lost just such a sister."

*Eighth.* An old woman came from spirit life, and stood by us, giving the name of Thankful Haines. She was at once recognized.

*Ninth.* To Mrs. D. Hass came her grandfather, giving words of cheer—fully recognized.

These tests were given during the day and evening, and were fully identified. One other came:

*Tenth.* Mary Rhodes, who stated that she had relatives in the hall, and that her father was present. We gave her name. Her father arose and stated that this daughter died one year ago the 17th of May, and that "Mr. W. has not been here since."

Thus the testimony increases. On every hand we hear of their coming, these angel helpers of ours, with words of comfort and cheer.

## CHAPTER XLII.

The Seance — The Blow — Lieut. Charley H. — The Denial — The Approval — The Railroad Accident — The Wife and Six Children — The Parents' Desire Disappointed — The Child Came — Satisfaction — A Day in New York.

### *OUR EASTERN TOUR.*

Monday, January 8, 1872. We gave a seance this evening, and there were full three hundred present. Thirty-nine tests were given — thirty-four fully identified — among which, the following may interest our readers:

*First.* To a man. "I see behind you a spare, dark-complexioned man; he holds in his hand a club; he approaches, and deals you a sturdy blow; you fall before it, and when you get up the would-be assassin has fled. You know the man; he entered the army, and lost his life in 1862. This assault was in 1859. The blow was given on the right side of the head, and from behind, and he intended to kill you."

"What time of the year was this?" inquired the stranger.

"In June, 1859," we replied.

"Correct, in every particular," said the stranger.

*Second.* Walking to the rear of the room, we pointed out a man, to whom we said:

"There stands by this man a spirit, who says that his name is Charley; that he was acquainted with him in 1859–60; worked with him, in the shop and otherwise; he entered the army in 1861, late in the year, and was killed in 1863—shot through the chest, the ball entering the right breast a little forward of, and under, the right arm. This spirit, when in the form, entered the army as second lieutenant, and was acting captain when killed."

We then fully described the man, repeating his name. "Yes, or no?" we asked.

"I really would like to approve of what you say, but, for my life, I cannot identify a word of what you have told me as true," replied the man.

"We do not desire you to identify, unless true," we answered.

"Well it certainly is not correct in my case," was the reply.

After the meeting was over, there gathered around us many of the audience, and, among them, the man to whom we had given the test that had not been identified.

"I really desire to identify the communication you gave me, but cannot," said he.

Instantly, the spirit was with us, saying:

"I am C. H——, who worked with you in 1860, and enlisted, in October, in a New Jersey regiment. Is it possible you have forgotten me, and the impression made upon you when you heard of my death?"

With a sudden start, he exclaimed, excitedly:

"I knew him well. Poor Charley! He entered the service as second lieutenant, was promoted to a captaincy, and killed in 1863—shot through the body, as you have stated."

*Third.* To a lady. "There stands by you a young man, a friend and old acquaintance. He was killed by accident, on the railroad, several years ago. He says he is your old friend, and was killed near your house."

We then gave a full description of the man, his age, and first name.

The lady answered: "I knew the man well; he has been correctly described; he was an old friend of ours, and was killed near my house; he passed our house a few moments before he was killed. As he passed our house, he waved his handkerchief to us. In a few moments more, in passing from one car to the other, he fell through between the cars, and was cut all to pieces. The statement is strictly true."

*Fourth.* To an old man. "We see by this man that which we doubt. There stands by him a woman and six children — four boys and two girls — and the woman says, 'I am this man's former wife, and these are his children.'"

We then gave a minute description of the woman, and the children with her, and when they died. The old man arose, and, with much feeling, said:

"This woman and these children are mine. My wife and our children came to me to-night! Oh, I am paid — well paid for coming here. It is true; every word of it is true."

*Fifth.* There came to our meeting a lady and gentleman, who had not been to a Spiritual meeting since the division took place, some two or three years ago, in the Philadelphia Society of Spiritualists, before coming to our meeting on Sunday. We heard that the spirits had told him he should hear from his child, and all day he patiently waited for the test. They had taken seats, on Sunday evening, near the desk. The meeting was over, and the test had not been given.

Said Mr. B. to his wife: "Thus it ever is — again a failure. There is no reliance whatever on these spirit communications. I am disappointed. Come, let us go home."

We were standing some feet from the parties referred to, and heard not a word of what he was saying, when we felt an influence. Turning, to see from whence it came, we saw, standing by these two people, a woman, holding in her arms a beautiful little boy, presenting it to them, with the remark:

"I have kept my promise; here is your little Franky baby."

They were very much affected, and, after we had fully described the child, they declared its full identity.

These are but few of the many tests given at the Sunday morning circle and evening meetings. Our audiences have been very large — on Sunday afternoon and evening reaching between four and five hundred souls.

Tuesday, January 9, we left Philadelphia in search of our brother — the oldest of our family — whom we had not seen but once in five and thirty years. It had been whispered to us from spirit-life that he was dead, or a spirit. When last we heard from him, he was in Perth Amboy, New Jersey. Following up the whisperings from spirit-life, we found it true. Our brother Samuel had passed on into spirit-life two years ago last October. The skeptic may ask us why this brother had not informed us of his departure. We answer, because, all our lives, we had been strangers, not seeing each other but twice in forty-three years, and writing but seldom to each other. Again we asked why his wife and son had not written to us of his death. She answered: "For the simple reason that we did not know where you were."

And here let me say, dear readers, that there are many men and women, friends and acquaintances we form after leaving the old home, who are as near and dear to us as members of the old home, and especially with one who has been estranged from his father's home over forty years.

### *A DAY IN NEW YORK.*

Thursday, January 11, 1872, we passed in New York City with the mediums. Our first call was upon J. V. Mansfield, 361 Sixth avenue. While we were talking of old times — the time we knew each other in Boston — Brother Mansfield's hand was influenced, and the following communications were given:

*First.* "My Brother Wilson, I thank you for the good work done at Goldsboro, North Carolina, last winter, in the family of my son-in-law, Wm. R. Barrinner; he married my daughter. Your labors in Goldsboro have been of great use to many of my friends, especially to my daughter and her husband.

I have two daughters in spirit-life with me; their names are Mary and Sarah. Will you publish this communication? I am Mary Lawrens, the mother-in-law of Wm. R. Barringer, of Goldsboro, North Carolina."

Will Wm. R. Barringer write us when he reads this, if the above statement is true? We know of Wm. R. B., and have been in his house.

*Second.* "How is Hannah?" asked a spirit.

"Very well," we replied.

"Is Eugene doing well?"

"Yes; so far as we know."

"Well, I am glad to hear it. You will remember me to her. I thank you and yours for the kindness extended to her. I am Captain Jacob Black, of Maine."

This is a fine test, and one that was very unexpected. We know Hannah and Eugene well, and, when her name was mentioned, we felt very sure that we were going to hear from her late husband, our old and tried friend, the late Ingraham Gould, Esq., of Beaver Dam, Wisconsin, but were disappointed; and yet, the test from Captain Black was really a better one than the one from Mr. Gould, for we never knew Captain Black.

*Third.* "Oh, my children, my daughters, my husband! I thank you! I thank Mary. Oh! oh!! I must speak to them. The fire! I — am — your — their — Mary. I can't continue the control any longer. M-A-T-D-A—"

This spirit was one of three from whom I most

desired to hear — my sister-in-law, Matilda, wife of Phineas Eames, who, with his two daughters, is at my house, in Illinois. The line of communication was here broken.

Mr. Mansfield is an old and tried medium, and one through whom we have received many, many fine tests in the past.

We next called on Sister Emma Hardinge-Britten, who is now speaking in New York City, at Apollo Hall. We found her looking well; in fact, we do not remember ever having seen her look better. Her answers to our questions were as follows, and, by her permission, we give them in substance:

"I am not doing as well here as I wish; there are two societies, Sister Tappan speaking to one, admission free; I, before the Apollo Hall Society — fee, ten cents, at the door. I am glad, and thank my God every day of my life, that I took the course I did in my marriage with my husband, and that I was married in the manner I was, and in the Episcopal Church. I am happy in my marriage, and love my husband, and he loves me. We have a little house and three acres of land, which we are cultivating; my husband works it himself. I have known him long, and, although a gentleman born, he is willing to work; he is willing to do anything that is honorable and just. We are poor, for I lost everything in the publishing of my book. I have secured an annuity for my mother, who is with me at our home in Massachusetts."

We next proceeded to the quiet and elegant house

of our old friend, Dr. H. Slade, Clairvoyant. While there, the following communication and physical phenomena occurred:

A slate was held between Dr. Slade and us, he holding one end and we the other, and close to the table, when we heard the pencil write the words:

"MY DEAR BROTHER: I am glad to meet you thus again. God bless, and spirits help and guide you in your good work. Go on, my dear friend, continue the work you have in hand, and fear not. The angels are with you, and will help you. I well remember the talk I had with you on the cars, coming up Grand River from Nunica to Grand Rapids. If I had heeded your advice, I might have been with you, and others, working in the earth form. It is well, however. All is well. A. W. S."

The above was written, without contact, on the slate with a piece of pencil not to exceed the sixteenth of an inch in length. The writer was our old acquaintance and co-laborer, Alinda Wilhelm Slade.

The slate was then laid on the table, and under it a piece of pencil the sixteenth of an inch long and one-thirty-second part of an inch thick, between the slate and table, and full fifteen inches from Slade or myself. Dr. Slade then took us by the hand with both of his hands, when the pencil began to write; and for nearly forty seconds we could hear the writing very distinctly, when it ceased. On looking at the slate, we found the following written thereon:

"My son, hold high your banner of truth; let its folds float out upon the breeze of progression. Your work is a great one. I am pleased with the work you are doing. Go on! Be true to God, Spiritualism, and yourself. SAMUEL WILSON."

After which, the right hand of a woman came up, between the table and us, to our beard — took hold of it and gave a pull. Then came the dusky hand of an Indian, who took hold of our coat and pulled it; this was repeated several times. We then took a large slate pencil, full six inches long, in our hand, and held it under the table; instantly, two hands came — one soft and velvety, and one large and coarse, with heavy touch; this hand clasped our wrist, holding it firmly, when the other took the pencil out of our hand. The reader will remember that both of Dr. Slade's hands were on the top of the table, as was our left hand. After the pencil had been taken out of our hand, we were requested to look under the table for the pencil. We did so, and the pencil was not found on the floor, or about the room. We joined hands, and, in a little time — say twenty seconds — we saw the pencil in the air descending slowly to the table, and lightly falling on our hand.

Dr. Slade was then influenced by the Indian brave Wasso, who spoke to us words of cheer, and bid us return at eight o'clock in the evening, saying:

"Big speak, come wait little time, and when me call, come up, and me give big speak — big see. Old brave, squaw, and some pappoose come."

Dr. Slade, after this influence, asked us to tell him what the Indian had said to us. We did so.

"Well, come and see what comes of it; but I

frankly tell you that every hour of the evening is fully engaged up to ten o'clock."

Our friends will bear in mind that everything recorded above took place in broad daylight, and independent of any human agency, save the presence of Dr. Slade and ourself in the room. We got no test from those we desired to, either through Mansfield or Slade, showing, conclusively, that the human mind has nothing to do, whatever, with the presentation of the phenomena.

---

## CHAPTER XLIII.

Sitting with Dr. Slade — We had not Taken our Seat a Minute before the Immortals were With Us — "Oh, my God, I Can't Stand This" — "Be Quiet, Doctor" — "Yes, That's my Wife's Hand and Arm" — "Yes, I am Your Father."

*OUR EASTERN TOUR.*

Returned again precisely at eight o'clock, to Dr. Slade's house, waiting for our summons to a council with the spirits. At half-past nine o'clock, we were called to the room. The table by which we sat is a common three-foot, fall leaf one, and was near the center of the room. Before sitting down, Dr. Slade stretched a line across the room between the table and the door. The room is about sixteen feet square, more or less, and well filled with furniture. This line, about the size of a good stout fish line, was six feet from the floor, hung slack; and in the center of this was a black cambric curtain about two yards wide and two to three yards long; between this curtain and the door through which we entered the room, there was a space full four feet with nothing in it. In the center of this curtain there is an aperture eight by ten inches, cut on three sides thus |__| the flap pinned up to the line. The table stood against the curtain which trailed on the floor. We had not taken our seats a minute before the immortals were with us. First came three spirits whom we did not know; then came Mrs. Alinda Wilhelm Slade and others. These we saw clairvoyantly. Soon came a hand from under the table, up between us and it, fully visible to the physical sense. This hand patted our coat sharply. It was the right hand of a woman. A chair was then moved visibly. Then the curtain was lifted up and let down; then shaken. During all this time the room was well lighted with gas—full head. It was then written on the slate, "Turn down the gas to half head." This was done. We now give our experience, or what we saw and felt.

First, we felt a cold chilly current of air. Then all over us a full galvanic current, causing a very peculiar prickling sensation. The hair on our head, which is long and fine, as well as silvery gray, became very lively—each particular hair felt as though alive. We have felt this sensation very frequently. Then there was a feeling as of cold water, the whole length of the nervous spinal column. Then came several electric shocks, clear and distinct, in quick succession — after which we were as in ordinary life, without any unusual feelings. During all this time, Dr. Slade was in an intense state of excitement — frequently exclaiming, "Oh, my God, I can't stand this! How can you sit there so still? Oh, my God, see them!" And then catching hold of us exclaiming, "How can you sit so quiet, with these things going on all about us? See them?"

"Be quiet, Brother Slade," we replied. "If we make our bed in hell, God is there, and he being love, we can't be harmed, for he is here with his angels, and I guess we shall see him pretty soon. Let us wait and watch."

"Great God, see there!" cried Slade.

And we saw the black cambric curtain sharply shaken. Saw the thumb and part of the hand and wrist of a man's right hand. Then the curtain became still — the man's thumb and part of a hand disappeared, and all was quiet. We were at this time seated at the table, Dr. Slade on the left side. We were on the right side — our hands clasped in each other's — Slade's left in our right; our left in Slade's right; the room light enough to see to read long primer type. When Slade exclaimed: "Good God, look at the gas!"

Turning our head, looking over our right shoulder, saw a large right hand — and arm below the elbow — of an Indian, turning down the gas until it was barely visible. We again felt a sharp electric shock. Turning our eyes toward the cambric curtain, we saw very white lines of light along the aperture and on the line; the room all the time growing lighter. All at once we were in a beautiful white light, everything was radiant. We turned to look at Dr. Slade, his face shone, his garments were white and glistening. We turned our eyes to the curtain and at the same moment Dr. Slade exclaimed in great excitement, "Oh, see! see!! My God, Wilson, do you see that?"

"Yes, Doctor, we see it; be quiet." There before us, was a woman's left hand and arm, from the shoulder down — the thumb, fingers, hand, and wrist, as perfect as life, but white as alabaster, and in a halo that we cannot describe. The arm was clothed in a fine lace sleeve, fastened at the wrist with a fine worked band and ruffles, in which sparkled a gem that reflected like the dew-drop under the rays of a June morning's sunlight. There was also a bracelet of jewels around the wrist that sparkled and shone even brighter than the light in which the arm and hand appeared. On the third and second fingers there were very fine-looking rings.

Here Dr. Slade exclaimed, "I can't stand it — I cannot. Oh, oh! what is that," partially rising and leaning toward the arm. At this the arm turned over showing the back of the hand, and we saw clearly the stones in the rings on the fingers. The hand then took hold of the cambric curtain moving it to and fro and disappeared, we exclaiming, "That was the hand, arm, sleeve, and rings that belonged to our sister, Alinda Wilhelm Slade. We should know that hand and the ring with the dark stone, at any time and anywhere!"

"Yes, that is my wife's arm, hand, and rings," said Dr. Slade.

The arm and hand continued in slow, graceful motion, waving to and fro, bending the elbow, the wrist, and finally the fingers. The appearing and disappearing of the hand, arm, and light, was gradual, easy, and graceful; there was no flitting or flashing hither and thither or other eccentric action, but a genuine spirit exhibition of power, will, and forethought, bringing vividly to our mind that Biblical exhibition of the parts of a man's hand that wrote on the wall of Belshazzar's reception room, "*Mene, Mene, Tekel Upharsin.*" With this highly gratifying difference, Belshazzar and his witnesses were drunk -- we were not.

A little later, sharp raps came on the table; a chair was moved; then the table; the curtain was violently shaken, lifted up and let down. We heard steps in the room. Then the room was filled with a light — such as we had never seen — unlike that in which the arm had appeared; that light was an alabaster white; this light was a golden one. A strange thrill of joy came over us — Dr. Slade exclaiming, "Great God, what is coming now?"

"Be quiet, Doctor, let us wait, and the angels will do their work well, and we shall see the Messenger from the Summer Land, and some of the glory thereof."

At this moment our mind was fully concentrated on first, our son, who was killed in the battle of Jonesboro; second, our sister-in-law, Mrs. Matilda Eames, who was burned to death at Birch Creek, in the Green Bay fire. We desired them to come. In our soul we said, Edwin, come. Come, Matilda. But one who died in September, 1844, who, at the time was not in our thoughts, came unbidden—and the manner of his coming was in this wise:

First: There came onto the black cambric curtain, white lines of light; then the aperture in the curtain was filled with this soft, beautiful light, sitting in a sea of golden light; then there came up from the floor the top or crown of a head, covered with short white hair; then the forehead, the eyes, nose, mouth, chin, neck and shoulders of a man. The chin and face covered with a white beard about four inches long. Reader, that man was my father in every respect as we last saw him on the third day of November, 1843, save the beard. We never saw on his face a beard of one week's growth. There he stood before us, head, face, beard, neck and shoulders. He looked at us; we at him. We first broke the silence. "Father, my father, do I see you—is it you—speak; my father, speak." He bowed three times, and then his lips moved, and we heard, (whether *clairaudial*, or with our natural ears, we are not prepared to say.)

"Yes, I am your father, and I meet you, my son. Though in your early life there was a gulf between us"—neither understanding the other—"let that gulf be bridged. You the mortal, and I the immortal man, meeting midway on the archway of eternal life. Hold high your standard: stand beneath its waving folds in truth — never again bow to the wrong; fearlessly stand in the breach and defend the right."

Our father then rose up full head above the curtain, bowed to us, stepping back a little, and disappeared. Thus he came; thus he left. We saw him; we knew him. "Our father who art in heaven, hallowed be thy name." The gulf is bridged, and I love thee, my father.

For a moment we sat in silence. Then Dr. Slade spoke, saying, "How like you your father is, in every respect, save size, and length of hair and beard. Your hair and beard is not as white as his; and how grand he appeared!"

"Yes," we replied, "there is a striking resemblance in that immortal father to his son."

Readers, our memory of our father is as follows: He was six feet in height at forty; weight at the heaviest, one hundred and ninety or two hundred pounds; well and compactly built, with strong arms, full sized hands, a thinking and hard-working man. When last we saw him, his face was somewhat wrinkled, his hair was short, and face cleanly shaved. He stood five feet eleven inches, and weighed not to exceed one hundred and seventy pounds. We had not supposed there was so marked a resemblance between our father and us, as appeared in this spiritual being.

Readers, what we have here related is strictly true; we saw it; Dr. Slade saw it, and we know whereof we write — and in the language of John, when on the isle called Patmos, "I John saw and heard these things." We, E. V. Wilson, Dr. Henry Slade, saw and heard these things, and as in the past, so in the present, these immortals exclaim: "I am he that liveth, and was dead; and, behold, I am alive forevermore, Amen; and have the keys of hell and of death."

"Write the things which thou hast seen, and the things which are, and the things which shall be hereafter." Rev. i: 18, 19.

After these things, Dr. Slade was influenced by the spirit of the Indian Brave Wassa, who spoke words of cheer to us, and among other things said to us, "Big Preach and Big Light is here from your wigwam." Then halting for a moment he said, "Say to squaws in Speak Brave's wigwam to come by and by, to the City of Many Wigwams, and with my media and yours, we will drive preach devils out of Big City." Then taking us by the right hand with his right hand, he laid his left hand (not tightly) on us saying, "Speak Brave, great work; great pow-wow by-and-by. Long Beard, big medium, much write. Speak Brave, Big Think, with many braves and squaws will hold big council, and then big work will begin. Good bye."

We asked who were the parties he named, but were too late, he was gone.

Thus closed our day in New York City. We shall never forget it.

# CHAPTER XLIV.

Return to Philadelphia — The New Yorker and Jim Fisk — The Lady Passenger — You lie, sir! — Jim's Charity — The Minister — How do you know? — Will you quote the Scriptures correctly? — Are you satisfied? Yes, sir — That person was a Christian.

*OUR EASTERN TOUR.*

Friday, January 12. We left the St. Cloud Hotel at nine o'clock A. M., for Philadelphia. For the first time in our life, we went to bed by steam; that is, instead of climbing up five stories, by flights of stairs, we stepped on a platform and were quietly sent to our room by steam. "Such a getting up stairs we never did see," and we question if many of our Western readers ever went to bed in this way.

On the street-cars, going to Jersey City Ferry, we fell in with a talkative New Yorker, with whom we conversed, thusly:

*E. V. W.* You have had great excitement here over the death of Jim Fisk, Jr.

*New Yorker.* Yes, sir; James Fisk is dead — murdered in cold blood, sir; a downright assassination. James Fisk had faults, sir, but he was not a murderer; and, with all his faults, many a poor family in New York and Jersey City will miss him. Sir, I know of many families who were dependent on him for their living.

*E. V. W.* You seem to think well of him, with all his faults.

*New Yorker.* Yes, sir; and James Fisk's name will live in the memory of many families after his assassin's name has been forgotten in the grave.

*E. V. W.* Will Stokes be hung for his crime?

*New Yorker.* Yes, sir; and, if he escapes the halter, he will be assassinated within five hours.

*A Lady Passenger.* Fisk deserved his fate, sir, and died as he had lived — a villain.

*New Yorker.* How do you know, madam, that he was a villain? Has he done you any wrong?

*Lady.* No! for he never had the opportunity; but everyone knows that James Fisk was an immoral, wicked, bad man, and kept his mistress, to the disgrace of his family and society, and, hence, deserved his fate.

*E. V. W.* You see, sir, there are two opinions in regard to this man Fisk.

*New Yorker.* (To the lady.) Madam, did James Fisk ever do you any wrong?

*Lady.* No, sir; and for the very good reason, he 's never had the opportunity, sir.

*New Yorker.* So, madam, James Fisk's offense, in your estimation, is that he did you no wrong, for the reason that you had no opportunity to accept the wrong from him.

*Lady.* Sir, what do you mean?

*New Yorker.* That your language warranted the comment I made, and that you, in taking part in the conversation between this gentleman and myself, opened the door for the retort made. I believe in woman's rights. You assumed the right to speak on this occasion, and are entitled to the answer you invoked. James Fisk had his faults, madam; but he never slandered a woman. He would go, in his carriage, in open day, and in the face of the world, to his mistress' house; his calumniators, with a lie on their tongues to their wives, would go to theirs in the dark.

*E. V. W.* Were you personally acquainted with Fisk?

*New Yorker.* Yes, sir; and know that there was a systematic plan on foot to rob him, and this woman is one of them.

*Lady.* You lie, sir!

*New Yorker.* Thank you; you have proved all I have stated. Good morning.

And we left the car for Jersey City; and having friends near the Erie Depot, we called on them, when we found that the dastardly murder of Fisk was the topic of conversation.

Again we heard of his charities, and of families, where the father and husband had been killed in the service of the Erie Railroad, that were receiving full pay, as when the heads of the families were living.

This certainly speaks well for his charity, but did it warrant him in doing wrong? But we can afford to let his ashes rest in peace, for the chaplain of his regiment assures us he has gone to glory, through the blood of Jesus Christ.

At one o'clock P. M., we found ourself seated in the

cars of the Camden and Amboy Railroad, and on our way to Philadelphia. On the opposite side of the car, a little in front of us, we noticed a group of three men, who seemed to be talking of us, from their looks, and nods, and motions of their hands. Soon one of them arose and came to us, saying:

"I believe this is E. V. Wilson, the Spiritualist, who lectured in Philadelphia last Sunday."

"Yes, sir; your belief is founded on facts; you are right."

"Well, I am not a Spiritualist!"

"You need not tell us that, sir; your looks determine the fact."

"Well, sir, what is there in my looks whereby you judge me?"

"Well, you are thin; well dried from contact with heat; you are wrinkled, and look sad; you have fear of God and the Devil in your features; besides, you are a Presbyterian minister, and in which creed we 'take no stock,' whatever. Sir, we are not Christians, but possess a practical religion, full of joy, whose axiom is knowledge. We know that we are immortal. Do you?

"No, sir; but we are taught to believe in God and his Christ, in the repentance of sin, and the remission thereof through the blood of God's crucified Son."

"I know you are, sir; but what an idea; only think for one moment, that the I Am, with whom all things are possible, who made the earth and all there is in it in six days, and pronounced it good, could not keep it in goodness; but losing it, through evil, is, and was, compelled, in order to save his own handiwork, to kill a man, and damn a man, in order to save a man. Jesus said to those Jews who believed on him: 'Ye seek to kill me, a man that hath told you the truth which I have heard of God.'"

"Will you quote the Scriptures correctly, sir?"

"Yes, sir; we have quoted them correctly."

"Will you give me the chapter and verse?"

"Yes, sir; you will find it in the eighth chapter of St. John, part of the thirty-first and fortieth verses. Here it is," we said, presenting him our Testament.

Taking it, he turned at once to the title page, to see if it was "The New Testament of our Lord and Savior, Jesus Christ, translated out of the original Greek, and with the former translations dilligently compared and revised. New York: American Bible Society, instituted in the year MDCCCXVI—1850."

"There, sir, are you satisfied that the church for whom you preach published that Testament?"

"Yes, sir; but I confess I doubted the correctness of your quotations."

"Of course you did; and you are not the first man who is afraid of the revolver he has placed in the hands of his enemy. Will you turn to the fly-leaf and read the inscription written there?"

"What is the object?"

"When you have read it, I will tell you."

"Well, sir, it reads: 'Presented to Mr. E. V. Wilson, of Toronto, by his new acquaintance and friend, Roberto, of Virginia.'"

"Read on, will you?"

"Yes; if you wish it."

"We do; for it is important in connection with what we have to say."

> "There are a few on this bleak earth,
> Whose friendship I would claim,
> And on that list of sacred worth
> I have plainly traced thy name."

"*September* 13, '53."

"There, sir; that person was a Christian; came on a visit to Toronto to friends; was thrown off by them; came to my house; gave me this Testament, and asked me to believe it; borrowed of me forty dollars, besides owing me sixty dollars' board bill, and then left. This person believes that, through the blood of Jesus Christ, she will be saved and I will be damned."

"My friend, you are in a bitter mood; you should learn to be calm, as well as generous. I came to you in friendship, and with a desire to persuade you from the evils of Spiritualism."

"You did; and in your first remark you insulted us, by telling us to our face, 'that you took no stock in Spiritualism'—virtually saying that it is a humbug; and that all who teach its truths are imposters; and then you insult me by doubting the authenticity of the New Testament, as you did when you turned to the title page, to see if it was a genuine one or not; and your closing remarks are abusive, inasmuch as you seek to convert us from our evil ways, or 'the evils of Spiritualism.' Now, sir, we offer you a discussion on the following resolution:

*Resolved*, That the Christian religion, as taught, had its conception and birth in evil, and that the serpent of Genesis, is really the great founder of your Christiaity, he foreseeing the necessity of a redeemer.

"Will you discuss this resolution with us in Philadelphia, next week, or, beginning to-morrow, at half past seven o'clock P. M., under strict parliamentary rules? Yes, or no; answer?"

"No; I will not!"

This caused a great sensation with the passengers, who cried, "Coward!" "Back out!" "Bah!" and we were left alone for the balance of the way to Philadelphia.

Saturday, Sunday, and Monday, January 13, 14, and 15, we were in Philadelphia. On Sunday, our hall was filled in the morning; full five hundred at Dr. Child's circle, and every inch of the sitting room was occupied in the evening, and many were obliged to stand. On Monday evening we had over three hundred persons present, with an admission fee at the door.

During the four meetings, we gave forty-seven tests, forty-one of which were fully identified on the spot.

*First.* To Mr. De Hass. "There is with you a little boy—your son." We fully described him, and gave his name.

*Second.* To Mr. Bush. "There is with you a spirit, who gives his name as Captain Waters, and who informs me that he knew you in early life, when you lived in Ashtabula, Ohio."

This spirit mentioned many names familiar to him, but the spirit was not identified, and, hence, counted out. Mr. B., however, wrote his brother, in Ohio, for information in regard to the matter, and every statement has since been corroborated.

*Third.* To a lady. "There is with you a spirit." We fully described her and gave her name, but she was not identified.

After the meeting was over, there came to us a lady, who stated that "the spirit you saw by the lady whom she could not identify, I knew well; and every incident, name, and place, is in my history."

The same thing occurred in a second case, with a gentleman, the man behind him being fully cognizant of every fact given the first party.

We know that, at times, when two parties of similar temperament are sitting side by side, or one behind the other, and the spirit stands between them, it is difficult, indeed, for us to determine to which the spirit comes. But the work goes bravely on, and all is well.

# CHAPTER XLV.

Our Visit to Hammonton — The Excellent Mother and Child — Step forward, Brother! — The Home of Brother Peebles — A Startling Test — Return to Philadelphia — Mrs. A., the Medium.

*OUR EASTERN TOUR.*

Tuesday, January 16. We left Philadelphia for Hammonton, New Jersey, at eight o'clock A. M. Arriving at Hammonton at a quarter before ten o'clock A. M., we were met by Brother Bradley, and conducted to the quiet home of Brother Wooley, the silversmith, who, with his excellent companion, ever strives to make the wanderer at home.

Brother Wooley has just returned from a trip to California, Oregon, and Washington Territory. He was in the snow blockade for many days, and has come to the very sensible conclusion of remaining where he is.

In this city, we made the acquaintance of an excellent woman and mother, who is toiling on, "stitching, stitching," on shirts and pants, for the support of herself and child — the deserted wife and daughter of one who claims to preach the gospel of truth and Spiritualism. A few short years ago, this woman was in a happy home, unencumbered, and was taken from it under the professions of love, to be deserted and left, a little later, to care for herself and child — *his child.* And oh! how sweet and winsome are the ways of the little darling, so pretty and gentle — the "little Birdie." God judge you, brother; we shall not. We write in no spleen, but in the spirit of duty and love, with good will to all. But, as we understand Spiritualism, we cannot sanction this desertion of a wife and child, without a home or means of support, save woman's last resort — "shirt-making, or dishonor." Step forward, brother, and be a man! Free this woman from the bond that hath made her your property. Give to her the darling child, and set her free; or come to her support, like a man!

There are two societies of Spiritualists in Hammonton — one is called the Conservative, and the other the Radicals. The very conservative of the Conservative Society do not, nor did not, countenance us, or our meetings. The more liberal of the Conservatives were among our friends. There is a hall, or church, here, built by members of both societies, controlled by the Conservatives, who made the Radicals pay for the use of the hall they helped to build. This is the direct fruit of organization with stakes and chains, fencing in the righteous and out the wicked. Thus did not Jesus.

The Radicals, referred to above, are, in our estimation, the saving element of Hammonton; and we question if there can be found the same number of men and women, in any community, who are purer in thought, deed, or act, than these so-called Radicals. We love them — the Presseys. Bradleys, Wooleys, and others.

Hammonton is the home of Brother J. M. Peebles; and here lives his wife, a noble woman and true, of whom all speak well. We did not meet her, hence could not greet her with the good will of a brother, and co-worker with her companion and mate. May the harmony of their lives be like the summer's sunshine and spring water — pure, warm, and eternal.

We lectured in this place four times, and held one seance, giving, in all, over one hundred fine tests, most of which were fully identified on the spot. Some that were denied at first, were afterward fully approved. Of these, we mention the case of Dr. N——, to whom we described two spirits, and fixed five dates in his life, which he could not identify. On returning to his home, and reviewing the statements, he confirmed everything.

Mr. R. Bradley received a startling test of past life, which brought him to his feet in such a manner that all conceded its sharp points.

Our attendance was not large, yet good, the Conservatives refusing to come out, because Brother Peebles and ourself switch each other occasionally, though this very switching is good for both of us. "Whom the Lord loveth he chasteneth," and the truly brave and honorable man ever loves the brave, who dares to act in the battle of life. The Conservative Society refused to come to our meetings. We say it fearlessly! We advised our society to go and hear Brother Dean Clark, who was to speak for the Conservatives on Sunday, the 21st instant. We are willing to let the world judge us.

Saturday, Sunday, and Monday, January 20, 21, and 22, we filled the desk in Philadelphia, speaking to crowded houses; in fact, our mission to the City of Brotherly Love has been a success, and the tests were simply wonderful.

Dr. Child's Sunday afternoon circle is the best thing we ever attended in the form of a Spiritual meeting; and on the occasion of the afternoon of Sunday, the 21st, we had full five hundred present, and many fine tests were given by the different mediums in the hall. The following tests may be of interest to our readers:

*First.* Mrs. A., the medium, said: "I see by this woman," pointing out the woman, "an old man about seventy-five; he is stooping; has very gray hair; has been in the spirit world nineteen years; he says this woman is his daughter Sarah."

The lady affirmed the statement to be correct.

*Second.* To a young man, Mrs. A. pointed out a soldier, who was killed at the battle of Gettysburg, describing him so minutely that he was at once recognized.

Mrs. De H. then gave several fine tests — one to us, which we fully recognized.

Our turn then came, and, for forty minutes, we mingled with the people, walking from one end of the hall to the other, giving dates and incidents in the lives of over twenty men and women; also, locating disease, hurts, deaths, likeness to parents, number of members of the family to whom the subject belonged, as well as describing many spirits. To one we said: "In September, when you were nineteen years old, you were nearly killed by the falling of a heavy stick of timber. It looks to us like a round, long log, or tree, but see no limbs nor bark."

"Can you give the day of the month and week?"

"Yes! on Thursday, the 17th."

"You are correct, sir. I came near losing my life by the fall of a derrick, in a shipyard, on Thursday, the 17th of September — the year I was nineteen, in my twentieth."

To a lady. "We find in your father's family, and entailed on his children — not from your mother's side — many sudden deaths, by accident or disease, in early life. On your mother's side of the house, we find well-defined pulmonary difficulties."

The lady replied: "You are remarkably correct. How did you get these things?"

"Your aunt, with whom you were a favorite, telegraphed them to us."

"On which side of the house did this aunt belong?"

"The mother's."

"You are right again."

To a man, we described a spirit woman minutely, giving her name in full, her age, and when he knew her; described her house, and their relations to each other. Then, stepping to the man, we said: "This woman stands here, between these two men, and we believe her to be an old sweetheart of this gentleman. She subsequently married a worthless fellow, who made a shipwreck of life, and this woman went down to the grave through troubles brought on by the husband. Will you answer, yes or no, to this reading?"

"No!" promptly replied the man.

"Then you know nothing about this statement?"

"No, sir! It is not true. There has nothing of the kind occurred in my life."

"We have been very frank with you, sir, and this is an important statement. We see her now. She stands between you and this man, and affirms the facts in the face of your denial, and your word will be taken before ours."

"Well, sir, I can assure you it is not true of me!"

The other man then said: "Mr. Wilson, your statement is true in every respect, and belongs to *my* history, instead of this man's. It is literally true."

"We leave the matter in the hands of the audience; they must decide on its merits," we replied.

---

## CHAPTER XLVI.

Royer's Ford — Schuylkill Valley — Valley Forge — The Keeper of the Village Tavern — A Christian Man — "I never had a Sister" — "Yes, but she is Dead."

*OUR EASTERN TOUR.*

Tuesday, January 26th. Royer's Ford, on the bank of the Schuylkill River, thirty-two miles from Philadelphia, *via* the Philadelphia and Reading Railroad, on which we had a pleasant ride up the Schuylkill valley, one of the finest in the United States, dotted with villages, beautiful country residences and parks, and abounding in fine natural scenery, as well as being one of the finest farming countries in the world. We were in a sort of dream, looking forth from the windows of our soul, drinking in the beautiful winter views of this truly beautiful valley — when we were startled out of our dream by the brakeman's shout of "Valley Forge!"

Oh! what recollections of the past rushed through our brain on hearing this name called. In a moment we were with the heroes of the Revolution, with the hungry, frozen and ragged army of Washington. We saw those old veterans tramping through the snow barefooted, nearly naked; on short rations — some starving, watching, waiting for the beacon-star of Liberty to take its place in the New World, as one more in the great family of nations. Then the sons of the North and South were brothers in arms under a Virginia leader — fighting for freedom. Then swiftly gliding back over the clairvoyant currents of life, how changed to-day! The sons and daughters of the North and South — unlike their fathers and mothers — are watching, waiting for separation, for the setting of the star of Liberty! Then may we exclaim in the language of Walt Whitman:

"Blow again, trumpeter; — conjure war's wild alarms!
Swift to thy spell, a shuddering hum like distant thunder rolls.
Lo! where the armed men hasten — ho! mid the clouds of dust, the glint of bayonets —
I see the grim-faced cannoniers — I mark the rosy flash amid the smoke — I hear the cracking of the guns!

Nor war alone:—thy fearful music-song wild player, brings every sight of fear—
The deeds of ruthless brigands—rapine—murder! I hear the cries for help!
I see ships foundering at sea—I behold on deck and below deck the terrible tableaux."

All is gone, when one of those grand old stars—the noble thirteen—drop out of their brilliant constellation. The setting broken, their glory gone, the Union lost! The Gods forbid! "The Union must and shall be preserved!"

"Royer's Ford!" shouted the brakeman, disturbing our dream, bringing us to a sense of our position. We grasped our satchel and hurried out. On the depot platform, we were met by Captain Samuel Egoff, who greeted us with a brother's welcome—then taking us to the pleasant and happy home of Mary Buckwalter, in which we felt that we were welcome. We gave two lectures in this place—we believe the first on the subject of Spiritualism ever spoken here. The hall was well filled each night, and we gave several fine tests, of which the following will be of interest to our readers:

*First.* To a man, the keeper of the village tavern, we gave a close reading of character, marking the likeness to his father and mother; also giving three dates in his life, of marked importance. We then called for approval from those who knew him. All conceded that it was strictly true; and the man himself said "It is correct in every respect."

"Save one," said a friend of ours.

"And what is that?" we asked.

"He sells whisky."

"Does he?"

"Yes, sir!"

"Has he a license to sell?"

"Yes, sir!"

"His license is granted him by the officers legally elected for that purpose?"

"Yes, sir!"

"Very well, sir, we would sell whisky, if we were in his place. And you have no right to find fault with him. You, sir, and every other sovereign voter who voted a license law, or for officers to grant this man and others the right to sell whisky, or other intoxicating drinks to your sons, brothers, fathers, or to yourselves—have no right to find fault with him! You are to blame; you, the sovereign voters, and none else! Put the ballot into the hands of your women, and this crying evil will be done away with at once."

*Second.* An old man, a Christian (we believe an exhorter in the church), got up to leave, and as he arose, there stood with him a woman and little boy, and as he stepped into the aisle to go out, we said, "The man now leaving, please wait a little." He stopped reluctantly, and with a defiant look of disapproval, turned toward us. As he did so, we said: "There is a woman from spirit life standing with you, and she has with her a little boy, who has been in spirit life some time. This woman died very early in life, and is your sister, and has with her your son." Then we gave a full and minute description of them, again stating this woman has been long in spirit life. What do you know of this?

"I never had a sister, sir."

"Then you had no sister."

"I never had a sister, and have none now."

"Did your mother ever bury any children?"

"Yes; but they are dead, and I have no sister."

"Was one of those children your mother buried, a girl?"

"I had no sister, I tell you!"

"We do not care whether you had a sister or not; was one of those children buried by your mother, a girl? Answer us; yes, or no!"

"But she is dead."

"The girl?"

"Yes."

"Then your mother buried a girl — a daughter."

"Yes, but she is dead — died long ago, and was buried, hence she can't be here."

"Then you had a sister?"

"Yes, but she is dead."

"That will do, so far as the sister is concerned. Now how is it about the boy, your son? Please answer."

Then, readers, this Christian wheeled on his heel and left the hall. A man then spoke, saying, "He has lost a son, such as you have described, and I put up a fence around his grave."

Thus this Christian man sought to, and did avoid the truth. Why? Because it conflicted with his religious dogmas.

Ah, Christianity! you have many sins of omission and commission to answer for in that day, when you stand before the soul-mirror of your future!

Two boys were seen and identified, who were drowned some years ago.

---

## CHAPTER XLVII.

Seance in Camden, New Jersey—On it we read: "The Last Will and Testament"—I am Mr. H.—Mind Reading—He is Dr. Henry.

*OUR EASTERN TOUR.*

On Thursday and Saturday evenings, January 25 and 27, we gave seances in Camden, New Jersey, to good audiences, giving many fine tests, among which are the following:

To a man, we said: "We see by you the spirit of an old man. He is tall, spare, and of dark complexion; his hair is iron-gray; his brow is broad and receding; he died many years ago. We also see a hillside, or country, home. It is a fine estate; the mansion is a fine one, standing in a fine park of trees." We then described the building, gates, walks, etc., "This spirit now shows us a package of papers. He takes one of them out of the package and holds it out to us. On it we read: 'The Last Will and Testament of ——, 1781.' On the second paper, we read: 'Covenant and Bond, 1804, with ——.' These papers are of value to you, and you are looking after them. They are far from here, in another part of the world. They are secreted in an attic room, in the mansion on the hillside, that we saw and have described."

"I am Mr. H——. Many here know who I am. I recognize the spirit. All the statements are strictly true. The Will was dated 1781, and the Covenant and Bond, in 1804. They are of great value to me, and others, and the suppositions of all concerned are, these papers are secreted in the mansion on the hillside."

"Mind reading," said a voice.

To which Mr. H—— replied: "Not by any means, sir, for I was thinking of a matter entirely foreign to the communication just given by Mr. Wilson."

To a lady, we said: "Here is with you a man," describing him. "He was a physician. He is Dr. Henry."

"I recognize him well. You are right in your statement, sir."

To a man came two spirit sisters, who were fully described and readily identified.

To an old man came a lovely little girl, just as she was in health and life, before death called her home. Then she stood forth in all the pride of well-developed womanhood of spirit-life, exclaiming, "My father, I live to love you, and will meet you with joy, ere long, in the Summer Land!"

The spirit was fully recognized.

To a young man, we said: "We see you when twenty years old. It is afternoon of the 16th of August. There is a heavy blow given you from behind; it looks to us like a handspike, in the hands of another man. The blow is a glancing one, hurting your head and left shoulder, as well as arm."

"You are right, sir; and the blow came near killing me; had it fallen fully on me, I should not have been here to-night."

"What day of the month, and what month of the year, did this accident occur to you, sir?"

"On the 16th of August, in the afternoon of the day; I remember well the time."

"We see, by this man, a boy — his son; this son, when fourteen years old, was drowned; he would be twenty-six years old, if living to-day."

"You are correct," replied the man.

These are but a few out of seventy-two tests given on these evenings in Camden. Thus the work goes bravely on.

Our meetings have been a grand success in the City of Brotherly Love, beginning with one hundred and seventy-four hearers, and concluding our engagement with a full house.

# CHAPTER XLVIII.

We leave Harrisburg, Pa.—The Drowning—The Gallon of Whisky—Davy Couch's Spirit—Disturbed—You are a Set of Thieves—Put him Out—York, Pa.—May I Kiss You—My Name is Nellie—Ma, Don't Cry for Me—Not Alone in Death.

*OUR EASTERN TOUR.*

Tuesday, January 30th, we left for Harrisburg, Pa., where we gave three lectures, closing February 1st. At Fairview we had a small audience, it being a place where Spiritualism is but little known and less understood. During our lecture, we gave nine tests, of which we mention the following as worthy of attention:

To a man we gave the following test: We see you at seventeen, with two others, in a drowning condition, describing it, the place and the parties with him.

"How do you get this?" he asked.

"Your sister, a spirit, gives it to us."

"You are right, and this is the second time you have given me this same communication. The first time two years ago, and to-night."

A man challenged us to read him, with a "You can't do it!" "Come and touch our hand with your fingers," we replied.

He did so.

We then gave him a detailed account of his life,

history, and his character, and the audience, with one voice, declared the reading correct.

We were somewhat troubled, during our meeting, with the spirit of one gallon of whisky that had control of one of our audience; but we are not disposed to find fault. Both the man and the whisky were true to themselves, and acted under the law.

Wednesday, January 30th, we lectured in Barr's Hall, Harrisburg, to an intelligent audience. We gave eighteen tests, twelve of which were identified on the spot; three subsequently.

To Davy Couch: There came seven spirits — three sisters, one brother, and "sweetheart," the grandfather and his mother — all of whom were fully described, and they mentioned many traits and incidents in the old man's life. He is the last of his tribe, and will soon go home to those he loved, all identified.

To Mr. Potts came his wife and brother, who were so fully described that they were at once fully recognized.

To a stranger: At seventeen years of age, you take great responsibilities, acting for others as well as yourself. At twenty, you make another remarkable change, affecting your whole life. Nine years ago the twenty-eighth day of next June, and continuing to the afternoon of the fifth of September, you are in continual excitement and danger, but on the third of July, at six o'clock A. M., you are in the very jaws of death. I get this statement from one who was a soldier, and who was with you most of the time. He was killed at the battle of Gettysburg. The man answered,

"You are correct in every particular; it is very remarkable!"

To a lady we gave a very remarkable diagnosis of her ailments. This reading was, in every feature, considered one of the best we had ever given in the city of Harrisburg.

Then came a spirit and stood by a man and related to us his character, as well as the incidents in his life, and then turning to us, told us just what the man had said of us and Spiritualism that afternoon, as well as the number of persons who were present. The man arose and declared it all correct.

Thursday, February 1st, we held a sceance at three o'clock, and lectured at half-past seven P. M. We gave, during the day, fifty-two tests, fourteen of which were not fully identified. Our evening was seriously disturbed by a man professing love for, and belief in, Jesus Christ, and the Bible as the Word of God. He frequently interrupted us during our lecture — we continually treating him kindly. At last his abuse became unbearable. Dr. Barr, the owner of the hall, had frequently called him to order; told him to be still or leave the hall. He declared that he had paid his money (which, by the way, was false, for certain parties paid his fee for him), and should stay as long as he pleased, and say what he pleased. At this, Dr. Barr went for him and started him for the door. He resenting and threatening the doctor with blows and such pleasant words out of Christian teachings as these: "You are all a set of G—d d—m thieves! You hounds of hell! you have robbed me of my money (fifteen cents fee at the door), and now undertake to put me out of doors! You sons of hell!" At this point two or three of his friends came to his rescue, and there was a clinch. We hurried to the scene of action, and it was soon over. But this we will say, Dr. Barr is not easily lifted off his feet.

We here present our readers with two articles, clipped from that excellent daily, "The Evening Mercury," Harrisburg, Friday, Feb. 1st and 2d. These articles speak for themselves:

"SPIRITS OF THE DEPARTED 'INTERVIEWED.' Mr. E. V. Wilson, the great test medium, lectured in Barr's Hall last evening to a large audience. The lecture was very generally pronounced superior, in delivery and argument, to any previous one on the same subject in Harrisburg. His manner and address were such as to command the closest attention of his auditors. He held them, as it were, spell-bound for an hour and fifteen minutes. The tendency of his argument was rather convincing than otherwise. During his lecture he gave the details of a very interesting visit he had made to Dr. Slade's, in New York. How he went there hoping to see and have an interview with the spirits of several of his relatives who perished in the great Wisconsin fires last fall, but to his delight and great surprise his father, who had passed away or died thirty years ago, entered the room where they were assembled and gave his name and the name of the lecturer, E. V. Wilson, in full, which names were unknown to any one present, and held a long converse with them. At the close of the lecture, Mr. Wilson gave several tests of the presence of spirits. To one gentleman present he gave seven, testifying to the presence of his two sisters, one brother, one that had been a 'sweetheart' in early life, his mother and father and a sister that died lately, describing these persons, whom he had never seen nor heard of in the flesh, so accurately that the gentleman at once recognized them. To another person he described his wife, his brother and aunt, with whom he had been a great favorite. To another, three important events in his life. To another, a lady, her descendants. In all he gave eighteen tests, thirteen of which were fully identified."

Friday, February 2d, we were very unwell, not able to leave our room until two o'clock, P. M., and then, weak and sick, we left for the old and conservative town of York, Pa., where but few lectures have been given. We lectured at night, expecting only a score of hearers, and had full five hundred. Our meeting was again disturbed by a crazy man, whose course was universally deprecated by all present. We gave several fine tests — all of which were fully accepted. Our audience were so well pleased that we were re-engaged to give two more lectures on the next Thursday and Friday evenings, February 8th and 9th, which we accepted.

Brother Jacob Kuehn, (pronounced Keen) secretary and managing officer of the city of York gas works, is the head and front of every spiritual movement in old York. There are others who are now his helpers — among whom are his father, Mr. Brown, and several young men of sterling worth and ability. One of those pleasing little incidents occurred at the pleasant home of Jacob Kuehn, that always cheers the wanderer. Nellie, a sweet little girl, met us at the foot of the stairs as we came down from our room, putting out her little hands, saying, "You will be my uncle and I will be your good little girl. May I kiss you?"

The little darling; we took her up and held her close to our soul — all the time thinking of our own dear little ones so far away in the West.

"Have you a little girl?" she asked.

"Yes, darling, just about your own age; and we have a bright-eyed little boy also — our Lois and Willie."

"Well," she said, "My name is Nellie, and my little brother has gone to heaven," and then her little head rested against our shoulder, and we heard an ominous rattle in her lungs, that foreboded her no good. We turned to the mother, calling her attention to the fact. She observed that she had noticed the rattling since Nellie had had the scarlet fever. On the Monday following, February 5th, in the afternoon, little Nellie left her happy earth-home for one in the Summer Land; and a little before she died, she called her mother (Mrs. Kuehn was her aunt — in fact, Nellie's mother being also in the spirit land,) to her, saying, "Ma, don't cry for me, for I am not going to be alone. Brother Herbert and my ma are with me, and they are going to take me with them this evening;" and then her eyes would follow these Immortals around the room, while a smile of heavenly joy rested on her little face. Later, she left, saying, "Mother, do not weep for Nellie, for I am not alone."

Blessed thought—not alone in death! The dear ones who have preceded us, are ever near—taking us by the hand and lifting us up out of the valley of darkness, into the home of life and light. O spirits! O eternity! Cheered by the sweet influence of angel friends—may all of us realize, as did this little girl, child Nellie, that death has no terror to the true soul, and the God-loving man.

Saturday, February 3d, also the 4th, 5th, 10th, 11th and 12th, we lectured in Baltimore to good audiences on Sunday evenings, and small audiences on week-day evenings. The First Society of Spiritualists is really the only society now in Baltimore. At the head of this society stands our friend and brother, Wash. A. Danskin, Esq. —a man and scholar, true to Spiritualism, and all that pertains thereto. His work in Baltimore has been a herculean one, never halting, never turning aside—with an eye single to the interests of the cause he loved so well—he has toiled on, and what has he gained? Enmity, contempt, abuse, and desertion! Those who should have stood by him, have been the first to desert him. What has he lost by his defense of Spiritualism? A princely home and property by the thousands, and is to-day comparatively a poor man to what he was twenty years ago. Faithfully by his side, firm as the rock, stands his charming wife, companion, and helper indeed, a true medium and one of superior worth. May God and the angels bless and ever be near these faithful workers in the cause of Spiritualism. There are some sweet singers in this society, under the lead of Brother Jones, who is a medium of superior ability, and we predict that, ere long, our Brother Jones will fill a place in the front ranks of our speakers. May the day be hastened, when he shall take his place among us.

---

## CHAPTER XLIX.

We found ourself in Washington, D. C — "Sir, we go back thirty years in your life history!"—"Remarkable! I have that sermon now!" — Brother Davis is here — We read Brother Davis — All Mind Reading — Let us now decide this Mind Reading — The German Spirit not Identified — It is True — Junius Unmasked — Thos. Paine acknowledged the authorship of Junius.

*WASHINGTON.*

Tuesday, February 6, 1872, we found ourself in Washington, the capital of the United States, at two o'clock. It was a dark, stormy day — the elements against us — and we expected no gain from our meeting. Night came; it was dark and cloudy, and wet and sloppy under foot. We were disappointed; the people came out, and we were greeted with a good and paying audience. We spoke again on Wednesday evening, by request. We gave, during the two evenings, ninety-two test statements, of which many were identified on the spot, as follows:

To. Dr. H——. "Sir, we go back in your history thirty years this past fall. We find you then in the midst of marked and strong religious influences and surroundings; you conflicted with others and their views; you stepped out of their influences, and put on record these words: 'God, man, or demon, has no right heretofore, or now, or hereafter, to mar or bar my soul in its right to progress.' There is here a spirit with you, who tells me this. Is it true, or false? You only can determine the matter. Now, sir, we are an entire stranger to you; what say you?"

The doctor arose, exclaiming, "Remarkable! Thirty years ago this past fall, I was preparing for the ministry; my family thoroughly conservative members of the church; I became dissatisfied, and wrote out a discourse, and read it before our people, in which I used the words he has spoken, or language equivalent thereto. I have that sermon in my possession now, and will bring it here to-morrow night, proving his and my statement true."

"It was most remarkable, for we were utter strangers."

On Wednesday evening the doctor came with his sermon, proving the statement.

While standing at the door, taking change, there came a crowd of men and women, completely filling up the doorway, and we felt an influence, saying to us, "Davis." We looked up into the faces of the crowd, but saw no one that we identified. After a little, we felt it again, saying, "Brother Davis is here."

"What Davis?" we mentally asked.

"A. J. Davis," came in answer.

Turning to Brother Williams, who was assisting us, we asked, "Is A. J. Davis in the house?"

"Yes; do n't you know him? He came in the crowd a short time ago."

"Did you take pay of him?"

"Yes."

"Where is he?" we asked at once.

Williams pointed him out to us, and we went to him and handed back the twenty-five cents he had paid at the door. He declined receiving it, saying: "Give it to your Brother Eames, who was so badly burned."

During the lecture and reading, Brother Davis got up and moved from our left to a position in front of us, and some thirty feet away. We said: "Brother A. J. Davis, the seer, is present to-night. For fifteen years, we have been reaching out our hand and soul to him, and yet have not been able to reach him. He has repelled us — held himself aloof. We have loved him as a man and a brother — not worshiping him. He has not returned this love; he has said in his soul, 'This man is not worthy, hence I reject him; not in hate, but for the reason that I do not believe in him; hence, I will hold him aloof.' I have met him three times — once in Boston, in October, 1858; again in New York City, in June, 1860, in the street; on the third occasion, in Cleveland, Ohio, in September, 1866.

On each of these occasions, we went to him holding out both hands, and with our soul full of love for him. On each occasion, he took our hand coldly — really gave us the cold shoulder, and turned away from us saying, by his actions: 'We do not want to make your acquaintance;' and yet we loved his spirit, and knew he did not understand us. At Cleveland, we were in the midst of a storm. Our cause was betrayed. The traitors were on the platform in force. We met them. It was a hard-fought battle. The victory was ours; and the traitors who then declared our mediums cheats and imposters, are double-dyed traitors to our cause to-day. You saw us stop some time ago, and, taking out our watch, looking at it, thus: Then, just thirty-four minutes ago, this very night, we reached Brother A. J. Davis — reached his spirit — and he has, this night, at the time referred to, thirty-four minutes ago, changed his mind, saying to himself, 'I have not understood this man; I am mistaken; I shall tell Mary that I am mistaken in him. I am surprised.'

"There stands with Brother Davis a spirit from the Summer Land, in many respects very like him, but is not his brother. This spirit informs me that Brother Davis knows him as one of the inhabitants of the Summer Land. The spirit says to me: 'On the morning of December 24, 1871, early in the morning, I called, or signaled, Brother Davis to be ready, for there is a great work to be given.' Brother Davis awoke, and has been waiting for the call to be given; it has not been, but will be in June next."

I then said: "Brother Davis, with a full sense of

our position, I have spoken of you and myself, in the past and present, as I have been directed by the spirit seen by me, with you this evening. I now demand of you an answer. This audience the jury, and you the witness; my statement to be declared true, or false, as you shall testify. Do not spare us, but let the people have the truth. What say you? Is the statement true, or false?"

There was a marked commotion and excitement, all looking toward Brother Davis, and we confess, and deny not, that we felt that we were in a critical position, and were about to be judged by a very intelligent and critical audience, on the testimony of one who had not believed on us. There was a moment, and but a moment, of delay in the answer; then Brother Davis said:

"Yes; it is true; Brother Wilson is right. I have held him at a distance, keeping myself aloof from him, and just about the time he named the change took place, I moved. I saw him in a different light, and resolved to tell Mary of the change. Brother Wilson has reached me this evening, and I cordially acknowledge the fact. I fully recognize the being — a spirit, or one of the inhabitants of what I call the Summer Land. I know him well. I did receive a call, or notice, to be ready, on the morning of the 24th of December last, but have not heard anything more from that time to this. But my mind is changed. I see my brother in another light; and, Brother Wilson, I will report you to Mary, as I now know you and see you."

After this event, the excitement with the audience was intense. When the meeting closed, Brother Davis and I shook hands over the past, each promising to tell his mate and companion how they saw each other.

Brother McEwen came forward, extending the hand of a true man, and took us to his home, where we were made welcome by his companion and their children.

Wednesday, February 7. "All mind reading!" exclaimed a voice, on the conclusion of our remarks to Brother Davis.

Turning to Mr. Mason, of Missouri, we said: "Sir, your memory of facts and dates are good?"

"Yes, sir."

"Very well; let us now decide this matter of mind-reading. Will you tell this audience what took place with you the year you were twenty, in August and September, dating from the 10th of August to the 25th of September?"

After a few moments' reflection, Mr. Mason replied:

"I do not remember of any remarkable event occurring to me at the time you refer to. On reflection, I cannot tell you anything."

"Well, sir, we will tell you what took place."

We then related a remarkable fact, giving a full description of persons, incidents, and cause, and asked, "Is it true, or false?"

"Yes, sir, it is true; literally true."

"Where is your mind-reading?"

"It was not my mind, sir," replied Mr. Mason.

"No, sir; we are well aware of that; we received the fact from a spirit," which we fully described, and who was as fully identified.

Turning to a German, we said: "There is with you a spirit; he has on a peculiar uniform: on his right shoulder hangs, or rests, an eagle, like the eagle worn by a colonel of the American Army. He pictures to me a foreign scene. [We fully described it.] The death of this man was a violent one; we hold that he was drowned. What do you know of these facts?"

"Nothing, sir, whatever."

After questioning him a little further, we became satisfied that he knew nothing of the matter; and yet, the spirit insisted that his statement was correct. Giving a name, again our German subject failed to sustain us, and there was an exhibition of satisfaction at our seeming defeat. These statements and facts occurred on the evening of Tuesday, the 6th. On the evening of the 7th, our German subject sent us word, by several parties, that the statement was literally true in date, the eagle, the uniform, the property, the death by drowning — in every fact true.

We found on our desk a book, "Junius Unmasked; or, Thomas Paine, the Author of the Letters of Junius, and of the Declaration of Independence. Washington, D. C.: John Gray & Co., Publishers. 1872." Accompanying the book was a note:

"E. V. Wilson, Esq.—*Dear Sir:* It is said that, before this book was published, you publicly prophesied, or stated, that Thomas Paine was the author of

'The Junius Letters,' as well as 'The Declaration of Independence.' Will you be kind enough to state, before your audience, the facts in this matter?

"Truly, your friend,

"——— ———."

We answered: In 1859, on the second Sunday in December, in Melodeon Hall, Cincinnati, Ohio, before full three hundred people, we stated, under influence: "I, Thomas Paine, declare to this audience, and acknowledge the authorship of 'The Junius Letters,' and I drew the first draft of the 'Declaration of Independence.'" Again, in March, 1865, in Metropolitan Hall, it was declared; also, in 1867, in Cincinnati.

In the spring of 1862, on the evening of the third Sunday in May, we again spoke the fact in Chicago, Illinois.

In September, 1862, while standing in the office of Judge James H. Knowlton, in Chicago, we took from a shelf of books "Junius Letters," and "Thomas Paine's Age of Reason." Looking at them, we spoke to ourself, as if answering a question, "Yes; two great mental efforts — great works, indeed; and by the same mind. Thomas Paine was the author of each!"

"What is that? What did you say, Wilson? that the authors of these two books are one and the same, and his name Thomas Paine, sir? What are your reasons for this statement; have you read and carefully compared these books — the 'Works of Thomas Paine,' and 'Junius'?"

"No, sir; but Mr. Paine says he is the author; and that, ere ten years have passed away, the positive proof shall be given to the world. Will you lend me these books?"

"Yes; and any other works in my library. Are you going to write up the matter?"

"No, sir; I am not capable of the task; but it will be done!"

For a moment the Judge reflected, then looking up, said:

"Wilson, I have often remarked the similarity of ideas, and style of writing, and, some time ago, came to the conclusion you have just now uttered. I believe you are right."

In 1869, on the 4th of July, at Algonquin, Illinois, under influence, speaking on the subject, "Who, and what, am I?" and "My work in the body, and as a spirit," the spirit again stated: "I wrote 'The Crisis,' 'The Age of Reason,' 'Junius Letters,' and, now that the overthrow of African slavery hath been accomplished, I turn my attention, as an agitator, to the Old World. And now, let the skeptic take note. We shall at once move upon Rome and France — the strongholds of religious and political despotism. Both powers must fall. And on the 1st of January, 1872, the power of France shall be broken; Napoleon III. without a throne, and the Pope a prisoner in the Vatican. England and the United States shall shake hands in friendship over the Alabama claims; England will bluster, and threaten to go behind her bond and pledge; the United States will not retreat or abate, but will stand firm by her claim. Judgment will be rendered. Will England abide by the judgment? I doubt it, but trust she will. I, Thomas Paine, prophetically declare these things."

We have here written out more fully the details of the prophecy than we declared then in Washington.

We now declare to our readers that, after a careful examination, and critical reading, of "Junius Unmasked," we feel that it amounts to a demonstration upon psychometrical principles. The soul of "Junius" is compared and measured with the soul of Thomas Paine; and in every conceivable point, wherever we have any record, they are found alike. In no particular do they disagree. There is no theft of language or ideas, but both are the genuine effusions of the soul, in every particular alike. Full three hundred parallels are given — not of language alone, which might have been stolen, but of opinion, style, character, composition, throughout the whole realm of politics, religion, metaphysics, together with special and private opinions, peculiar to the two.

We hold that, so far as the "Declaration of Independence" may be concerned, it is forever settled (at least, in our opinion), that the genius of Thomas Paine's inspiration gave it to the world. For a truth, we feel that "Junius Unmasked" is a work of merit, and adds one more proof of the good there is in Spiritualism, and that the immortal spirit of the earthly Thomas Paine has kept his promise to us, proving his power to control our mind. Our prophecy has been sustained. The slave power is broken, and the slave is a free man; "Junius" is unmasked, Thomas Paine the author; Austria has been subdued, and the unity of Germany established; France is a conquered nation, and Napoleon III. is without a throne, and Pio Nino virtually a prisoner in the Vatican, with his political power gone. Will England stand by her treaty, or will she back down?

"And the spirits of the prophets are subject to the prophets."

"I am he that liveth, and was dead; and, behold, I am alive forevermore. Amen."

"To another, the gift of prophecy; to another, discerning of spirits."

"Should not a people seek unto their God for the living to the dead; to the law and the testimony? and if they speak not according to this word, it is because there is no light in them."

And we, the Spiritualists, believe not, but know that we are immortal.

# CHAPTER L.

We leave Washington—Wilmington, Del.—A Night in Philadelphia—New York City—Troy, N. Y.

*OUR EASTERN TOUR.*

On our second visit to York, Penn., 1872, gave two lectures to crowded houses, full seven hundred or more present, our lecture commanded the most marked attention. We gave many very fine tests.

To a young man: "There is with you a spirit, in a captain's uniform," fully describing him. "He was your personal friend, and was killed at Gettysburg, on the 3d of July, 1863. He calls you Lieutenant ——, and manifests marked friendship for you. What are the facts, sir?"

"They are correct in every particular, sir."

To a lady we said: "We see you in trouble. You took a stand five years ago, from which you have not revived. This stand affects your whole life, and that of others. Your mother and sister sustain you, as well as other friends. The spirit of your little girl gives me this." This was a remarkable case, all the parties being present, and was fully appreciated.

To a man who sat near us, we said: "Sir, you said on entering this meeting, 'You could overthrow our position completely;' thirty minutes afterwards you said; 'I cannot do it, the verdict is his.' Are we right?"

"Yes, sir."

Thus the work goes on. We spent the 10th, 11th, and 12th in Baltimore—our home being at the Mansion House.

We spoke in Wilmington, Del., to good audiences, giving many fine tests, on the evenings of Tuesday and Wednesday, February 13th and 14th. Among the tests we gave are the following:

A boy came forward, was described, gave time when he was drowned, and described the place—fully identified.

A woman who died two years ago, July, 1871, aged 30 years. This was a fine test given to a man and woman who readily identified the fact. Then came the third test—the sister of a man—gave her age, time of death—all the particulars.

Next came the old sweetheart and spoke of the past, giving such perfect history of by-gone days, that identity was full and complete.

Turning to a man by whom stood the wife of former years, who gave a pathetic history of her sorrows and afflictions, claiming that death was a release to her.

To Dr. C. A. Kanney, a Scotchman, came an old aunt in all the character of Scottish women, manifesting her former liking for her bairn.

The Spiritualists of Wilmington are doing a good work, and are getting along finely under the management of our friend S. D. Forbes and his very excellent lady, assisted by Bros. Fogg, Way, Smith and others. The ladies are earnest workers here, helping on our cause with might and main.

Thursday, February 15th, we reached the City of

Brotherly Love, at 10 o'clock A. M. Called on Dr. Child; found him very unwell, indeed, and we fear that he is ticketed for many days confinement. We gave a seance at night to a large audience, and gave many fine tests. And at the close of our meeting, received the congratulations of many who were present. We met Bro. Thomas Gales Forster. He is looking fresh, hale and hearty, and is good for many more campaigns. We went direct from the desk to the cars, and away on the rail for New York City, arriving in the early morning of February 16th. We leave New York City for Troy, at 10:30 A. M., on fast train. We like the fast train, there is something like God, in flying through the country at 2:40. How we like swift thoughts, fast horses, quick-witted people, and a swift ride on the cars. We once rode sixty-two miles in sixty-one minutes, on the Michigan Central Railroad. We cheered the iron horse, the engineer, and everything around us. In the midst of our exultation some one touched us on the shoulder. Turning our head and looking behind us, we saw an elderly man and woman in the seat next to us. They were alarmed and exhibited great fear.

"What do you want?" we asked.

"Arn't you afeared?" asked the old lady.

"Afraid, by no means; and instead of fear, I am perfectly delighted! O! how I should like to ride on forever, straight ahead, into the very arcana of God's Holy Kingdom."

"Oh! oh! what a man. I say, Mr., are you a Christian?"

"Am I what?"

"Are ye a Christian? Have you got 'ligion?"

"No, I am not a Christian; nor have I got 'ligion, nor any other cutaneous difficulty."

"I don't mean measles, nor the itch. I asked a proper question. Have you got religion?"

"No! no!! no!!!" we shouted.

"Well, Mr.," said she, "you will land in hell!"

"At this speed, Madam, we will make the fire fly and give the imps a scare as we go in."

Too-o-o-oo-oo-o-ooo! shrieked the engine whistle, and we were at a stand still on a side track, waiting for the western train to pass us. We made the run from New York City to Albany, a distance of one hundred and twenty-nine miles, in four hours and fifteen minutes, or at a speed of thirty miles an hour, reaching Troy at 4:15 P. M. We found comfortable quarters at the Troy House. We gave a seance at Lyceum Hall, on Third street, to one hundred and ten persons, giving fifty-one tests, of which forty-seven were fully identified, and may be of interest to our readers.

To a lady: "Madam, there is with you a spirit, once a woman in this earth-life;" fully describing her. "She calls you Nellie, and was your tried friend and schoolmate, Rosa."

A spirit gave Bro. Starbuck a statement which was not identified. After a little we called Bro. Starbuck to us and in a whisper related a fact—history to him which fully identified every feature of the communication.

To a man we gave his very thoughts, word for word,

just as he thought and said to himself of us, the cause and its effects, on man.

We left Troy at 10 o'clock P. M., via West Troy, for Albany, at which place we found ourselves nicely stowed away in a sleeping car at 11:30, and ten minutes later we were under way for Watertown, Jefferson county, N. Y.

The Spiritualists of Troy are in a progressive condition, occupying a good hall, and are being ministered to by Bro. J. M. Peebles, who, we believe, has been engaged for six months, commencing April 1st.

---

## CHAPTER LI.

Detroit, Mich. — Gen. John E. Swartze — Governor Crapo — The Soldier — At Nunica — Laura, the Friend of Mrs. P. — The Sailor — Mike Fanning — This is My Son William — The Wife-Meetings — It is Father and My First Wife — Father, we are not Dead — Mary Pearsall — Farewell.

*DETROIT, MICHIGAN.*

Here we are, dear readers, in the old city of Detroit. After a ride of 284 miles at lightning speed, on the fast train of the Michigan Central Railroad, occupying eight and a half hours, including stoppages, eleven in number, averaging five minutes at the very least, leaving seven and a half hours actual traveling time, making about thirty-eight miles an hour. Only think of a ball weighing seventy-five tons, flying through the air at the rate of thirty-eight miles an hour, and you will have some idea of our condition, sitting in the splendid car of this superior railroad. The motion was easy and the ride a pleasant one. There was a double acting motion in the car that we never felt before—it was a horizontal and perpendicular tremble combined. We felt it in every nerve, and there was a language in it, not to be misunderstood. It said, "I am a fast thing—Dexter is nowhere compared with me. Be not afraid, for if my driver knows his business and holds me well in hand, I will carry you safely to your destination at the rate of one thirty-six," and we resignedly put ourself into the hands of the railroad agent, and sped on our way to entertain "a nice society," for five Sundays.

Well, at 8 o'clock we found ourself in Detroit—eight hours and thirty minutes from Chicago. Twenty-six years ago this very fall, we made this same journey from Detroit to Chicago on foot, and were ten days in accomplishing it. Detroit was then the largest city. We were then unknown to the world, a day laborer, and engaged as a hostler in the old New York House, situated on Lake street, North side, between La Salle and Wells streets. Times have changed since then, dear readers; we are older now, yet still living, moving much faster, for we are nearer God to-day, than twenty-six years ago, and the nearer we approach to Him, the faster we go and the wiser we become.

We feel a conservative element in Detroit, not felt in Chicago or St Louis. Spiritualism is more organic here than in Chicago, and we were greeted on Sunday morning with a good house, and in the evening, the house was full, and our meeting was a great success. We gave tests that were at once recognized.

*First.* Adgt. General John E. Swartze came, gave his name and was fully identified from description of his person.

*Second.* A child, a little girl, came and stood by a relative, and was identified.

*Third.* Governor Crapo came, presented himself, and we described him so minutely that the audience said this is our late Governor Crapo.

*Fourth.* A soldier came and stood by a man. We described him carefully, and the man informed us and others that it was correct in every particular, and this stranger was so deeply interested, that he followed us to our home, conversing on the soul's future. We gave four readings of character to entire strangers, and they testified to their correctness.

### *OUR ENGAGEMENT IN MICHIGAN.*

On Thursday, October 7th, at Nunica, after lecture, we went home with Brother Spencer, Sister Pearsall accompanying us. After a little our influences came, when the following interesting facts were given. First, by Mrs. P., we saw a beautiful girl standing, who had been in the Spirit World many years — full twenty. We described her carefully and gave the name of Laura.

Mrs P. was much surprised; identified the spirit as an old friend and schoolmate of her girlhood days, and the daughter of a Methodist Minister. This was an interesting test, and the spirit held in her hand an exquisite little bouquet of beautiful flowers from the garden of the Summer Land, and holding them out to Sister P., spoke in beautiful language of by-gone days and of future reunions in the Summer Land.

O! this blessed immortality! This actual knowledge of our immortality, how grand the thought that we shall live forever, and all the old relations and incidents of our earth-life talked over in our spirit homes.

We turned to Mr. Spencer, and said: There stands by you a sailor, fully describing him. His arms are bare, and on the right one there is tattoed a brig in full sail on a rough sea; under it we see the letters "H. C. M., 1849." This spirit says that he sailed with you on a brig in 1854, and that in the fall of the year, you had the fore topsail yard carried away, precipitating two men to the deck, or one of them to the deck and one into the water.

Mr. Spencer answered, "I remember the brig and the accident of carrying away the topsail yard, and the fall of the two men. The name of the brig was the Black Warrior. I have a faint recollection of this man you have described."

Soon after this there came a spirit and gave his name as Mike Fanning, stating, "I lived with Mr. Spencer several years ago, and worked for him." We then fully described the spirit. This spirit told how he died, and when; all of which proved true.

Surely, this answers the question of Job, "If a man die, shall he live again?" And settles the skepticism of Solomon, for now we know where the spirit of man goes to — the land is discovered and we know the way there, too, and all is well.

We lectured at night in a school house, to an attentive and large audience. While lecturing there came into the room an old man who had once lived in the neighborhood, now an inhabitant of the Spirit World. We described him, but no one responded. The spirit turned to us and said, "Never mind, Mr. Medium, we will demonstrate who we are before you leave." Soldiers came also — none of them identified. We were assured by them that they would be. Mr. Horace Scott was then called for delineation of character, after which the audience conceded that it was correct.

Friday, October 8th, was a clear, fresh morning — all nature full of joy; the autumn hue of the leaves spoke joyously, and praised God in beautiful colors as they left the parent stem and fell to the ground. We lectured at night to a full house, during which several spirits came and identified themselves and their relatives.

The old man of the night before came and went to the rear of the room, placed his hands on a large man's head, saying, "This is my son William," after which we again described him. The spirit then said, "yet a little longer, William, and I will take with me my earth companion, now low and prostrated in your home. You are blessed, my son, in the care rendered her."

Then came another, a woman, full of joy and truth. She was beautiful beyond language to describe — her soul full of joy. Came to the man, William, by whom the father stood, enveloping him in a mantle of light, and we heard her say:

"Husband, mine, I greet thee from the Summer Land, from my beautiful home beyond the rolling river, and bless thee for thy kindness and love; bless you in your new joy, with your young companion. May your house be a house of love, full of peace. Wait a little, and mother will come from you to us," and then this spirit woman cast her light upon a sister of hers, Mrs. Charles Hunter, after which we gave a minute description of both the man and woman, asking,

"Sir, do you identify these spirits?"

The strong man, in a subdued voice, replied:

"It is father and my first wife;" and there came from the audience that long, intensified, cautiously expressed breath of relief, that spoke louder than words, "Thank God, it is true."

There was no noisy demonstration. It was too sacred. We felt and knew that the angels were present with us, and heaven was close at hand.

*Second.* There came two soldiers; those that came last night. This time they came in full uniform — the sergeants of their company, and full of joy. They stood by the side of their earth father, saying:

"Father, we are not dead, but living and full of joy. Arza and William are with you, loving you as of old. Blessings we will shower around you, and your old age will fill with joy. Bless you, father and mother."

And the father and mother wept.

We then described the two sergeants carefully, and the people said, "We knew them."

*Third.* There came a beautiful girl, the spirit of Mary Pearsall. We identified her mother, gave her age when she left the form, and the time she has been there.

This communication was one of those thrilling, sensation facts, that moves human nature into the acceptance of principles.

Mary, the spirit, bade us say to her mother, as near as we can recollect:

"Mother, mine, the merry laugh of the little child, the patter of little feet, are no longer heard along the royal walks of my heavenly home. The memory of the seven bright summers I stayed with you in your earth home, are bright and fresh in my youthful mind. Now the thoughts of a woman fill my soul, for the child of the past, the loved of former days, now budding into womanhood, greets you with love from her home divine. Carry to the dear ones in the old home, sweet memories and love from me, for my soul goes forth to them in the fullness of its heaven cultured nature, this evening, and the angel, once the loving little child, now the fully developed woman from the spheres of angel life, thy child and daughter, yet remembers the loved ones of the old earth home — mother, father, sister mine, blessings gather around you, making your earth life true and beautiful, and by and by, reunited in the Summer Land, our joy will be the joy of angels; and now, farewell — not forever, but for a little while farewell, f-a-r-e-w-e-l-l," came floating back from her angel home, like the last cadence of the æolian lyre, moved by the impulse of the retreating air, and Mary had gone home; and after which from the people came the long breath of satisfaction, the unspoken wish that it may be true, and then the call upon Mrs. Pearsall:

"Madam, is this true? Have you lost a daughter? Was her name Mary? and do the dates agree with your knowledge of the girl?"

Then the mother stood forth, full of womanly joy and love, and in a clear, ringing voice, said:

"Men and women, it is true — my child, my Mary, and the holy memories of her baby days, the seven bright summers she was with us in our earth home. I came many miles for this test, and thank God, I have it." And the people were full of the spirit of heaven.

There came a little boy standing by Dr. Worden, whom we fully described. He called his name Willie. Dr. W. affirmed that it was correct in every feature.

# CHAPTER LII.

Away on the Rail — Arrive at Detroit—A Glorious Fresh Morning — From the Immortal Thomas Paine — God Save Great Thomas Paine — The Vision — The Treasure.

*OUR ENGAGEMENTS IN MICHIGAN.*

Saturday, October 9th. Up before the dawn of day, and away for Detroit, on the train drawn by the iron horse, breathing fire, shrieking, thundering along the plain. At Berlin, our gentle Sister Slade, who has been lecturing in that vicinity, came on to the cars, bound for Grand Rapids, to attend their Quarterly Conference. Greeting passed between us — words of cheer for absent friends, a thought for the cause we love so well, and then the pleasant good-bye, and we parted.

On we went, reaching Detroit at 5:30 P. M., riding 180 miles, and at the post office found twenty letters demanding our attention.

Sunday, October 10th. Glorious, fresh and fair, this beautiful autumn morning! Lectured at 10:45 A. M. in Carter Hall. Our subject was, "The rich man and the unjust steward. The rich man and the beggar."—Luke 16th. The singing was good, the people orderly, the attention marked, and we felt that the angel of inspiration was very near unto us. No tests were given at the morning lecture.

Lectured again at 7:45 P. M., to a large audience.

Our discourse was from the immortal soul of Thos. Paine, of whom Washington wrote:

"Your presence may remind Congress of your past services to this country, and if it is within my power to impress them, command my best exertions with freedom, as they will be rendered cheerfully by one who entertains a lively sense of the importance of your works," and on this occasion, the influence of the sacred spirit of our illustrious patriot commanded the attention and respect of the large and intelligent assembly present — the sainted patriot, of whom the Republicans and Reformers of England in 1792 looked upon as the true "Apostle of Freedom." They circulated a song to his praise, commencing:

"God save Great Thomas Paine!<br>
His rights of man proclaim,<br>
From pole to pole."

(See Preface of Catham's Life of Paine.)

He spoke of his feelings on entering spirit life, of his interview with his mother; of his views of the spirit life; of its floral kingdom, mountains, rivers, lakes, homes, and the employments of the angels; of the interest he takes in the affairs of our world, and especially of our great Republic, of which he justly prides himself, as being one of its founders. He then went into a careful review of the struggle for the emancipation of the slave, referring to historical names and dates, over whom and in which, the spirit world held control and directed the affairs of state.

# CHAPTER LIII.

Call on Capt. Ward — Three Men Think — Go to Lyons, Mich.— Mrs. Holmes — The Trial — The Drowned Boy — Lieut. H. — Mrs. L.— I Lost a Sister — The Stranger — The Man's Name was Gardner.

*OUR ENGAGEMENT IN MICHIGAN.*

Monday, October 11th. A cool, fair morning — all is well. Called on Capt. E. B. Ward in the afternoon, had a very pleasant conversation. We gave a seance at night in Carter's Hall — one hundred and thirty present. Gave many fine tests, dates and readings of character. These were received with marked approval, among them the following, which we trust will interest our readers:

*First.* We stated, these three men, (pointing them them out) have felt, thought and reflected thus: No. 1 has followed our remarks closely, approving of certain points, and disapproving of others. No. 2 has tried his best to affect us with his will-power, thus seeking to experiment at our expense. No. 3 has been listless, paying but little attention to what was said or taking place about him. We then called on them to affirm or deny our statements. They separately affirmed.

Tuesday, October 12th. Left Detroit for Lyons, Michigan, at 10 A. M. Arrived at Lyons at 4 P. M. Went to the quiet home of Dr. J. R. Jewett. Lectured at night to ninety people. Gave a reading to Mrs. Holmes, of Iowa, giving three incidents of her life, one at ten years of age, and one at nineteen. "Seven years ago, you passed through a trial, sharp and severe. There is with you a young girl, sixteen years of age, who was a schoolmate of yours, and has been in the spirit life many years."

Then there came and stood by her a boy, who was drowned when eleven years old, and would be now, over twenty-two years of age, all of which was true.

Wednesday, October 13th. Lectured at night to a good audience on "The effect of revival meetings and spiritual circles."

At the conclusion we called the attention of the audience to the fact that it had been reported that there was a collusion between us and the lady from Iowa. We now proposed to the audience to call out a man and woman for delineation and tests.

After a little, Lieutenant Hitchcock was called out by the gentleman, and he came forward. Mrs. Lewis was put forward by the ladies for reading. We first read Lieutenant H., carefully giving the temperament, traits of character, as well as habits of life.

"At nineteen years of age, you are in imminent danger. There is a rush or fall of ponderable matter. There is a rush of feet — commotion; you escape. At the age of twenty-three, you change, take upon you new associations, affecting you socially, locally and pecuniarily. It is an era in your life. Five years ago you are surrounded by enemies, are in trouble, and are aroused by them to excitement. There is with you a First Lieutenant (describing him). This Lieutenant tells me of trouble you had with your Colonel, and other incidents of your life. There is with you the spirit of a woman. She has been in the spirit world a long time. Passed away very young. She is your sister." We then described his father and mother, giving many fine antecedents in their lives. The friends and relatives of Lieutenant H. affirmed that the reading was correct. He said of the incidents:

"The first I do not recognize as marking my life. I joined the Baptist church, and was nearly killed by a run-away team. At twenty-three, nothing important, save that I married and began life then. Seven years ago, I knew several Lieutenants, who would answer your description. I know of nothing marked five years ago that I can identify."

"What about your arrest and being taken to Detroit, five years ago?" said a voice from the audience.

"Oh, yes," said the Lieutenant. "And what about the difficulty referred to in the communication of the spirit, Lieutenant?" said another voice.

"Well, there was some trouble.

"And about the spirit sister?" he asked.

"Yes, I lost a sister, the only sister I ever lost. She died very young."

Mrs. L. was then read, after touching her hand. We saw her grandfather, who referred to property belonging to her, but which she had never received. We then said:

"There is with you the spirit of a young woman, who was your young friend, and you loved her as a sister. She died early in womanhood; died in childbirth. She knew you well."

We read many incidents in her life, all of which on careful reflection were fully identified, and the people were very much surprised, and the scandal mongers were confounded. After lecture we took the cars for St. Johns, arriving at 1 o'clock.

Thursday, October 14th. A cloudy, wet morning. Delivered a funeral discourse over the remains of Brother Elisha Abbott, who left his earth form at midnight on the 11th, at 11 o'clock A. M., and at forty-five minutes past twelve, we laid his inanimate form in the grave, and we saw his spirit take leave for a little season of the dear friends in the earth form. We know he is not dead.

Returning at 4 P. M., we found our friends waiting for us. Lectured at 7:30 P. M. This lecture was full of sharp points, and made a deep impression. At the conclusion we gave the following tests:

*First.* To a stranger, we said: "You are from a distance. Came many miles to hear our lecture. The young lady at your side is your daughter. You have never seen us. Twenty-one years ago there was a great change socially and locally with you and yours. We speak the name, Mary Rogers."

The man answered:

"I am an entire stranger to the speaker, never saw him before. I am from a distance, living in Maple Rapids. This is my daughter by my side. I came to hear these lectures. My name is Rogers. This is very strange."

*Second.* To a man in the centre of the hall, we said (pointing him out from the desk), "Thirteen, twelve, and eleven years ago, you were imposed upon by two men (describing them minutely). Financially you suffered at their hands, the taller one of the two being the greater rascal."

"That's so," said the man.

The man's name was Gardner, to whom this communication was given.

*Third.* We turned to ladies, sitting on our right, and said:

"There is the spirit of a young man with you. He was a soldier; died in the service of his country. The first lady is his aunt, the second one is his mother."

This proved true.

We gave Dr. Jewett several dates and incidents of the past, but from the fact of our making our home with him, they were of no importance as marked tests. Thus closed a very important evening's work. Surely we are in the midst of a wonderful era. Come, let us investigate this phenomenal life.

Friday, October 15th. A fine, cold morning; ground white with frost. Winter is just over the border, and will soon be with us. May we be prepared, both in body and soul for the storms of nature, and all will be well.

Gave a seance at 2:45 P. M. to one hundred souls, and many fine tests were given, among which are the following:

To Mrs. K., we spoke of her thoughts, social condition, giving incidents in her life. All proved correct.

*Second.* Mrs. H. Read her mental condition very carefully.

*Third.* Saw by a man (Mr. R.) his wife, a spirit, fully identified.

*Fourth.* A boy from spirit life, told when and where he was drowned, and his age. This was a remarkable test and proved correct in every particular, and was identified by full a score of people.

*Fifth.* Mr. S., a skeptic, called up by the audience for a test character. He was an entire stranger to us. We first touched the end of his fingers, then walked from him some ten feet, and with our back toward him, gave a careful reading of his physical and mental manhood, entering into minutia. We then drew a word picture of his father and mother, giving a likeness to each, after which, we said:

" We now come to an incident he knows nothing of personally, but from tradition and hearsay. It belongs to his father's household, and occurred before he was born, some two or three months. It is an ante-natal condition; its effect is on his mother, it is in the form of great excitement, fear and anxiety, caused by great loss, either of life by accident, or loss of property and position. You know the history. Twelve years ago, financial and social trouble of a marked character; seven years ago, sorrow, grief, and mourning; you lost a female relative very dear to you," (fully describing her.)

The audience testified to the correct reading of the man's character.

He then said, " This is remarkable. The ante-natal

incident is correct, the trouble caused by loss of property and death from accident. The incident of twelve years ago is true. The grief and sorrow of seven years ago was the loss of my wife, and he has described her accurately."

And the people felt that they were in the presence of the Lord.

---

## CHAPTER LIV.

Our Visit to Keokuk, Iowa — The Test — The Prophecy — Its Fulfillment — Marion, Iowa — Burlington, Iowa — Madison — Dallas City, Ill.--The $4 Brought Through the Air.

*OUR WESTERN ENGAGEMENTS.*

Friday, May 10th, 1872, we reached Keokuk, Iowa, to fill an engagement for three lectures. Keokuk, the Gate City, is an important railroad point, as well as steamboat landing, situated on the Mississippi river, about two hundred miles south of west from Chicago, and forty-three miles by railroad below Burlington. It is a fine town, full of enterprise and progress. We like Keokuk, and predict a great future for this fair city of the West.

We spoke to fair audiences while there, giving many fine tests, of which the following are a sample of all:

*First.* The spirit of a man and little girl came to a lady, and was fully described and identified.

*Second.* A sister came to her brother, speaking words of cheer from her home in the Summer Land. The sister being fully described, was at once identified.

*Third.* This test we gave was not identified, at which the skeptical portion of our audience laughed; but there was never a laugh when startling tests were given. Is it not strange that Christians will preach a future existence, and sneer at any testimony pointing to a future life — not coming from the pulpit of the church of their Christ and him crucified?

*Fourth.* The fourth test was to Mr. B. "Sir, sixteen years ago we find you sinking as if into cold water or snow. You are suffocating as from snow, or your head being held in snow and water, and it is in the winter time."

The answer was — "It is true, sir, to the letter, in date and cause."

*Fifth.* This test came to Judge M. "Sir, we see a man approach you (fully describing him); you will be called upon in a very short time to defend a case. The parties are a man, woman and child; an estate will be at stake. This suit will soon be in hand, and down for trial in September."

Judge M. replied: "I know of such a suit soon to come off, and expect to be retained by the parties."

Subsequently the Judge met us and said: "Friend W., your prophecy has come to pass since you made it. A man, answering to your description, called on us and put the very suit you named into my hands, and I am going to take hold of it."

Friday, May 17th, we were preparing for our Wheaton Convention to be held over Sunday, the 19th.

Monday, May 20th. Our Convention is over, and has been a grand success, and well reported by our Secretary, Bro. Howard, and we shall, in all human probability, convene our association in St. Charles, next.

At Marion, Iowa, May 27th, we concluded a three days' meeting. It is a beautiful inland town. We had good audiences, gave many fine tests, and found many warm friends. There are but few here who declare themselves to be Spiritualists. There are many very liberal Christians (?) here, and have a fine church and good congregations. Amongst those who are workers, we found Mrs. House to be a fine medium, with good clairvoyant power. Bros. Mitchell, House, Noble, and others, came well up to time as workers and helpers.

May 30th, we spoke in Burlington, Iowa, to a full house, giving some fine tests. A few Spiritualists are striving to establish a society in this fine western city. We spoke three times, but were cut short by change of railroad time. We shall yet go to Burlington and stir up the Soul-Sleepers one of these days. Bros. Forbs, Webster, Giles, and others, are striving to open the way for a society and lyceum. May they succeed.

Monday, June 2d. We have just closed a course of four lectures in Fort Madison, Iowa. This place is on the west bank of the Mississippi, twenty-four miles above Keokuk, and nineteen miles below Burlington, by way of the Burlington and Keokuk railroad, and presents to the vision of the traveler one of the loveliest places for a home on the banks of the "Great Father of Rivers." We found many tried and true Spiritualists here — more by far than we expected. Bro. Hazen Wilson took the lead and responsibility of our coming, as did Bro. Miller, of Keokuk; Judge Vezee also helping, as did many others. We gave many very fine tests in Fort Madison, and especially fine ones to Judge Vezee. Our work in Fort Madison proved a success, creating thought, developing truth, and ennobling man. Many of the friends accompanied us to the depot, bidding us God speed on parting — a pay to us very precious. May angels of God continue to minister to our friends in Fort Madison.

Dallas City, Ill., June 7th, 8th and 9th, we lectured in this little town to full houses. We found the interest marked and progressive. The true workers in Dallas are Bros. Porter, Weaver, and Asa Moon, and their good wives. We had a good time here, and gave many tests. Mrs. Weaver possesses fine mediumistic powers; is a writing, seeing, and speaking medium, and yet this woman cannot write a word from education. Mrs. Weaver possesses a "spiritual gift" that would be very dangerous to the church if it could be imparted to its members. At various times and in sundry places, money in coin and paper in various sums has been brought her by her controlling spirit — the aggregate amounting to some thirty dollars. There seems to be a peculiarity in this money matter; it comes just in the nick of time when wanted by the family to meet their necessities. The evidence in their case is so complete that to deny it would be to deny our senses.

While in Dallas, we made the acquaintance of Dr. Pekill and lady, of Pontoosock, two miles below Dallas City.

On Sunday evening, the 9th, when closing up the accounts current of our meeting, there was due from Bro. W. four dollars. Bro. W. saying, "I have not the money with me."

Turning to Dr. Pekill, he asked him to lend him the money.

Dr. Pekill replied: "I have not the money with me, but have it at home in my desk, if we could only get it."

Now, the Doctor has a familiar spirit, by the name of "Peter," who is one of his helpers. Instantly Peter gave the Doctor to understand that he was present and would help him out of the matter. The Doctor turned to the friends, saying, "Wait a little, and we will see what can be done."

Doctor Pekill.—"Peter, can you get me four dollars out of my desk in my house in Pontoosock?"

Peter.—"I will try."

The Doctor, turning to the friends present, said: "Come, let us go into the house."

All started for the house. We were all at the house of Asa Moon. It is a one story frame house, with one large front room, a second or rear room, then a shed or slight building attached for summer work. On passing through the shed into the rear room there was present Mr. Weaver, Dr. Pekill, Asa Moon, Mrs. Moon, her two daughters, and others. Dr. Pekill said: "Peter is here."

Asa Moon saw a small package of paper in the air over Dr. Pekill's head. Dr. P. felt it hit the hat brim. A lady saw it in the air, falling to the floor. Mr. Moon and his daughter saw it on the floor. One of the parties present picked it up and found two two-dollar bills; Peter, the spirit, informing Pekill that he (the spirit) had been to the Doctor's house, in Pontoosock, and taken the money from his desk, in order to loan it to Weaver. Dr. Pekill stated: "I had these bills in my desk at home, and if not there when I go home to-morrow, then Mr. W., will this money be as a loan from me, and return it, and if my two two-dollar bills are at home as when I left home, then the money is not mine, and Bro. W. will not pay it back to me." This statement was made public before a full house the same evening.

# CHAPTER LV.

Spiritualism in Buffalo—Its Condition—The Tests.

## *SPIRITUALISM IN BUFFALO, NEW YORK.*

We spoke nine Sundays in Buffalo, during December, 1868, and January, 1869, giving eighteen lectures, and spending two hours each Sunday in the Children's Lyceum, making our work on each Sunday equal to six hours per day.

We found the Society inharmonious and full of discord, poorly attended, and in debt. We left them with a crowded house, growing interest, and out of debt, but wanting in harmony.

There was at our first lecture in the city, but ninety persons; at our last, over five hundred. Every seat was filled, the platform covered, the standing room all occupied, and full five hundred people in a three hundred hall.

The first Lyceum we attended had sixty-three children present; the last one, eighty-seven. We formed an adult group that was full every Sunday, and there were present many persons to witness the interesting exercises of the Lyceum. The Lyceum is very well officered, and the children attentive and well behaved. Many of them giving evidence of fine talent as speakers, declaimers and singers.

Bro. Henry Fitzgerald is eminently qualified for the position of conductor, and fills the office with credit to the Lyceum as well as to himself, and he has some good helpers in the cause as leaders and guards. In fact, the Lyceum is a good one and well managed. Spiritualism is alive in Buffalo, and needs but a little more harmony to become a grand Society, numbering thousands instead of hundreds. They need a first class hall, with plenty of room for the children.

Bro. Fish is to succeed me in ministering to the Buffaloans, and may the angels help him in his labors with the people. The angels helped us in our labors in Buffalo, and through them we were enabled to give many fine tests.

On the evening of Monday, February 1st, we gave a seance, of which the *Express* published the enclosed, clipped from its columns:

*First.* A spirit calling himself Charles Edwards, bartender in a hotel six years ago, stood by Mrs. S. and thanked her for her kind care and attention to him.

*Second.* Mr. Gibson fully described, came and told how he committed suicide some years ago, pointing out many he knew in life, saying, "The crime is forgiven, the offense not forgotten."

*Third.* A spirit came who declined to give his name, saying: "Describe me, for there are many here who know me." We described him minutely, and the people said, "This is Judge Stevens, some time ago our neighbor, and formerly, Mayor of our city."

*Fourth.* There came and stood by a lady, one calling her mother. The description was carefully given, and the woman said, weeping at the time, "It is my dear son."

*Fifth.* A man came, was fully described, and told us he was murdered in this city, fourteen years ago, and that the man who murdered him was in the hall last night, but not present to-night. I do not wish him to be brought to trial. I am on his track, and he remembers his crime, and this hell of conscience is all that any needs here, or hereafter.

*Sixth.* Two boys came, hand in hand, and told how they were drowned in the river, nine years ago; told of their death trials, and leaving words of cheer for those they had left behind.

*Seventh.* A man, fully described, standing by a stranger, showing us how he was killed — when and where.

*Eighth.* A soldier stood by his old friend — told how he was killed — when and where.

*Ninth.* A beautiful child came and placed her hand on the knees of an old man and called him father; told of the time of her death, and of her happy life in the spirit world.

*Tenth.* A sailor came and stated, "I am Captain Wiltsey, and sailed the topsail schooner George W. Willis, of Oswego; foundered and sunk in 1836, off Madison dock, below Cleveland, Ohio. The vessel was raised subsequently and taken into Ashtabula harbor. I was found in her cabin, and those who raised her took from the desk in her cabin $800 in bills."

*Eleventh.* There stands by that lady Mrs. S., a

spirit who shows us the letter J. We then entered into a full and minute description of him, and he says: "Tell my wife, for me, that she is a foolish woman to put up with the abuse and oppression she is enduring at present, for the man who married only for money."

*Twelfth.* A sailor, Joe W——, came and told of many wild pranks he had been in, and gave an account of a Bacchanalian row he had been in, in a saloon, with many lake captains, in 1840.

*Thirteenth.* Captain Walker, of the Great Western steamer, was fully described and identified.

All of the above tests were fully identified. Besides these, we gave many readings of character, and located over thirty dates, and only one single case unidentified, and he was a confirmed Spiritualist.

Are we not surrounded with a great cloud of witnesses? Thus God, through his angels, as in the past, continues to be our helper.

---

## CHAPTER LVI.

Rochelle, Ill.—Elder Miles Grant—Rev. H. S. Weller—His Views on Spiritualism.

### *INCIDENTS OF OUR LECTURES, ETC.*

On the evenings of August 8th, 9th, and 10th, 1870, we gave a course of three lectures in the prosperous and progressive little town of Rochelle, Ogle county, Ill., on subjects pertaining to Spiritualism—giving also many well defined and identified tests from spirit life. Our audiences were good, attention marked, and a demand on the part of the people for more spiritual food of the same sort.

Last year Elder Miles Grant visited Rochelle with his message of false prophecies and slander of the true spirit, for the edification of such as have no souls, and "die all over,"—during which, he attacked us most bitterly. Hearing of his whereabouts, sayings and doings, we went for him, and when he heard we were coming, like the valorous Stephens, he hurled a volley of lies at our shadow—and left for parts unknown.

On reaching Rochelle, we picked the fellow up and unveiled his skeleton Theology, making the whole Church feel very much as Dr. Newman felt after a dose of Bible polygamy at the hands of Elder Pratt.

On the evenings above mentioned we visited Rochelle again, and once more unveiled the skeleton. On the first evening we challenged the Advents to meet us and go to trial before the people. They failed to put in an appearance. Of course, the people gave us judgment by default on their part.

On the next Sunday, August 14th, the Rev. S. H. Weller, in the Presbyterian church, gave us a benefit. He began by saying: "I do not intend to give an elaborate statement of this pretentious system of modern infidelity."(?)

*Answer.* Why do you touch it at all, Brother Weller, if it is only pretentious infidelity, (?) and modern at that. It strikes us very forcibly that there is a contradiction in your assertion — we shall see.

PLATFORM.

*First.* There is no uniformity in their creeds. Their discourses are alike coarse and illogical, and they adopt this mode to bring their system into notoriety.

*Your first position.* "No uniformity in their creeds" shows your utter and complete ignorance of our views and principles. As to creeds, we have none. We are a unit on the following points, viz.: "God is a spirit, in whom we live and move and have our being;" therefore a part of God — not outside of Him as you are. Our God is love intensified, and is our friend and father. Your God is love, whose creed is revenge and hate. He gets his Ebenezer up, and blows down his own house, knocks his minister's eyes out, kills little babies, burns temples dedicated to his name, and is just now destroying his Cathedral at Strasbourg, and lately killed many thousand Americans to get rid of one of his own institutions — human slavery.

*Second.* We hold that every man, woman and child is immortal, even down to the fashionable fœticide, and that angel guardians and nurses are frequently in attendance on a mother who has committed a high crime against her nature, sustaining her weakened constitution, and at the same time holding the young life she has sought to destroy near her mortal form, in order to give it strength in its spirit-life hereaftar.

*Third.* We hold to one God and no more, infinite in matter and space—seen in the sunshine, felt in the storm, and that He is this side the blue as well as beyond it, and "His kingdom is within us," hence He is ever with us. Your God is a great big man, a creature full of short comings, and has to keep a big hell always on hand to make his followers obey him.

*Fourth.* We hold there is no personal devil, or local hell or heaven; hence, in the future as here, there is good and evil side by side; that we are subject to the evil influences as well as the good, and that in the future life as in this when the evil man desires to reform, the good are on hand to help him, while on your side of the question there are but two conditions or estates in the future life—hell and heaven—from which, and out of which, there can be no progression.

Your second position:

"Their discourses are alike coarse and illogical, and they adopt this mode to bring their system into notoriety."

This sentence contains an argument "what is an argument." Brother Weller, do you read the Spiritual papers, the chaste and beautiful lectures of Sisters Hardinge, Doten, Cora L. V. Tappan, Foster, Brittan, Peebles, Whiting, Chase, and our late eloquent and noble brothers, Henry C. Wright and Jesse B. Ferguson, now immortals, whose lectures have thrilled the souls of millions, listening with upturned faces, whose lectures, as published in our papers, have fed the souls of millions who could not hear them from the rostrum ; and are you aware, brother, that your brethren and yourself, "ministers of the meek and loving Jesus," through your coarse and vulgar sermons on the conditions of the damned ; your insulting expressions to Almighty God, such as are commonly used in your revival meetings, have disgusted the millions and drove them from you ? If not, it is time you were told, for of all people in the world, you ministers of the gospel of Christ are the most coarse and vulgar when appealing to people's passions — men crying with all of their might, "Come right down now, God ! now, God ! ! now, God ! ! ! And crush out the wicked ! God, shake the sinners over hell ! Oh, God, slay the wicked, hip and thigh."

There is refinement and logic which we trust may never be found in our "coarse and illogical" lectures.

"And they adopt this mode to bring their system into notoriety."

Verily, verily, I say thou art logical beyond thy measure, oh, Brother Weller !

"I admit the phenomena of Spiritualism."

Thank you, my reverend brother. Is there not uniformity with Spiritualists in this admission, and you, a minister of God (?) in this admission — avowed that you were wrong a few years ago, when you fully denied it. Being wrong in a former judgment, may you not be altogether wrong in other conclusions ?

"As the Spiritualists hold it, the name is false. It is, in fact, materialism."

Brother Weller, do you know what constitutes a paradox ? Spiritualism is materialism; a shadowy vapor is a solid substance; an invisible thing is a visible fact; an unheard sound is a loud noise; when we do see, we don't see; when in the devil's employ we are working for God, and when we are God's angels we are the devil's servants. Slightly paradoxical! Now, my brother, your religion is as thorough a materialism as was ever taught. You resurrect the old body from the grave, and take it with you into heaven. We leave it behind, and enter the future a spiritual being, refined and beautiful. You, with all of your old filth of body, with broken limb or eyeless socket, and festering sore, appear before your God, for the old sore existing on your person at the time of your death, is as much a part of the man proper as the sound arm, and equally entitled to be resurrected. We leave all these things behind us, and appear a purified spiritual being.

I am really afraid, my brother, that you are ignorant of spiritual things, or you would never have committed yourself to this contradiction.

"They give God a prominent place in their theology."

What ails you, Brother Weller? We "have no uniformity;" and yet we all give God a prominent place in our theology. We "are infidels," giving God a prominent place in our teachings. Do you know the meaning of the word infidelity? If you do not, we refer you to Webster. We believe the Bible, but deny your conclusions drawn from the Bible. We hold that there is spirit inspiration in the Bible, but that it is not plenary inspired—you do, hence we are materialistic and infidels.

"With them, spirit is only matter in the highest state of organism."

Will Brother Weller tell us what spirit is with him? With Presbyterianism? Dare you deny God's personality and materiality? What manner of hand was that which hid Moses beneath its palm? Was the hinder part of God, seen by Moses, substance or spirit? Did the "judge of all the earth" dine with Abraham on veal, bread and butter? Is it true as Jacob says, that he saw God face to face and lived, (Gen. xxxii: 20), and was this God an athlete—a man, and could not handle or throw—"prevailing against Jacob"? (Gen. xxxii: 24). Now, sir, is your God a material fact? Where in the name of all that is true, have you a spiritual idea, and yet you tell your hearers that "with them, spirit is only matter in the highest state of organism?" Well, this indeed excels your estimate, and is not as coarse, besides our spirits are modest and appear to us in comely apparel.

You are right for once, brother. As spiritual beings, we are refined matter in its superior state, or highest organism; and God is a Spirit, in whom we live and move and have our being, and not a coarse, vulgar, material being, pleased one day, and showing his face, and angry the next, and showing us his hinder parts, and that to *sans culotte*.

"Christ's ascension is the highest proof of the materialism of the soul."

Where Brother W. gets this idea from, we are at a loss to determine. Certainly it is not a spiritual one, but thoroughly Christian. We take no stock whatever in the old mutilated body of Jesus, or in his wasted blood, but in his philosophy, his teachings and his great humanity. We love Him as our elder brother—we do not worship Him as a God. He forbade us, after his ascension in spirit life, to do so. Rev. xx: 8, 9.

"The world is God's body—you are not a man, but a thing, a brute."

Will our brother give the authority for this statement? Remember, Brother W., you have said that we have no uniformity in our creeds, and here, for the fifth time you declare a uniformity, wonderful, if it were true! You cannot find among any of our writers a sentence declaring man a brute. We hold that the kingdom of God is in man. You hold that it is outside of man, and that man cannot enter the kingdom, save by the shedding of the blood of God, through Jesus Christ. We hold the blood of Jesus as we do the blood of Judas—only useful while warm and in the body of the man it belongs to.

"Spiritualism is old Paganism revived."

Paradox after paradox! Much preaching hath made the Rev. Weller mad! Your first position is as follows:

"I do not intend to give an elaborate statement of this pretentious system of modern infidelity," and here you declare it to be old Paganism revived. Do you know the meaning of the word infidelity? for in your use of the word, you are at fault with its meaning.

"It claims a new revelation. It has always been the enemy of God and man."

We challenge the Reverened Weller to find in the vast field of Spiritual literature, a sentence conflicting with men's rights or liberties, or in which causation and formation are denied. Our God, like the God of Jesus, is a spirit, and they that worship Him must worship in spirit and in truth. John iv: 24.

Your God, a material being, fully described in one hundred and fifty passages, evidences all the bitterness of a human being, as described by Moses and the prophets. He is a failure—He is the author of divorce, laws of slavery, of polygamy, of blood offering. Nation after nation He has slaughtered, saving the virgins that had not known a man, that is, that had not consociated with a man, for the use of his soldiers.

He taxed the people to build him a house, such as the world had never seen, and then sent the enemy to destroy it.

Our religion opposes slavery in every form—has one God—not three; bows not to the cross or the scaffold; demands no blood offering. Our God was not born of a woman against whom every door was shut. He has never repented him He ever made man. He is love, truth and fidelity combined, and men and angel men are his agents. Your God declares that He has anger, hate, revenge, scorn, and that He hateth a lie. He repenteth He ever made man. In the mountains He was mighty; in the valley, where He hath nothing to hide behind, He could not prevail. He deprived man of immortality, and then put Himself into the hands of man to be killed, that man might be immortal. You, the Reverend Weller, ask us to be on friendly terms with such a being as your God—the old Moses God—a God whose snakes knew more than his man Adam; who eats bread, butter, and veal; who could not throw Jacob; who used a liar to kill Ahab; who sends his people strong delusions; who was carried around on the shoulders of men; who chose the Hebrews as his favored people, who are a miserable failure,—and you to-day are by God used to abuse the Jews.

---

## CHAPTER LVII.

Seance at Hannibal, Mo.—Palmyra, Mo.—Chapter of Facts at Oskaloosa—A new sensation—Names of Spirits given—Light and Darkness—A remarkable opening up of Soul Light.

### *SEANCE AT HANNIBAL, MO.*

*First.* At Hannibal, Mo., on Tuesday night, Feb. 11th, 1868, we lectured before a full house, and gave the following test: There is an influence here of a man crushed, broken to pieces. It is here, with this group of men (there were four men sitting together) on my left. Will you please step out, sir, (addressing one of them,) so that I can determine which of you may be associated with this fact? He did so. That will do, sir; I have got it. There is a man with you (describing him) who is crushed and mangled very much, and I find you in a smash-up on the cars and barely escaping with your life. I can find no date whatever with this fact, and yet I know it is a fact, and took place with you, but cannot get the date of the incident, and the spirit seems bewildered.

*Answer.* I live in Brookfield, Mo. To-day, about 9 o'clock, west of this, on the St. Jo. Railroad, I was in a smash-up, and the man described was killed, and we had a narrow escape.

I never saw this man before, and he could know nothing about this whatever.

*Note.* No data.

*Reason.* Not a day had passed since the accident.

This is one of the most remarkable incidents on record, for prompt return of spirits, I have ever met.

*Second.* At Palmyra, Mo., February 13th instant, I lectured before a full house. While lecturing, there came a coarse-looking negro spirit, who in life was a stout and well-made physical man, but with a low, vicious animal organization. He troubled me a good deal during my lecture, and finally I said, mentally, "What do you want?" "'Scribe me." "When did you die?" "Done gone and hung me, twenty years 'bout gone." "Why did they hang you?" "'Cause dey could." "Did you live here?" "Sartin' I did." "Do you know anyone in the audience?" "I knows lots on 'em." "Point out some two or three that you know." He did so. "What is your name?" "Tom." I then called the attention of the audience to the fact, describing the character, action, and peculiarities of this spirit, and called on one of the parties he had pointed out, and asked if he knew of any such incident in the history of Palmyra.

*Answer*. I knew the fellow, and saw him executed, and your description is correct in everything but one, and that is his name. His name was Ben. ["Yah! yah! yah!" laughed the black spirit, "dat was de name dey hung, but my first mars' called me Tom."]

What of it, says the church? They are but devils, evil men let out by Satan to decoy souls down to perdition. Very good, my Christian friends; you admit, then, that evil spirits, and the spirits of men and women can, if evil, demonstrate their immortality. That is one point gained, and a concession on your part, that those who are foolish enough to join your churches are so controlled by church rule that when they get into Eden they do not know enough to return unless helped by the serpent.

## *FACTS AND TESTS.*

At Oskaloosa, Iowa, May 2d, 1870, we turned to Mr. C., saying: "We see you in a very excited state. You are very angry. There are before you three boys," fully describing them. "You defend the larger boy, and are blamed by your neighbors, they taking sides against you; but you were not to blame. The lesser boy was the aggressor; you were right."

We were tarrying at the very pleasant home of Brother and Sister Garritsen's. On the morning of the 3d Dr. S. called on us, and in a respectful manner asked for a repetition of what we had seen, observing:

"I am the father of the lesser boy, and if my boy is at fault I am willing to make amends for the wrong and blame I attached to Mr. C."

Just then I looked up through the door, which was open, and saw Mr. C. He came to the gate and asked Mr. G. if Wilson was in. We arose and went to the gate, saying:

"Good morning, Mr. C., will you come in?"

"No, Mr. Wilson; I came this morning to brand as a falsehood the statement you made last night in regard to me. You have wronged me, and you had no business to repeat the story."

This was spoken in bitterness.

"What statement did we make?"

"You stated, that in the matter of difference about the boys, I was to blame, which is false; and the party that told you told you a falsehood; and it is that which I have come to brand as a falsehood."

"Come in, sir."

"No."

"Yes you will, for I am prepared to settle this matter right here."

So he came into the house.

"Now, sir, let me fully understand you. You say, first, that we said you were to blame in the matter of the boys?"

"Yes."

"Second, that some one told us, and we related it to you for the purpose of injuring you in this place?"

"Yes."

"Now, sir, who told us?"

"I don't know; how should I? You claim that spirits told you, which I don't believe a word of, for I have no faith in Spiritualism."

"Now, sir, you are just where I want you; and every word you have uttered is false, and you know it is so. In the first place, we never said that you were to blame, but that you were not to blame, and you could not misunderstand us; hence you have uttered that which is false, for here is Dr. S. who did blame you, and is now here on this same affair, asking why he was to blame."

"Yes," said the doctor, "I came on purpose; for Wilson blamed me, and not you."

Mr. and Mrs. G. confirmed Dr. S.

"Second, in regard to the story retailed by me, as charged by you, I answer that the man who utters it, or says that the statement was second hand from me—that is, that some person in the form told us, and we retailed it, that man, whether you, or anyone else, utters that which is not true, and means to tell a lie; and, as a minister of God, you have no right to suspicion your neighbor, or accuse him falsely; and I am prepared to prove that every statement made by you this morning is incorrect, and every person with whom we have talked are here, and can answer for themselves;" and then an appeal was taken to the parties present, and we were sustained.

"As to your belief in Spiritualism, what care we for it. You can have no less belief in Spiritualism than we have in theology, from either the Christian or Universalist stand-point; and we here affirm that no minister can be relied on, where testifying to that which conflicts with his orders as a minister."

### *A SPIRITUAL SENSATION.*

The *Troy Daily Whig* of March 14, 1870, notices our lectures as follows:

March 5, 1870, a new spiritual medium suddenly manifested himself in our community. He came unheralded, but promises to produce a spiritual revival here, such as we have not had since the advent of the new and strange doctrine of which the medium is such a powerful exponent. His name is E. V. Wilson, and he held forth yesterday at Apollo Hall to large and interested audiences. We were not present, but are told of some wonderful feats performed by him. After the lecture in the evening, which was a very sensible production, Mr. Wilson introduced some tests to prove the truth of Spiritualism. To a gentleman sitting in the hall he said:

" I see standing by that young man the spirit of a second lieutenant in the army, who was his friend, and who died from the effects of a wound in his side."

The gentleman admitted that he had lost such a friend 'n the army

"That lady," said Mr. Wilson, referring to a person sitting near the aisle, nearly half-way back from the stage, in the hall, "has lost a young lady friend. The spirit now stands beside her. The deceased was about eighteen or nineteen years of age when she departed this life. Am I correct?"

The lady said, "The statements are correct."

Several tests of this kind were given, and in nearly every instance were pronounced correct. It is impossible that there could have been any collusion between the speaker and the subjects he selected as means of testing his powers, and the wonder and excitement among the audience at times were very great.

### *SPIRITUALISM — LECTURE — NAMES OF SPIRITS GIVEN—GHOSTS DESCRIBED.*

Apollo Hall was densely packed last evening by people drawn thither by the wonderful stories afloat in regard to E. V. Wilson, who described and gave the names of spirits present in the hall, outside of the body. The hall was so crowded that over two hundred persons were unable to obtain seats. Mr. Wilson took his text from an incident which occurred in his hearing on Saturday, when he was pointed out in the street as the Spiritualistic medium, at which a conversation arose between a couple of gentlemen in regard to Spiritualism. One asserted that it was true, but it was of the devil. From this the lecturer took his text: "The Devil and Diabolism." Space forbids a report of the lecture, but in the way of illustrative testimony and powerful eloquence, the lecturer is one of the best exponents of the so-called Spiritual philosophy that has ever been in our midst. At the close of the lecture, Mr. Wilson said that he saw near him a tall gentleman, of dark complexion, with black hair, who gave his name as Lansing, who once lived in the 'burg by that name, and who would be now ninety years of age. Description of habits and life given; recognized by many in the audience. Description of life and peculiarities of Mr. Benedict, who removed to Albany fifteen years ago, but died in this city; recognized. Mr. Delaware, of West Troy — life, business, and time of death given; recognized by many. Mr. Bennett, once of the Troy House. We do not know whether this person was recognized by any one or not.'

## *LIGHT AND DARKNESS.*

On the evening of Thursday, Oct. 12th, 1871, we lectured is Esgate schoolhouse, Jackson county, Iowa. It is a wayside schoolhouse, in the edge of the woods. Before leaving the comfortable farm house of my friends, the Bradways, we observed that we had a strange and peculiar feeling, such as we never before passed through. During the lecture we felt our usual speaking influence. Our discourse was earnest, and we entered with zeal into our text. The text was as follows: "Ante-natal and post-natal laws, and their influence on mankind."

There were a hundred and twelve earnest men and women present. After the lecture we gave several fine readings of character, and dismissed the audience.

Now, it was very dark out doors; not a star to be seen, for it was cloudy overhead, and within two days of the new of the moon. As we came toward the door we heard such remarks as these: "How dark it is." "Oh! how dark; how shall we get home?" "I do believe it will rain before we get home."

On stepping out of the house into the open air, everything was in a golden mellow light; not daylight or moonlight; it was light. We looked up and down the road for the cause; there was no apparent cause. We turned to a friend, and said: "Can you see, Charley; is it very dark?"

He replied, "I can see nothing; why do you ask?"

"Because everything is perfectly clear to me. I can see the buttons on that lady's coat; the curls in that lady's hair; I can see the color of your hair."

And this light accompanied me to the door of the Bradways, full a half mile from the schoolhouse. I called the attention of the Bradways, the Stevens, and others to the phenomenon. I heard no voice, or saw any spirits.

On the 16th of October I met my friend Dr. Pratt, of Wheaton, Ill., at Turner Junction; called his attention to the fact. On reaching my house Mrs. W. informed me of the burning to death of her sister Matilda and her two children, Lincoln and the baby; and instantly I heard a voice speaking out of the air, "Remember the light, and send for my husband and children." And we answered from the very depths of our soul, "We will."

FINIS.

www.ingramcontent.com/pod-product-compliance
Lightning Source LLC
LaVergne TN
LVHW020115110826
845151LV00001B/163

* 9 7 8 1 4 2 5 5 4 3 1 6 7 *